The Liberal Ideal and the Demons of Empire

The Liberal Ideal
and the Demons of Empire

Theories of Imperialism
from Adam Smith to Lenin

Bernard Semmel

The Johns Hopkins University Press *Baltimore and London*

© 1993 The Johns Hopkins University Press
All rights reserved
Printed in the United States of America on acid-free paper

The Johns Hopkins University Press
2715 North Charles Street
Baltimore, Maryland 21218-4319
The Johns Hopkins Press Ltd., London

Library of Congress Cataloging-in-Publication Data

Semmel, Bernard.
  The liberal ideal and the demons of empire : theories of
imperialism from Adam Smith to Lenin / Bernard Semmel.
      p.   cm.
  Includes bibliographical references and indexes.
  ISBN 0-8018-4540-8 (alk. paper)
  1. Imperialism. 2. Liberalism. 3. Free trade. 4. Marxian
economics. I. Title.
JC359.S5734   1993
325′.32—dc20   92-36270

A catalog record for this book is available from the British Library.

For Maxine

Of all malice, which gains hatred in Heaven, the end is injury; and every such end, either by force or by fraud, aggrieveth others. But because fraud is a vice peculiar to man, it more displeases God; and therefore the fraudulent are placed beneath, and more pain assails them. . . . By force, death and painful wounds may be inflicted upon one's neighbour; and upon his substance, devastation, burnings and injurious extortions. . . .

Behold the savage beast with the pointed tail, that passes mountains, and breaks through walls and weapons; behold him that pollutes the whole world . . . and that uncleanly image of Fraud came onward. . . . His face was the face of a just man, so mild an aspect had it outwardly; and the rest was a reptile's body.

Dante, *Divine Comedy*, cantos 11, 17

Men make their own history, but they do not make it just as they please; they do not make it under circumstances chosen by themselves, but under circumstances directly found, given and transmitted from the past. The tradition of all the dead generations weighs like a nightmare on the brain of the living. And just when they seem engaged in revolutionising themselves and things, in creating something entirely new, precisely in such epochs of revolutionary crisis they anxiously conjure up the spirits of the past to their service and borrow from them names, battle slogans and costumes in order to present the new scene or world history in this time-honoured disguise and this borrowed language.

Karl Marx, *The Eighteenth Brumaire of Louis Bonaparte*, 1852

Contents

Preface

This study attempts to uncover the dialectic between the liberal ideal that emerged in eighteenth-century Europe—Adam Smith described it as a utopia—and the theories of colonialism and imperialism that made their appearance when this ideal proved difficult to attain. Some readers may be familiar with other writings in which I have touched upon aspects of the subject of imperialism, particularly as they concerned British economists and politicians. This book brings sociological as well as economic theories into view, and includes Continental and American theorists along with British. I have tried not only to set down the ideas of the various theoretical schools but also to explain the preconceptions, modes of analysis, and social and political agenda of each.

The present work has occupied me, intermittently, for a considerable time. In the process I have incurred a number of debts. I would first of all like to thank the National Humanities Center, and particularly Charles Blitzer and Kent Mullikin, in Research Triangle Park, North Carolina, for a fellowship in the academic year 1986–87. Friends and colleagues have read the manuscript, all or in part, and have offered good advice, which I may not have always followed. Among these are Martin Albaum, Abraham Ascher, Daniel Gasman, Eric E. Lampard, Charles E. Staley, and Robert K. Webb. Thanks also are due to J. G. Goellner, Henry Y. K. Tom, and Carol Zimmerman, of the Johns Hopkins University Press, in speeding the completion of the study. I have benefited from the assistance of the British Library and the New York Public Library, as well as the libraries of Columbia, Harvard, the State University of New York at Stony Brook, and the Graduate School of the City University of New York.

As always, I feel most grateful to my wife, Maxine, for her help in bringing succeeding drafts of this study into existence. Her efforts were much more than editorial (or secretarial), but a few sentences cannot describe all I have drawn from her encouragement and companionship. I have been fortunate in receiving similar support from my son, Stuart, to whose sense of words and style as well as to whose grasp of the historical process I owe much.

The Liberal Ideal and the Demons of Empire

1 Imperialism and the Liberal Ideal

Commentators have praised or denounced the empires of the past as either the benefactors or the parasitic exploiters of mankind. Byron has told us that "the Assyrian came down like a wolf on the fold." This was certainly the view of the nations of the ancient Middle East, which contrasted Assyria's pernicious rule with the later beneficent dominion of Persia, which did not interfere with the economies or cultures of its subjects and maintained an efficient system of roads and mails. Both ancient and modern writers, at least to the mid-nineteenth century, preferred Sparta's military to Athens's exploitative commercial and maritime empire. Ancients distinguished similarly between the oppressive colonial domination exercised by Carthage's trade empire and the relative beneficence of Rome's later imperium. In the time of the Antonines, the Roman empire maintained not only roads but also a system of justice that led St. Paul to claim Roman citizenship in defense of his rights. In more recent times, Spain's empire of the sixteenth and seventeenth centuries signified for the Protestant Dutch and English the flames of the Inquisition, an Armada poised for a bloody invasion of England, the brutal domination of the Low Countries, and the enslavement of a good part of the native population of the New World. Spaniards and some modern scholars have drawn a counterimage of ruthless English and Dutch pirates prepared to rob Spain of its gold and silver so that they might mount a profitable trade in African slaves, whom the Protestant heretics were less prepared than the Catholic Church to see as spiritual equals.

The successors to Spain's empire of force were the mercantilist systems of Holland and England. The Dutch and the English established plantations and trading posts in America and Asia and profited handsomely from their near monopolies of colonial produce. Amsterdam in the seventeenth century, and London by the mid-eighteenth century, became the leading centers of business for the merchants and bankers of the world. They used their vast capital resources to control the increasing trade between Europe and overseas colonial territories and among the European states themselves, as well as to exact a profit from their role as moneylenders. Spaniards contrasted the Dutch and English empires as those of fraudulent and parasitic traders and usurers, on the Athenian or Carthaginian model, with their own, based on the traditional and gentlemanly virtues of courage, loyalty, and honor.

There had been comparatively little theorizing concerning earlier empires. One took possession of land, perhaps killing or enslaving the proprietor and transferring ownership to a noble or soldier of the conquering nation; one reduced a vanquished people to some form of serfdom and exploited their labor for the profit of the victorious chieftain and his agents; one appropriated capital in the form of precious metals or goods by seizing them at the time of conquest or, in more sophisticated fashion, by erecting a system of taxation for tribute so as to have a milch cow for all times. The mercantilists of the seventeenth and eighteenth centuries, on the other hand, did begin to theorize, though more haphazardly than systematically.

The mercantilists attempted something more subtle than brute conquest and expropriation: they sought to fit colonial possessions, particularly those where emigrants from the homeland settled in overseas colonies, into a system that might work to the mutual benefit of the colonies and the mother country, though it was considered right that the advantage rest with the metropolis. According to the mercantilists, colonies would supply raw materials in exchange for the manufactured goods of the mother country, with each party having a monopoly position in the market of the other. The export of manufactured goods was believed to be more stable and more remunerative than the export of agricultural products, and each nation would erect tariffs to protect manufacturers of the metropolis against foreign rivals. Nations sought a preponderance of exports over imports; theorists called this a favorable balance of trade. Insofar as one nation might be persuaded to supply raw materials in exchange for manufactures of another, it was, in mercantilist reasoning, an informal colony: the position of eighteenth-century Portugal with respect to Britain was at times equated with that of a subjugated Ireland or of Britain's North American colonies. Mercantilist nations readily took up violent means to expand and retain their possessions, acting on the conviction that economics, like politics, was a zero-sum game, with one nation's gains possible only from the losses of another.

Adam Smith's *Wealth of Nations*, published in 1776, and the school of classical political economy that followed, countered such reasoning. Mercantilists had lived in a world of comparatively limited resources; in the new world that emerged in Britain at the end of the eighteenth century, it became more and more evident that it was possible, for the first time, to increase the world's wealth absolutely. This was the basis for a profound revolution in economic thinking. One no longer needed to regard the world in parochial national terms. The classical economists argued in favor of an international division of labor, with each nation or region producing what its climate, soil, and talents dictated. A competitive marketplace within and between nations would decide the terms of this international division. Operating under conditions of free trade, they argued, such a system could provide optimal conditions for increasing the wealth of all countries. In such a world, the possession of formal colonies provided no advantages and imposed the expense of governing.

The free-trade model of the classical economists was established on the sense of mankind's having newly arrived at rationality, a rationality seen in economic terms as based on an enlightened self-interest. The liberals of the nineteenth century, moreover, saw this new society as the immediate and ultimate stage of man's progressive historical development. If men were not exclusively, or even primarily, guided by economic rationality, and by a general benevolence, the system would fall apart.

In the eighteenth century, a free-market capitalism appeared to be the best solution to the problems besetting Europe. The seventeenth and eighteenth were centuries of warfare over dynastic power, religion, and trade. War had been seen as endemic to the human condition since the time of Cain. Now, however, new circumstances—the great expansion of commerce and industry and the decline of feudal institutions—presented a way out. Society must direct the aggressive passions to which men were subject (lust, a desire for dominance, avarice) into useful channels. If men exerted their energies to accumulate wealth peacefully, in ways that the new system made possible, an idyllic future seemed attainable.

The liberal writers and statesmen of the new age, among them Montesquieu and the economist Sir James Steuart, looked forward to the conversion of the aggressive passions into the single passion of greed, with men accumulating wealth rather than battle flags as trophies. "Passions" might be transformed into "interests," the irrational become rational, a worthy goal even if it meant that life would be less rich—narrower, more mechanical, and more alienated. The new political economy devoted itself to an analysis, both philosophical and practical, of the rules of the new game that the advanced nations of the West might now play, and of the best ways of winning it.[1]

The science of political economy bore the unmistakable stamp of eighteenth-century deism and the Newtonian world order. The age of reason pictured a universe constructed and set into motion by a Great Clockmaker and never afterward requiring His intervention. The mechanism continued in its orderly, consistent, and therefore predictable course and enabled the scientist to frame laws describing its movements. The classical economists' description of a self-regulating free market, automatically governed by the forces of supply and demand and fueled by self-interest, conformed to this model. Less mechanically certain was Adam Smith's view of an "invisible hand," a providence that, like the benign but absent God of the deists, translated individual selfishness into the common good. This was one of the almost utopian conceptions that lay behind the new science at the time of its birth, and which persisted among mainstream adherents of the classical view into the twentieth century. If only the state did not interfere with the economic mechanism, the advocates of the free market maintained, all would go well. To intervene would produce crippling distortions.

The German Enlightenment philosopher Immanuel Kant had in the 1780s and 1790s distilled the views of the liberal theorists of his time and anticipated those of the nineteenth century. Joining social theory to an argument derived from economic theory, Kant sought to prove that a modern commercial society, by its very nature, must turn from trade wars and colonial expansion to the establishment of a perpetual peace. Anticipating the union of Protestant conscience and laissez-faire economics that was to characterize the thinking of later (primarily British) liberals, Kant rejected the view that colonial conquests, with their oppression, wars, and famine, were justified because they brought an advanced culture to backward peoples. "Supposedly good intentions cannot wash away the stain of injustice from the means which are used to implement them," he declared, condemning the powers that had chosen to live on "the fruits of iniquity." Kant described the "unsocial sociability" that brought men into the harmonious relations with one another to which their natural propensities to secure power or property appeared hostile. This was a part of Nature's "hidden plan" enabling men to overcome selfish animal inclinations. At the stage of civilization at which Europe had arrived, all commerce and industry, and the armies and navies dependent on them for their effectiveness, were founded on the advance and diffusion of knowledge, and this intellectual progress was conditioned by a climate of freedom. Consequently, a ruler's "self-seeking schemes of expansion" were hostage to a regime of liberty. In Kant's model, much like that suggested in Adam Smith's "invisible hand," a selfish human nature would further the general welfare. A natural providence would insure the victory of a "practical moral reason," and a human nature "animated by respect for right and duty" and not too "deeply immersed in evil" would eliminate war.[2]

With a Promethean arrogance, then, the eighteenth-century liberal bourgeoisie, particularly in Britain, America, and France, became convinced that industrial, commercial, and scientific progress was creating a new society in which war and conquest would become obsolete, and that that society would produce a new man. Nineteenth-century social theorists and their disciples, as we shall see, made a distinction between the traditional and the modern when they described the passions of the aggressive, militant society of the past and compared it to the rationality of the pacific commercial and industrial society of contemporary Britain and France. In the 1880s, a German sociologist would describe the earlier European society, like traditional societies elsewhere, as a *Gemeinschaft,* a community in which emotions exercised full sway, whereas in the *Gesellschaft,* the modern commercial society, these were kept in check and reason prevailed.[3] In traditional societies, aggressive war was still to be encountered; in modern societies, dominated by a rational bourgeoisie that consulted its interests and not its emotions, war and colonial conquest were passing away. Even Friedrich Engels, in the *Anti-Dühring,* suggested that war in the advanced nations might be dialectically negating itself because its wholesale waste would be abhorrent to the capitalist's concern for frugality.[4]

Scholars have traced the meaning and uses of the political and economic term *imperialism* during the nineteenth and twentieth centuries. In the France of the Second Empire, those who saw the glories of Napoleon I revived in the regime of his nephew Louis Napoleon were called "Imperialists," and the suggestion of a similar policy of pomp and glory attached itself to Disraeli's Tory government of the 1870s. In the 1880s and 1890s, those who sought a federation of Great Britain's self-governing colonies were proud of their Imperialism; and in the first decade of the new century, both Tories who sought a system of imperial tariff preference and free-trade Liberals whose program of social reform envisioned making an "imperial race" of the British happily claimed the title. It was during the course of the Spanish-American War of 1898 and the Boer War of 1899–1902 that the term began to acquire an invidious meaning. Liberal opponents of these conflicts in both America and Britain charged their "imperialist" supporters with brutal aggression, willful malice, and cruel exploitation. Overseas enemies of the Anglo-Saxon countries were to convert the name into a slogan to describe a plot first by Great Britain and then by the United States to achieve world domination.[5]

Modern imperialism has been regarded as a phenomenon of late capitalism, exhibiting its characteristic form in the "new imperialism" of the 1880s that began the division of Africa and Asia among the chief European powers, soon to be joined by Japan and the United States. Scholars have usually credited the English sociologist and economist J. A. Hobson, in 1902, and the Austrian neo-Marxist Rudolf Hilferding, in 1910, with having set down the essentials of the analysis that the Bolshevik leader V. I. Lenin employed in establishing the model of imperialism of finance capital in his 1917 tract. For over half a century, not only the communist world but many of the leading politicians and intellectuals of the emerging nations of Africa, Asia, and Latin America as well believed implicitly that the Leninist model was an accurate formulation. And important sections of liberal opinion in Europe and America by and large accepted this view, although with some qualifications.

Since the 1960s there has been in the noncommunist world a decline in confidence in the Leninist theory, a greater readiness to accept an enlarged conception of the idea of imperialism, and an interest in earlier models. Social and economic theorists have written on the subject from the time of Adam Smith in the late eighteenth century onward. Yet studies of the development of the idea of imperialism have still tended to begin with Hobson, neglecting over a century and a quarter of the idea's earlier evolution. Nonetheless these earlier theories—notably those of the national economists and, to a lesser extent, the liberal sociologists—have become the building blocks of what we might call a post-Leninist formulation, one that seemed to approach a new consensus during the past generation.

There are four principal schools (or traditions) of analysis of imperialism. The first is that of the classical economists, both the Ricardian mainstream and the heterodox Malthusians. These economic theorists believed the persistence of wars and colonialism—despite the optimistic expectations of the liberal advocates of the new free-market economy—was due to difficulties within the new industrialism. Adam Smith, writing in the 1770s, even as he dismissed the mercantilist view of the necessity of colonies, saw them as a sometimes useful market for the surplus production of the manufacturers of the metropolis. A little more than a generation later, mainstream classical economists were even more optimistic, having formulated Say's Law, which denied the possibility of overproduction, and the law of comparative advantage, which argued both the economic advantages and justice of free trade and an international division of labor. On the other hand, a heterodox school of British political economists (in the first third of the nineteenth century), largely under the influence of the clergyman-economist T. R. Malthus, saw the new system as tending almost inevitably to both overpopulation and overproduction and the accumulation of a surplus of capital that would substantially lower the rate of profit and bring on economic crises. The Scottish minister Thomas Chalmers wrote along these lines, as did the economist Robert Torrens and, intermittently, the utilitarian philosopher Jeremy Bentham. Even the father of orthodoxy, the stockbroker David Ricardo, foresaw an inevitable decline in the rate of profit, and his ally James Mill wrote of the advantages of colonization in overcoming this and similar problems engendered by the industrial system. The most articulate and influential exponent of the heterodox pessimistic position was Edward Gibbon Wakefield, who, in the 1830s and 1840s, argued that only by developing the lands of overseas colonies (like Australia, New Zealand, and Canada) could an industrial Britain overcome gluts of people, production, and capital—and avoid social revolution.

James Mill's son John Stuart, the leading economist of the 1850s and 1860s, accepted large parts of Wakefield's analysis and remedy, notably the usefulness of fresh lands as an antidote to a glut of capital. In the early 1860s, during the American Civil War, J. S. Mill joined the American writer F. L. Olmsted and the Irish economist J. E. Cairnes in seeing the slave economy of the American South as so destructive of the soil as to make necessary continual imperial expansion onto previously untilled acres. Here was an economic theory of imperialism drawing on the classical principle of the declining returns from agriculture and joined to what we will call a sociological theory (already presented by earlier writers) which saw the Southern slaveholders as a quasi-feudal caste perhaps concerned as much with maintaining their power and prestige as with economic returns.

This brings us to the second tradition of theorizing, that of the sociological school, which held that the spirit of the new society was at core opposed to the militarism and colonial expansionism of the preceding mercantilism. Insofar as the ethos of the past militant society survived, this school reasoned, it was an aberration, an atavism proceeding from the interests of the premodern governing classes striving to maintain their previous prestige and power, as well as the rewards stemming from their economic base in the land, mercantilist enterprise, and remunerative colonial and military offices. (These classes were described as the selfish "vested interests.") For liberal writers, not capitalism but the still potent heirs of the feudal spirit and mercantilist privilege motored colonial and military enterprise. In the decade after Waterloo, a number of French social theorists, most notably Henri Saint-Simon, presented early versions of this argument, to be followed, more systematically, in the second quarter of the century, by Saint-Simon's disciple, the positivist founder of the "science" of sociology, Auguste Comte; in the 1850s and 1860s, the liberal British sociological historians H. T. Buckle and W. E. H. Lecky supported and in certain particulars extended this position. The Radical wing of the Liberal party in Britain, under the leadership of Richard Cobden and John Bright, made the struggle against the landed classes (whom it described as the "feudal" governing classes), and their policies of protectionism, militarism, and colonialism, the central thrust of its program. The Radicals were convinced that the tide of history made victory inevitable.

In the last quarter of the century, the English philosopher and social theorist Herbert Spencer, who had earlier maintained this Radical faith, worried that the premodern militant ethos was reasserting itself. For Spencer, state intervention in the economy and society was the principal culprit. A more socialist-leaning Hobson, one of Spencer's admirers and similarly convinced that free-trade industrial capitalism was blameless, saw the growing influence of finance, and a reversion to a mercantilist protectionism, as making possible the persistence and strengthening of the spirit of militarism. As 1914 approached, the American sociologist and economist Thorstein Veblen, also a disciple of Spencer's sociology, saw the primary source of war in the acquisition of a modern industrial machine by a still feudal class of German Junkers. As World War I was drawing to a close, the Austrian economist J. A. Schumpeter brought the sociological theory to its most sophisticated formulation in a reply to the neo-Marxist theory that had been developed in the first two decades of the century.

A third stream of analysis was that of the national economists. One of the earliest writers of this school was the first U.S. secretary of the treasury, Alexander Hamilton, who in the 1790s warned his countrymen that the terms of trade would always favor an industrial Britain over an agricultural United States and urged the erection of a tariff to foster American manufactures. (A discussion of a similar question some decades earlier by the British clergyman Josiah Tucker, in an encounter with the philosopher David Hume, had already led Tucker to put forward protection as the only means by which a less advanced industrial country could successfully confront a more advanced one.) Other American writers, notably Daniel Raymond, adopted Hamilton's protectionist program. A German writer, Friedrich List, was confirmed in his neomercantilist views by a long stay in America and a study of Hamilton's ideas. He returned to his country to campaign for a German Zollverein and high German tariffs. The Philadelphia economist and publisher Henry Carey—whose writings deserve more attention than they have received—following the position of Hamilton and List, also subscribed to protection of industry as necessary to America's well-being and its full freedom from British predominance.

The national economists viewed Great Britain very much as Napoleon had when he constructed the Continental System: as an aggressive state that threatened the independence of all others. Both List and Carey saw Britain (the leading industrial, commercial, and financial power of the first three-quarters of the nineteenth century) as determined to make all nations perpetually subservient to its free-trade empire; they depicted the powerful Bank of England as an insidious mechanism to exploit other nations.

We may see in the portrait of the international usury of finance capital—which would play a significant role in the evolution of the idea of imperialism—a subcategory of the school of the national economists. The leading national economists were American and German, and these nations would become the chief manufacturing rivals of Great Britain by the end of the nineteenth century. France, lagging behind in industrial development and still in the first half of the century in a stage of what has been called primitive accumulation, was the primary home of another group of writers. These drew on the long medieval revulsion at usury to attack Britain, the Jews, the Protestant bankers, and the Freemasons as masters of finance determined to bleed less economically advanced nations. The utopian socialist Charles Fourier wrote in this fashion as early as the first decade of the century. His disciple Alphonse Toussenel would follow these lines in the 1840s, and Toussenel's disciple Edouard Drumont gave even greater attention to Jewish financiers in the 1880s. All these writers described the links of this international finance to colonialism. By the end of the century, American and German writers would take up these themes in their discussions of imperialism; among them were both Brooks and his brother Henry Adams (of the well-known American political family) and the German economic historian Werner Sombart.

The Marxists constitute a fourth tradition, one that synthesized the views of their three (or three and a half) predecessors and gave them a characteristic turn. (The Marxist position on the declining rate of profit, for example, would be quite different from those of the orthodox Ricardo or the heterodox Wakefield.) In the 1840s and 1850s, Marx and Engels intermittently considered, with approval, the views of the sociological theorists and the national economists. By the end

---

of the century, they would stress the special role of a usurious finance capital, as would their neo-Marxist followers. The best-known of the neo-Marxists, Hilferding, formulated the most subtle and complex Marxist discussion of the new imperialism; the Polish-German economist Rosa Luxemburg's view was more original, and probably less Marxist in conception. With the Bolshevik economist N. I. Bukharin, and even more with Lenin, we will find the subordination of analysis to polemic, with the special goal of seeing the imperialism of finance capital (with its ceaseless warfare) as the ultimate stage of a disintegrating capitalism. This was a reply to the "reformist" views of the German Marxist Karl Kautsky and his revisionist rival Eduard Bernstein, both of whom prophesied the coming of a relatively pacific "ultra-imperialism."

The idea of imperialism, one may argue, became in the early twentieth century an essential element in realizing the Marxist utopia. The liberal ideal, the Marxists (following Lenin) asserted, was a vain dream, for wars were inevitable so long as nations competed for the empires that a moribund capitalism absolutely required to counter the declining rate of profit. These imperialist struggles, accompanied as they would be by the growing immiseration of the proletariat, were the ineradicable reality of capitalism and would bring to pass the revolution that would usher in the dictatorship of the proletariat, a classless society, and a perpetual peace. If capitalist wars did not continue, as Marxists like Kautsky suggested, it would call into question the overthrow of the capitalist system and the victory of socialism.

This book will survey all these theoretical schools of the period—roughly, between Adam Smith's classic work of 1776 and the publication in 1919 of Schumpeter's work on imperialism. Another, considerably thicker volume would be necessary to discuss the immense literature published during the past seventy years, particularly that produced since 1945. A few such volumes have already appeared. By the first twenty years of our century, however, the shape of the leading theories of imperialism had already been arrived at, and what followed was a somewhat qualified reproduction of the earlier models, or efforts to combine their features.

Since human beings were not merely calculating animals but also subject to irrational sexual drives, as the clergyman Malthus understood, and to such motives as individual or national prestige and power, the rational foundations for the new system of capitalist industrialism were unsure. If humans were, as many of the religious continued to insist, irremediably tainted by sin, matters assumed an even more dubious complexion. Finally, if historical development was more complex and more difficult to direct than liberals believed, all certainty was gone. Under such adverse conditions, the "science" of political economy became just another doctrine whose inner logic, though flawless, might have little touch with reality—perhaps another utopia.

A number of the theories of colonialism and of imperialism which this study will discuss grew out of an effort to align the at times defective realities of the new system with the theoretical perfections of the most optimistic laws that purported to describe its operations. Free-market theorists saw themselves as having largely given up the theological and metaphysical preconceptions that had impeded thinkers of the past. They sought to avoid admitting that their ideal had been built on similarly uncertain foundations and might consequently be as deficient as all previous ones. While prepared to grant that certain classes (the aristocracy, the military class, and the landed gentry) continued to be marked by tendencies to violence and conquest and that the survivors of the older mercantile and financial classes might be given to parasitic avarice and demands for special protection, they saw these groups as atavisms soon to be extinguished. In the end, reason would triumph and a new era emerge.

There were still other difficulties. Though the doctrine of the classical economists appeared for a time triumphant, neomercantilist economists persisted in the views of the deposed system even while giving lip service to the new liberal dispensation. While agreeing with liberals that a universal free trade would ultimately benefit all nations, List and Carey argued that, so long as nations were at different stages of development, a free-trade policy would favor the advanced nations with more capital, better established commercial and financial facilities, and more efficient means of production. Those who maintained otherwise—the classical economists and their dupes or hirelings in other countries—were not friends of a cosmopolitan humanity and an impartial economic science, as they claimed, but advocates of parasitic traders and bankers who lived by fraud.

The social and economic writers with whom we are primarily concerned may have all believed themselves to be searching for an objective, "scientific" theory of colonialism and later imperialism. But in their efforts to secure an all-embracing synthesis, we may see a simplification of a complex phenomenon, usually in the interest of a political agenda. And beneath this synthesis, we may perceive the passions tapped by ideologies that endowed theory with the emotional force required to gain adherents.

In the late 1790s, a group of French liberals under the leadership of Destutt de Tracy established a "science of ideas," which they named ideology. Their goal was a natural history of ideas, grounded in a scientific biology, with traditional solutions to religious and moral questions dismissed as metaphysical illusions—in Destutt de Tracy's memorable words, illusions "destinées à nous satisfaire et non à nous instruire," designed to satisfy, not to instruct us. Reason guided by experience would vanquish what the empiricist philosopher Bacon had called "idols" and the Enlightenment *philosophes* "préjugés" which had supported the constraints and selfishness of the past societies dominated by despotic rulers and priests. Hegel and Marx would later agree that men might overcome the limitations of time and place and by reason gain access to the universal truths of an ultimately rational history. Marx defined ideology as "false consciousness," since he believed that only a few gifted with critical intelligence could seize the rationale of the historical process and present a "scientific" view of the conditions that shaped both thought and practice. When mankind achieved this triumph of comprehension, Marx wrote, it would no longer be a creature of historical necessity subject to unconscious historical "laws." No longer the victim of the illusions of Plato's cave, it would find truth and formulate its own conditions of living. It would thus triumph over the various and confused individual misunderstandings of history imposed by the economic processes of earlier stages of development.[6]

But, unfortunately, this was not to be. We may in fact argue that the several ideologies of imperialism, far from having unveiled the universal truths of an ultimately rational history, rather enlisted the primal demons of earlier stages of development to cloud the understanding. Beneath the various theories of colonialism and imperialism were political demonologies. For the great mass of people in nineteenth-century Europe, there were two primal forms of exploitation, both with deep roots in the Middle Ages—that of the feudal lord and landlord and that of the usurer. These were the serpents in Eden. These demons assumed mythic forms, drawing on popular legend and belief: the wicked feudal baron, despoiler of the daughters and lands of the peasantry; the greedy usurer, whose trade of making money from money seemed diabolical parasitism. Both the feudal lord and the usurer, moreover, were seen as sucking the blood of less elevated and more virtuous classes. One recent scholar has described the strong emotions accompanying anti-Semitism as in good part a consequence of the dread of bloodsucking, a term employed as both a metaphor for Jewish moneylending and present in the widespread acceptance of the supposed fact of the Jewish drinking of Gentile blood for ritual purposes.[7] Another writer has discussed the folklore of the vampire, who from the time of Vlad the Impaler has more often than not been seen as a demon aristocrat.[8]

Many liberals believed they had exorcised the demons of the old regime but continued to wonder if ghosts of the previous system might still remain as active forces, perhaps somewhat disguised, in the new society. In one form or another, these legendary figures of evil persisted in the popular mentality and, we shall see, in the thinking of some of the leading economists and social theorists of the time as well. Such myths appeared all the more plausible when a privileged aristocracy continued to play an important role in national affairs and when the lending of money at interest was central to the new industrial society. Certain French writers, among them Charles Fourier and his disciples, united the two images into one, a *féodalité de finance* under both British and Jewish control. Others on both sides of the Atlantic were to follow their example.[9]

Each of the schools discussed had its characteristic demons or groups of demons, and these frequently overlapped. The pacific defenders of the new system, both the economic and the sociological theorists, shared the fear of the return to dominance of the landed and mercantile classes, with their violent passions and policies that had fomented the trade wars of the century before the French Revolution. They wished to exclude what Bentham called the "sinister interests" from reclaiming the offices and economic perquisites they had enjoyed, at the expense of the nation, under the old colonial system. Then there was the demon of the all-devouring evil empire. A number of liberals would see this ogre in a militaristic and feudal Hohenzollern Germany, the successor of the evil empires of force of the Spanish Hapsburgs and the French Bourbons. The national economists (and their Fourierist sympathizers) believed the rapacious evil empire of fraud to be that of a free-trade Britain (and its Jewish allies) and depicted these antagonists as dreaded usurers. Borrowing almost as heavily from the demonology of medieval usury, the Marxists portrayed an avaricious and exploitative capitalism obsessively accumulating its gold like Balzac's moneylending Jewish miser, Gobseck, whom Marx invoked in his first volume of *Capital*,[10] and employing this hoard to exploit the industrial laborer much as the medieval usurer had the peasant. For later Marxists, there were the evil "usurer states" (Lenin's term) of an imperialist finance capital always requiring fresh blood to survive.

The Austrian economist and social theorist J. A. Schumpeter, writing in 1942, described "the fascination exerted by a synthesis" that "teaches mankind the hidden meaning of its struggles," a fascination to which intellectuals, especially young intellectuals, were particularly susceptible. "Panting with impatience to have their innings, longing to save the world . . . dissatisfied emotionally and intellectually, unable to achieve a synthesis by their own efforts," they find "what they crave for" in some ideologist. "There it is, the key to all the most intimate secrets, the magic wand that marshals both great events and small." And they now "no longer feel out of it in the great affairs of life" and can see "through the pompous marionettes of politics and business," who are ignorant of the key that those who master the synthesis possess.[11]

While understanding the important role played by political demonology, we cannot dismiss the writings of the social and economic theorists with whom we are concerned as merely manifestations of "false consciousness." The ideological aspect makes it more possible to see why the term *imperialism* has absorbed so much of the negative emotional force of such longtime villains as feudalism and usury— the first the spur to an empire of force, the other to one of fraud— and of capitalism, which has rarely enjoyed a good press. The theorists of imperialism have on the whole seen themselves as describing irredeemably evil empires rather than, as some writers would argue, the birth pangs of an international society and economy. Noting the presence of nonscientific factors in these theories does not, however, entirely invalidate them.

We will often (implicitly if not always explicitly) be dealing with abstractions: ideal-types of a Weberian character. There will appear, fully or partially, such types as feudalism, mercantilism, capitalism, the old colonial system, and imperialism (free-trade and protectionist), and so on. Social and economic theorizing requires such ideal-types, and the writers with whom we are concerned employed them, often despite their inapplicability in detail to actual circumstances. It is with these types in mind and against the general background of national and international politics and industrial and capitalist development that we will explore the ways in which certain of the leading European and American economic and social theorists (from Great Britain, France, Germany, the United States, Austria, and Russia) assisted in what we may call the evolution of the idea of imperialism.

The liberal ideal-type may very well be seen as a utopia, a dream whose realization human nature made impossible. This was apparently the view of Adam Smith. "To expect, indeed, that the freedom of trade should ever be entirely restored in Great Britain," he wrote in 1776, "is as absurd as to expect that an Oceana or Utopia should ever be established in it." The "prejudices" of public opinion and ("much more unconquerable") "the private interests of many individuals, irresistibly oppose it." Not only would "the most infamous abuse and detraction" be heaped upon proponents of free trade, but "real danger" to their persons would arise "from the insolent outrage" of the monopolists.[12]

And yet Britain in the mid-nineteenth century embarked on just such a utopian course. Convinced that reason was on its side, it expected to carry the rest of the world with it in the construction of an international division of labor based on free trade. Smith had forecast the difficulties: both public prejudice and private interest made their opposition felt, both in Britain and abroad. In Great Britain itself, the free trade pioneer where the new dispensation would prevail until the 1930s, even political economists, disciples of Smith, would see systemic difficulties in free trade as well as in other parts of the new order of the liberal ideal.

2 The Political Economists, Free Trade, and Empire

The most usual view of the difference between the mercantilist and free-trade ideals was that mercantilism pursued power while the free traders preferred plenty. Liberals regarded this distinction as grounds for their approval of free trade, while conservatives saw this as evidence of the failure of the liberals to set proper priorities. A perceptive student of economic policy has concluded that, in fact, eighteenth-century mercantilists had *both* plenty *and* power as objectives, though some scholars have argued that maritime and constitutional states like Britain and Holland were more concerned with profits than were absolutist landed states like Prussia.[1] But regardless of the predominant motive, wars for power and for profit were fought and colonies conquered as a matter of course, without risking the condemnation of most writers of that time.

By the late eighteenth century, opinion was shifting. For the German philosopher Kant, conscientious scruples were the major grounds for the rejection of war and colonialism; in the world-view of the classical economists, a universal free trade would remove the economic need for wars and colonial conquests. Mercantilist expansion, it was now argued, would only depress the economy, saddle the mother country with the expenses of governing an overseas colony, and expose the nation to the dangers of brutal and unnecessary wars. In the free-trade ideal of the classical mainstream, each nation would benefit from commerce in proportion to its capital and its ability to fulfill the requirements of other countries. If a nation lost one trade, it might easily turn to another, more profitable one. Gluts of goods or capital were logically inadmissable. This was the position of the more optimistic disciples of Adam Smith during, roughly, the first two decades of the nineteenth century.

17

This liberal ideal proved difficult to achieve in the real world, where glut proved an ever present problem; even in the realm of theory, political economists discovered disturbing doubts that actual circumstances appeared to confirm. The three decades following the defeat of Napoleon in 1815 were a time of widespread depression in Great Britain. This gave rise to questions concerning the viability of the new system and led to both theoretical and practical efforts to set matters right. Some radicals attributed these difficulties to the overvaluation of the pound sterling at the time the gold standard was restored in 1819. Others, liberals in the camp of Richard Cobden and his Anti–Corn Law League, blamed the Corn Laws, which imposed tariff protection of grain, for hard times. These Cobdenites raised the banner of Adam Smith and called for a free entry of foreign wheat, which would not only lower the price of bread for British workingmen (and consequently the costs of production, making British exports more competitive) but also provide foreign countries with the money to purchase British manufactures. This would make possible an international division of labor in accordance with the liberal ideal.

Very few among the writers on economic subjects were entirely sanguine about depending entirely on the new system. From the beginning, we find discussion of the possible need to retain, perhaps only temporarily, certain devices of the old colonial order. Some writers began to reconsider the usefulness of a tariff wall to protect British colonies against foreign manufactures. Others wished to enter upon extensive programs of colonization, with government cooperation. There were increasing doubts as to how long Britain's industrial superiority might last. Such theorizing seemed to herald a revival of the old mercantilism.

Adam Smith and the Optimists

Adam Smith, a professor of moral philosophy at the University of Glasgow, had acquired a European reputation on the publication of his *Theory of Moral Sentiments* in 1769. With the appearance in 1776 of his *Wealth of Nations,* the Scottish moral philosopher became the seminal authority for the classical political economy of the nineteenth century, the best-known and best-regarded proponent of the free market and free trade against an interventionist mercantilism and a system of colonial monopoly. In mounting his argument against colonialism, Smith often adapted the reasoning of the mid-eighteenth-century French physiocrats, who believed agriculture to be the only productive economic activity, with both manufacturing and commerce somewhat parasitic dependents. The French economists saw the profits of foreign trade procured by a kind of thievery. Smith knew too much about the contribution of manufacturing and overseas commerce to the wealth of Britain to accept so wide-ranging an indictment.[2]

In writing of the different employments of capital, Smith agreed, substantially though with qualification, with the physiocratic case against the commercial system. Like the French economists, he believed that agriculture was the most (but not the only, as the physiocrats had asserted) productive pursuit, that capital in domestic commerce was much more profitably employed than that engaged in overseas trade, and that foreign trade gave only half the encouragement to a country's productive labor as home trade. Such opinions, of course, struck forcibly at the leading conviction of the mercantilists, who elevated foreign trade above both agricultural and domestic commerce. Smith argued further that the capital engaged in the carrying trade supported the labor of foreign countries, not that of the country whose flag the ships flew; moreover, he added, the distances involved in overseas colonial trade (whose superior benefits mercantilists stressed) made for less frequent turnovers of capital, and therefore such trade was less remunerative to the nation. Despite his acceptance of much of the physiocratic case against the commercial system, Smith could not deny that individuals often found it to their greater advantage to invest in "the most distant carrying trades of Asia and America, than in the improvement and cultivation of the most fertile fields in their own neighborhood."[3]

When Smith wrote, Britain's North American colonies were in revolt against the old colonial system. Smith argued that, contrary to the mercantilist view, Britain would benefit if the restrictions of the commercial system were removed.[4] Britain could buy its tobacco more cheaply than could France under the prevailing arrangements, but it might have such goods more cheaply still under free trade. Privileged merchants and producers would suffer, of course, as the nation benefited, for the mercantile system had sacrificed the interest of the home consumer of colonial goods to the interest of the producer and the trader.[5] The Navigation Acts of the seventeenth century, though necessary to Britain's maritime defenses, had not so much increased British overseas trade as they had changed its direction from Europe to the colonies. The monopoly of the colonial carrying trade granted in those acts had raised the rate of profit to be got from such enterprise and, as a result, had diverted capital from supporting more productive labor and from the improvement of land. The high profits of the colonial monopoly had depressed domestic wages and rents and injured all trades in which no monopoly existed, thus breaking "altogether that natural balance" among the branches of the economy.[6]

Smith, while somewhat regretting that the planting of European colonies since the fifteenth century had raised the mercantile system to "splendour and glory," could yet delight (in marked contrast to the French physiocrats) in the stimulating effect that the opening of the American and Asian trade had had for Europe and for his country. Europe had become the manufacturer and carrier for all the continents. America was proving an "inexhaustible market" for Britain's surplus production, for which there had been no demand at home. (Here Smith clearly accepted the mercantilist argument for the usefulness of colonies.) These new markets had made possible further divisions of labor and thus had increased the productive powers of labor and the revenue and wealth of Europe as well. These benefits greatly outweighed the harmful consequences of the colonial monopoly. The new produce and capital created by the colonial trade supported more labor in Britain than might have been made unemployed by the distortions created by the artificially high profits of colonial monopoly.[7] Meanwhile, all Europe (not just the imperial nations who bore the expense of governing the colonies) enjoyed the benefits of the development of the overseas continents.[8]

Smith urged the British to abandon the colonial system. The yielding of the colonial monopoly might be "contrary to the private interest of the governing part" of the country, which would lose "many places of trust and profit," but all others would benefit if the colonies achieved independence under a free-trading system.[9] Smith sanguinely concluded that, after the colonies were granted their independence, there would continue to be a mutually profitable and harmonious trade between the less developed former colonies and their previous imperial masters.

It was left to Smith's contemporary, Josiah Tucker, the dean of Gloucester, to make the most far-reaching arguments for granting independence to colonies to assure their better exploitation.[10] "Trade is not carried on for the Sake of Friendship," Tucker observed in 1776, "but of Interest," and it was not in the interest of the American colonies to break off their trade with Britain.[11] If Britain gave up its colonies, he added in 1782, it could trust "solely to the Goodness and Cheapness" of its manufactures and "to the long Credit we can give." Indeed, if it merely relied on "the Strength of our great Capitals," Britain could command the goods of all the world.[12] On the other hand, the restrictions of the old colonial system compelled Britain to purchase raw materials from its colonies when it could obtain them more cheaply elsewhere. Colonial independence and a free trade, then, would be more profitable than mercantilist colonialism to Great Britain.[13]

But Tucker's prescription was valid for his country only because of Britain's lead in finance, in commerce, and in industry. Was there a more general argument in favor of the emancipation of colonies and free trade? The mercantilists believed, and Adam Smith had agreed, that agricultural regions overseas were useful markets for the surplus manufactured products of Europe. If this were true, would not metropolitan powers be wise to retain colonies as a privileged market? Another problem presented itself. The mercantilists insisted that the benefits of trade were distributed unequally, with the exporter of manufactured goods profiting to a greater extent than the exporter of food and raw materials. Would an agricultural America, free of imperial control, continue to trade under what were alleged to be disadvantageous conditions? The mainstream of classical economists provided optimistic solutions to each of these difficulties—the first was Say's Law and the second, the law of comparative advantage.

Both the eighteenth-century mercantilists and their physiocratic opponents had agreed that, though an increase in agricultural production—in food—would automatically call into being more people to consume this food, such reasoning did not apply to the production of industrial goods. Hence the need for foreign and colonial markets for an industrial surplus. In 1803, however, the French economist J. B. Say argued that a growth in a country's industrial production would likewise be accompanied by an increase in the markets for its consumption; since goods produced represented a demand as well as supply, goods exchanging for goods, a general overproduction or glut was impossible. The argument was logically impeccable, and greatly reassuring.[14]

The English physiocrat William Spence, in an 1808 tract, warned that an industrial system produced gluts of capital as well as of manufactures. In a reply that same year, James Mill restated Say's Law, as well as the doctrine of both Smith and Turgot that the accumulation of capital, far from being an impediment to a healthy economy, was a necessary basis for increasing the wealth of a nation.[15]

In this tract, Mill also presented a theory of the territorial division of labor that hinted at the law of comparative advantage; in another publication that year, a former major of marines, Robert Torrens, more precisely and forcefully anticipated the statement of the law. David Ricardo completed its elaboration in 1817, arguing that if Britain could manufacture cotton cloth of a superior quality and lesser price than Poland, while Poland had an analogous advantage in growing corn, both countries would benefit by an exchange of these products. Britain's industrial skill could then convert a given amount of capital into obtaining more corn than that same capital could have produced by investment in farming the most fertile lands in Britain; and Poland, without Britain's advantages in manufacturing, would similarly secure more industrial goods than it could by manufacturing for itself. Both countries would prosper through this mutually beneficial trade.[16]

In the following decades, there were writers on political economy with less technical proficiency, but possessing styles more suited to a wider public, who repeated the optimistic message of the free-trade ideal. They preached a harmonious economic system in which there was no danger of overproduction and in which the accumulation of capital served not to clog the arteries of the economy but to make for greater prosperity. These optimists believed that the free market within a country, and a free trade between nations, produced a mutually beneficial internal and international division of labor which would make possible an increasing progress and prosperity for all.

The Cobdenite Radicals saw an international division of labor established on free trade as embodying scriptural principle. They believed themselves to be waging a war against a colonial and mercantile system motored by a sinful avarice, feudal aggressiveness, and the devil. Despite evidence of an unredeemed spirit among some capitalists, a free-trade capitalism was viewed by Cobden and Bright as an approach to the Kingdom of God. Defending the repeal of the Corn Laws in 1846, Cobden denied "anything selfish" or "discordant with Christian principles" in the maxim "to buy in the cheapest market and sell in the dearest." What this meant was that "you take the article which you have in the greatest abundance, and with it obtain from others that of which they have the most to spare, so giving to mankind the means of enjoying the fullest abundance of earth's goods, and in doing so carrying out to the fullest extent the Christian doctrine of 'Do ye to all men as ye would they should do unto you.' "[17] A year earlier, John Bright spoke to the House of Commons of those members of the Dissenting, industrial classes "into whose hearts free-trade principles had sunk, and became, verily, a religious question." (There were some cries of protest from the benches of the Tory protectionists.)[18] When the French popular economist Frederic Bastiat described free trade as the solution to all social problems, Cobden described him in a letter to Bright as having "vindicated his favorite science from the charge of inhumanity with all the fervour of a religious devotee."[19] Free-market rationality was thus wed to the will of a benevolent Divinity.

Malthus and the Pessimists

Other, less optimistic British economists, some operating on physiocratic and others on mercantilist premises, continued to insist that a stultifying glut—a mounting surplus of goods and capital as well as of population—would plague a growing industrial system. The clergyman T. R. Malthus, very much under the influence of the physiocrats, had argued along these lines, as did his leading disciple, the Scottish minister Thomas Chalmers. Malthus is best known for his "law" that described population as increasing geometrically while food production increased only arithmetically; this imbalance necessarily brought into play the Four Horsemen of the Apocalypse, Famine, Death, Disease, and War. Malthus modified this conclusion of his first *Essay on Population,* published in 1798, in an expanded second essay some five years later in which he portrayed moral (sexual) restraint as making possible a less unhappy sequence of events. But appreciating the deep-rootedness of original sin, as the more hopeful writers of the eighteenth-century Enlightenment had not, the Anglican parson did not seem overly sanguine that such a course would be widely undertaken. Classical economists would accept his law of population, and the leading figure of the school, David Ricardo, put forward a so-called iron law of wages on the Malthusian model: since wages tended to be set at subsistence levels, they would fall if there were too many laborers, thus bringing the Four Horsemen onto the scene, and would rise again only when these nemeses had restored the balance.[20]

Malthus's pessimism extended to all parts of the commercial system, and he warned his contemporaries against overreliance on industry and trade. Alone among the classical economists, he even favored the Corn Laws protecting British agriculture, fearing a British dependence on foreigners for food, and complained that high commercial profits only diverted capital from agriculture, "that more essential and permanent source of wealth." Moreover, he held that a society that relied on foreign trade was built upon the most uncertain of foundations, for monopolies of capital and machinery, profitable while they lasted, could only be temporary. Foreign competition would soon doom them. Not only would commercial prosperity be short-lived, but it was also exploitative, belonging "a little to that worst feature of the commercial system, the rising by the depression of others."[21] Whereas the mainstream of classical economists delighted in the accumulation of capital, on which, they maintained, the expansion of trade depended, Malthus saw only the harmful effects of an oversupply of capital, which he believed would bring about falling prices and profits and a decline in the effective demand for goods. Rejecting Say's Law and reviving the arguments made by the physiocrats, Malthus warned that an industrial Britain faced gluts of population, of goods, and of capital. Only a balanced union of the agricultural and commercial systems, he argued, could insure national prosperity.[22]

In 1817, Malthus appeared, briefly, to have found another solution to the dilemma faced by a commercial society. Colonies might provide an answer to the decline in the rate of profit caused by the competition of a redundant capital. A country with colonial possessions had "a large *arena* for the employment of an increasing capital"; indeed, such a country could rely on its imperial provinces to supply it with food, which it could not do in the case of a foreign country. Malthus even speculated that the agricultural resources of the British empire might support three times Britain's population at the time.[23] In 1824, Malthus saw the difficulty of a commercial system not in the absolute amount of capital it generated but in the "relative difficulty of finding *profitable* employment for it" in a "limited territory."[24]

Malthus's disciple Thomas Chalmers's first contribution to economic thinking was in 1808, in a tract where he identified himself with the physiocrats as well as with Malthus. For him as for the French economists, foreign trade and manufacturers were nonessential. Only agriculture was genuinely productive.[25] In his *Political Economy* (1832), he supported the cause of the landed interest in all its aspects. Chalmers approved of primogeniture and condemned an electoral system that gave too large a voice to what ought to be a "subordinate and subservient" commercial middle class. The overaccumulation of capital was the chief flaw in a commercial society, he asserted, as had Malthus, and he urged expenditure (rather than the frugality advocated by Smith, Ricardo, and the mainstream economists) to avoid a fall in the rate of profit. Great Britain was capital-saturated, a condition to which older countries were particularly prone, and overinvestment and underspending caused gluts. Only in a new country where agriculture was expanding, as in the United States, might profits be high, for the "exuberance of capital may overflow" onto its uncultivated lands and "find profitable investment for generations to come."[26]

Though David Ricardo, a wealthy stockbroker who turned his attention to political economy and whose *Principles of Political Economy* of 1817 became the leading work of the classical mainstream, was a proponent of both the law of comparative advantage and Say's Law, his view of the commercial and industrial system was hardly one of naive optimism. We have already noted his pessimistic iron law of wages. In addition, his view of the division of the revenues of the new society implied a class struggle among capitalists, workers, and landlords. While Malthus explained declining profits as largely the result of the accumulation of capital and the lack of effective demand, Ricardo believed the inability of the land to support an increasing population to be a prime cause of such a decline.[27] In a tract of 1818, Ricardo observed that with the rise in corn prices, and therefore of wages, would come a fall in profits. When a country had brought its farming to its "highest state of cultivation, when more labour employed upon it will not yield in return more food than what is necessary to support the labourer so employed, that country is come to the limit of its increase both of capital and population." The operation of this law of diminishing returns from agriculture would bring about a crisis.[28] Britain, however, was far removed from such an eventuality, for the solution was immediately at hand. By establishing free trade, Ricardo argued, Britain might exchange its manufactured goods for food and raw materials produced abroad. It must become "a great manufacturing country"—what a future generation would call the workshop of the world.[29]

We have mentioned Robert Torrens as one of the formulators of the law of comparative advantage; he was also, like Ricardo, an opponent of the protectionist Corn Laws. Yet his economics sometimes appeared to owe more to mercantilism than to the mainstream of classicism. Though, in an 1808 tract, he opposed the granting of exclusive trading privileges to particular companies or ports, he favored making the metropolis the sole entrepôt for trade between the colonies and foreign countries and giving a monopoly of colonial markets to British manufactures. Unlike the mercantilists, however, who were prepared to grant a reciprocal advantage to colonial goods in the market of the mother country, he objected to the preferential treatment of Canadian over Norwegian timber, where British interests were "blindly sacrificed," making Great Britain a "tributary to her own colonies."[30]

In 1815, Torrens based his support of free trade in corn on the need to provide the resources for foreign exporters of corn to buy British manufactures. Torrens, indeed, amended Say's Law and argued that if Great Britain turned to a world market for its food, it could avoid glut by creating in foreign markets "an additional demand for the equivalents" (i.e., the British manufactures) "which purchased it." In such circumstances, commercial and industrial progress and prosperity had no real limits. A nation determined to supply all the needs of its home markets, on the other hand, would deprive itself of the benefits of foreign divisions of labor and would necessarily remain a largely agricultural state, stationary rather than progressive in character. Its high food costs, making necessary high wages, would enable foreign competitors to undersell it. However, a turning to overseas suppliers for cheap food would make Britain not only the "granary of Europe" but also "the emporium of the world." It might thus have a trade empire like those established in the past by Tyre, Athens, Carthage, Venice, and Holland.[31]

The utilitarian philosopher Jeremy Bentham is regarded as one of the fathers, along with his disciple James Mill, of what became known as Ricardian orthodoxy.[32] As early as 1790, Bentham set down one of the chief creeds of the classical economists: the anticolonial dictum that the trade of every nation was limited by the quantity of capital, not by the extent of the market. A liberal, Bentham also condemned the Navigation Acts, which even Smith had accepted as necessary since, in Smith's words, "defence is more important than opulence."[33] Three years later, in 1793, Bentham pointed to the prosperous trade with the United States as proving that it was not necessary to govern a people in order to enjoy a profitable exchange with them, and he denounced colonial monopolies as failing to allocate capital in the most productive manner. He repeated his earlier view: without an increase of capital "all the power on earth cannot give you more trade," and if a nation possessed capital, "all the power on earth cannot prevent your having the trade you have."[34] Colonies constituted a loss to the people, he observed in an unpublished work of 1818 entitled "Rid Yourselves of Ultramaria," though they undoubtedly were to the advantage of the "sinister interest" of the "ruling few."[35] On the whole, Bentham saw Britain free of its colonial burden and increasing in its wealth in decidedly optimistic terms.

But pessimistic strains were also present in his writings and would seem in the end to have proved decisive. In a manuscript dated 1801, Bentham attacked what would become the orthodox view of capital and investment: he insisted that expenditure, not savings, as Turgot and Smith had urged (and as Bentham had agreed some years earlier), was necessary if the economy were to operate successfully.[36] In another tract of 1801, Bentham wrote of colonies as a necessary "relief" for the "efflux of hands and mouths," and the "efflux of capital."[37] In 1804, he declared that the pressure of population on land in Britain would have resulted in "a severe sense of general poverty and distress," had it not been for past colonization.[38] When in 1811 he even wished to publish a repudiation of the principle of Say's Law, James Mill and Ricardo succeeded in discouraging him.[39]

James Mill remained orthodox in his devotion to Say's Law, but in 1820, in an article for the *Encyclopaedia Britannica*, he would nonetheless write approvingly of colonization as useful if not essential to Britain. While, as a good Radical, he decried colonies as the "grand source of wars" and as the provider of jobs and of sinecures for the

The Liberal Ideal and the Demons of Empire

aristocracy and wealthy mercantile classes—Bentham's "sinister interests"—Mill nonetheless criticized Smith's view of the relative unproductiveness of foreign and colonial trade when compared to a home trade. He believed that the overseas trade, and the carrying trade with which it was associated, were prime producers of net revenue. Mill presented colonization as the means of overcoming both the pressure of population on the land and the declining returns from agriculture, forces that would undermine civilization in advanced countries like Britain and produce "reduced wages, and a poor and starving people" unless colonists went overseas to cultivate fresh lands "yielding a greater return to their labour." If the cost of colonization was too great, of course, he concluded on a more orthodox note, the home population might suffer "more by the loss of [essential] capital" than it gained by "the diminution of numbers."[40]

We see that even such orthodox stalwarts as Bentham, James Mill, and Ricardo himself were pessimistic on the questions of population pressure and the declining returns from agriculture and that they saw the advantages of colonization. But they did not think expansion a pressing *necessity* to the existence of the new system. By the 1830s, Edward Gibbon Wakefield, a young economist in the Benthamite circle, was to preach that Britain immediately *required* both lands to settle a redundant population and overseas markets for surplus production and investment sites for superabundant capital. By establishing an informal trade empire that would include agrarian states overseas, as Torrens had urged, as well as by planting colonies, as Malthus and James Mill suggested, Great Britain might overcome the destructive contradictions inherent in the new commercial and industrial system and avoid a disastrous social revolution.

E. G. Wakefield

Wakefield was born in London in 1796, the son of a Pall Mall land agent who had written a highly regarded survey of Ireland and was an intimate of James Mill and other Benthamites. Always a rebel, he had by a strategem enticed an heiress into a Gretna Green marriage in 1826 and was sentenced to three years in Newgate Prison. During his imprisonment, he began a study of colonial affairs, seizing upon the principle of "systematic colonization" that he set forth in *A Letter from Sydney* in 1829.[41]

Previous efforts at colonization had failed, Wakefield suggested, because the man with capital to invest in colonial lands had been unable to hire laborers. The migrant had found it all too simple to obtain land free or at such a low price that he could set himself up as a proprietor almost immediately. But the most productive farming required the proper combination of capital and labor, and capital would not migrate unless assured of an adequate supply of labor. The answer for Wakefield was the setting of a "sufficient price" upon colonial lands so that the working-class migrant could not obtain land until he had served for some years as a laborer. The alternative to such a system, Wakefield stressed, was the slavery that was to be found in virtually all successful colonies producing exportable crops. Through such "systematic colonization," furthermore, one might have all the advantages of civilization which were products of the concentration of population (as opposed to the barbarous diffusion of, say, the American backwoods).[42] Marx devoted a chapter of *Capital* to demonstrating that the "bourgeois" Wakefield had in this theory inadvertently revealed the truth about the dependence of capitalism upon the exploitation of labor.[43] Of course, a sufficient price and the concentration of population would also mean that the organizers of the colony (to whom Wakefield expected the government to grant land) would gain considerably through the rise in real estate values and the sale of the land. Contemporaries criticized Wakefield as a land speculator, and a part of the Wakefield correspondence lends credence to this charge.[44]

Systematic colonization was only a corollary of what might be called Wakefield's "general theory" of empire, a theory rooted in his dismissal of Say's Law. Wakefield saw industrial Britain as chronically beset by the possession of more capital than it could profitably employ. The resulting competition among capitalists tended to drive down the rate of profit and was the cause of crisis, business failure, and widespread misery. During the Napoleonic Wars this "superabundance of capital" had been wasted and, consequently, the rate of profit had not been depressed; with peace, however, the more rapid accumulation of capital caused difficulties. Wakefield, in the manner of the Malthusian school, urged "expenditures" on the part of capitalists, instead of "investitures in trade." More particularly, he urged, as the method of absorbing the surplus of capital and the excess of production to which it gave rise, the expansion of the field of production and employment.[45]

The vital question, Wakefield explained, was "the proportion which population and capital bear to the land, or what may be termed, the field of employment" (or field of production) "for capital and labour." Production was limited not only by capital, as the orthodox insisted, but also by this field of production. Where, as in the United States, capital bore a large proportion to labor and a small proportion to land, wages and profits were both high. Where capital bore a small proportion to labor and a great proportion to the land, the result was, as in Britain and other advanced, densely populated commercial societies, both low wages and low profits. A remedy existed. An advanced commercial system that had outgrown its field of employment required new lands for its population and new fields in which to invest its rapidly accumulating capital—required, in short, an empire. Despite an increase of national wealth, "the state of capitalists and labourers may grow worse, provided that the field of production be not extended at the same rate with the increase of people and capital." An inadequate field of production had been the source of Britain's distress in the years between 1815 and 1830.[46]

In *England and America* (1833), Wakefield offered a program that would permit, and even encourage, a considerable increase of people and capital through the formation of colonies. In addition, he advocated the repeal of the Corn Laws to assure Great Britain of an informal trade empire as well as a formal colonial one. Repeal would make possible a permanent division of employment between Britain and America: "Americans would raise cheaper corn than has ever been raised; and, no longer wanting a tariff, might drive with the manufacturers of England the greatest trade ever known in the world." American agriculture would also prove a most useful opportunity for the investment of superabundant British capital.[47]

Wakefield's *England and America* anticipated portions of Marxist and neo-Marxist analyses. Wakefield observed that Great Britain possessed a more numerous working class than any other country, a working class "whose only property is their labour" and which was compelled to sell this in a market "overstocked with labour." Consequently, they earned "the minimum of wages" that "will barely supply the labourer with necessaries." This class, composing "the bulk," "the vast majority of the people," lived in a state of misery as "white slaves," and "if the English had been a martial people," the workers "would either have destroyed the classes whom they considered their oppressors or have perished in a servile war." In addition to the capitalist and the worker, there was what Wakefield called "the middle or uneasy class," consisting of "three-fourths, or rather perhaps nine-tenths of all who engaged in trades and professions," as well as the many smaller capitalists. All the professions, all the trades were overcrowded, and this middle class was especially hard pressed by the low rate of profit, which brought them to "ruin, or, at least the constant dread of ruin," and the haunting fear of submersion into the working class.[48]

Yet, Wakefield argued, though such painful and inequitable conditions were highly dangerous, they were necessary. Britain owed its riches to its inequitable economic organization, for if "the capital of the society was equally divided among all, it would be impossible to undertake any of those works which require the employment of many hands and a fixed capital." This gross inequality made social revolution an ever present peril. However, the structure of the nation's economic system was extremely delicate, so much depended "upon confidence and credit," that all would be lost in case of class violence. Democracy, consequently, would soon have to be granted; if it were granted immediately, however, the working-class majority would opt for "a revolution of property" disastrous to production. The solution to the dilemma was fortunately at hand. Parliament would have to act "to raise wages" by extending the field for the employment of British capital and laborers—that is, by establishing a trade empire and colonies.[49]

"The whole world is before you," Wakefield declared, in the accents adopted earlier by Torrens. "Open new channels for the most productive employment of English capital. Let the English buy bread from every people that has bread to sell cheap. Make England, for all that is produced by steam, the workshop of the world. If, after this, there be capital and people to spare, imitate the ancient Greeks; take a lesson from the Americans, who as their capital and population increase, find room for both by means of colonization." Only in this way could Britain resolve the contradictions of its economy and "escape from that corrupting and irritating state of political economy, which seems fit to precede the dissolution of empires!"[50] Dwelling upon questions of distribution made for "bad blood between the two classes," when by concentrating on production "we may prove that masters and servants have one and the same interest." Through a system of colonies, both formal and informal, capitalist and worker could prosper together.[51]

Wakefield's general theory became a part of the program of the leading Benthamite Radicals, who separated on the issue of colonization from their Cobdenite Radical allies. Wakefield converted Jeremy Bentham himself; Bentham's views on these questions were, to say the least, somewhat ambiguous, and he offered a fertile subject for conversion.[52] Earl Grey, the Whig-Liberal colonial secretary during the 1830s, defended Wakefield's ideas, as did the best known of the colonial reformers, Sir William Molesworth and Charles Buller, the formulators and advocates, along with Wakefield himself, of the celebrated Durham Report, which established the foundations for Canadian self-rule.

Molesworth served as the chief spokesman for Wakefield's views in the House of Commons. The Wakefieldian cadences of his speeches for repeal of the Corn Laws contrasted sharply with the free-trade optimism of Cobden. "There is a tendency in labour and capital to augment more rapidly than the means of employing them," Molesworth declared in 1837, and this produced "hurtful competition" that brought distress. "Labour and capital are superabundant compared to land," and "consequently both wages and profits are low."[53] In 1838, Molesworth depicted the ruin of "smaller capitalists" as a result of competition and the "general fall of profits," and he noted the fears of these ruined capitalists that they would be "absorbed in the labouring class." Soon the nation would "consist only of two classes— labourers and the possessors of immense capitals." The result might be social revolution. The solution for Molesworth, as for Wakefield, was "to augment . . . the field of employment," through colonization and repeal of the Corn Laws.[54] One point emerges clearly: much of what has been regarded as characteristically Marxist analysis was already common currency among certain Radicals over a decade before Marx came to England.

In Parliament in 1849, in the course of acknowledging his own debt to Wakefield, Molesworth observed that Wakefield had "produced a profound impression on the minds of some of the ablest men of our day, as for instance, John Mill."[55] In his *Principles of Political Economy* in 1848, John Stuart Mill, the son of James and the best known and most highly regarded of the British classical school during the middle decades of the nineteenth century, paid a generous tribute to Wakefield and his ideas.[56] Mill agreed with Wakefield that "colonization, in the present state of the world, is the best affair of business, in which the capital of an old and wealthy country can engage." In advanced countries, he observed (largely following Wakefield's analysis), not capital but fertile land was deficient, and the legislator ought not to promote "greater aggregate saving, but a greater return to savings . . . by access to the produce of more fertile land in other parts of the globe." In more specific terms, Mill argued that if one-tenth of Britain's workers and capital were "transferred to the colonies," wages and profits would benefit from "the diminished pressure of capital and population upon the fertility of the land." Noting that a glut of capital in Britain was pushing profits to the minimum, he asserted that one of "the counter-forces which check the downward tendency of profits" was "the perpetual overflow of capital" into colonies or foreign countries. This had "been for many years one of the principal causes by which the decline of profits in England has been arrested." Indeed, capital export for Mill was a precondition to the healthy functioning of advanced economies: "As long as there are old countries where capital increases very rapidly, and new countries where profit is still high, profits in the old countries will not sink to the rate which would put a stop to accumulation." "The exportation of capital" was "an agent of great efficacy in extending the field of employment" for the capital that remained at home and would help to put off the advent of what the classical economists called the "stationary state."[57]

For Wakefield and those who agreed with his analysis and his remedy, the old system of mercantilist restrictions was buried. By means of a universal free trade, they wished to preserve Britain's position as the workshop of the world, to maintain that trade empire which, as we shall see, the German protectionist Friedrich List and his American counterpart Henry Carey charged was designed to make the entire globe subservient to Great Britain. Britain, content with its technological superiority and immense productive capacities, wanted free access to the markets of the world and new fields for the investment of its surplus capital. It was no longer necessary to impose a rigid colonialism upon undeveloped areas, as it had been during the mercantile wars of the seventeenth and eighteenth centuries.

Still, the Wakefield party believed Britain needed a formal empire. Colonies would provide investment and market conditions of special safety. Wakefield's followers urged that such colonies of settlement as Canada, Australia, and New Zealand be given responsible government; they believed these colonies were tied securely by sentiment and economic necessity to a free-trading imperial metropolis that alone—along the lines of Tucker's model—could provide manufactured goods for their agricultural exports and offer them necessary credit facilities. Another convert to Wakefield's program, however, J. A. Roebuck, wished to prohibit the colonies from erecting tariffs against Britain;[58] and the economist Robert Torrens, who had in some matters anticipated Wakefield's argument, proclaimed, some sixty years before it became Tory policy, the necessity of an empirewide customs union, an imperial Zollverein.[59]

In his *Principles* (probably with continental and American mercantilist, national economists in mind), J. S. Mill sanguinely dismissed the view, widely accepted abroad, that Britain's welfare depended upon the continual acquisition of new markets for its manufactures. This was "a surviving relic of the Mercantile Theory," he declared. If for any reason Britain's foreign commerce failed, the capital and labor supplying overseas markets would be profitably employed (albeit with some loss to the consumer) in the home market.[60] Mill's thoroughly orthodox conclusion, based on Say's Law, suited the new optimistic mood of the late 1850s and 1860s. With the coming of the 1850s, for a combination of reasons (among them the 1846 repeal of the Corn Laws and the expansion of the currency after the discovery of new gold supplies in California in 1849), conditions improved and the memories of the hard times of the previous three decades faded. British politicians and writers on economic questions entertained the hope and expectation of an international free trade and international division of labor in which Britain enjoyed an economic advantage. The earlier problems of the industrial system that had threatened a return to a bellicose mercantilism were no longer pressing.

For Mill, and for his disciple the Irish economist J. E. Cairnes, there was another economic model that made aggressive expansion necessary. In the early 1860s, both Cairnes and Mill perceived in the slave society of the cotton-growing South an agricultural system doomed either to expand or to die. It had been brought to such a pass not only by its distorted economics but because of the social drives of a planter class attempting to reproduce all the abominations of a feudal, seigneurial society. But was it the slave system that led to Southern aggression, as Cairnes argued, or a defect in the liberal international economy being erected under British auspices?

Cairnes, Mill, and an Expansionist South

In the early months of the American Civil War, the professor of political economy at Trinity College, Dublin, J. E. Cairnes, joined a variation of the liberal-sociological view of war and expansion with pessimistic economic analysis in a book titled *The Slave Power*.[61] The Irish economist described what might be called, in twentieth-century terminology, a quasi-totalitarian agricultural system, based on slavery and under the control of a decadent landed aristocracy. It was a society that, if it were to survive, would be compelled to go onto a path of continuous aggression. Cairnes's subject was, of course, the slave-owning, plantation South of the Confederacy, an important sector of Britain's free-trade empire; indeed, it had been Southern influence in the Congress that kept American tariffs within reasonable bounds, permitting easier entrance of British manufactures in exchange for Southern cotton and Western wheat. Mill was impressed by Cairnes's analysis, parts of which he would adopt as his own.

Though Cairnes and Mill brought this theory of expansion to fullest development, it was the American writer Frederick Law Olmsted who had prepared the way.[62] In the 1850s, Olmsted, a New York farmer, traveler, and, in his later years, a prominent landscape architect among whose accomplishments would be New York's Central Park, distilled what was a common Northern view, at least since the 1846 war with Mexico. Many antislavery writers believed that the Mexican war had been brought about by the need for fresh lands of a cotton culture that rapidly exhausted the soil, as well as the Southern interest in new

---

slave states to maintain that region's influence in the Senate. When the war between North and South began in 1861, Olmsted published an abridgement of his earlier books describing travels through the South, *The Cotton Kingdom*; this compendium included a dedication to John Stuart Mill. Olmsted's principal purpose in abridging his earlier works was to persuade Britain, badly in need of cotton for its Manchester mills, to refuse assistance to the Confederacy.[63] At this time, we must note, a sizable segment of British opinion sympathized with Southern aspirations for national self-determination as well as with the South's devotion to free trade.

In this as in earlier volumes in 1856 and 1857, Olmsted described two villains, slavery and the Southern plantation aristocracy, and denounced the system of aggressive expansion to which the combination inexorably led.[64] Olmsted compared the Southern planters to the untamed British aristocrats of the days before the Reform Bill of 1832.[65] Plantation owners defended an immoral and economically inefficient system because it gave them "the power of exercising authority" over "a subject class," without submission to the "insolence of a laborer"; it gave "position and status," which Southerners prized "more than other wealth." It was as "fashionable" for Southerners to own slaves as it was for Englishmen to own land.[66] The Southern slaveowners wished to expand their holdings. The wealthier sugar planters of Louisiana, for example, moved by "a romantic excitement and enthusiasm" and "inflamed by senseless appeals to their patriotism and their combativeness," were interested in annexing Cuba so that they might secure larger estates and make use of their "greater skill," "better machinery," and "much cheaper [Cuban] land and labor." For similar reasons, Southerners supported annexations in Mexico and Central America and hoped to employ the United States army for their purpose, much as they had during the Mexican war.[67]

It was more than a romantic combativeness that led Southerners along the road to aggression. Expansion was necessary, Olmsted wrote, because both tobacco culture and cotton growing, as practised in the South, exhausted the soil.[68] Ten years of slave cultivation, he argued, took more of the natural elements out of the soil than two hundred years of free cultivation. Olmsted was vague in his explanation of this claim.

Olmsted took his indictment a step further. The slaveholding system, he declared, always threatened by insurrection, required a repressive regime, a government that must suppress all civil and political liberty.[69] If the Confederacy were permitted its independence, he warned his British audience, freedom would be submerged throughout the American continent.[70] A slave insurrection was inevitable in those circumstances; no level of expansion could prevent it. Great Britain should take note that the dislocation caused by such an insurrection would interfere with Manchester textile manufacture even more gravely than did the war in progress.[71]

In *The Slave Power*, in 1862, Cairnes, more precisely than Olmsted, linked slave cultivation to exhaustion of the soil and hence to Southern expansionism. Exhaustion of the soil for Cairnes was a necessary consequence of the "unskilfulness and want of versatility" of slave labor. Slaves could not be trusted with the more elaborate techniques needed to work inferior soils. A proper rotation of crops, which might replenish the fertility of the soil, was therefore impossible. A retrograde agricultural system, he argued, obliged the planter to seek fresh lands without which he could not employ the capital invested in slaves.[72] Slaveholders were like barbaric herdsmen ever driving their flocks to fresh pastures; the system was constantly driven "by exigencies, which it cannot control, to extend its territory, and by an ambition not less inevitable to augment its power." Cairnes's analysis was plausible, but like Olmsted he did not explain why free farmers of the United States appeared to follow a similar pattern of seeking fresh lands.[73]

Extending the sociological aspects of Olmsted's argument, Cairnes observed that it was not only for economic reasons that slavery was valued: it was also because the system upheld a society in which slaveholders were "the sole depositaries of social prestige and political power." Indeed, the slaveholder was "moulded to an intense craving for power." The relationship between master and slave had corrupted the character of the master class just as that between lord and serf had corrupted the feudal classes of medieval Europe.[74] The Southerner eulogized slavery and recommended its universal adoption; the permanent subordination of the Negro to the superior white race was regarded as a biological and a moral truth. The entire South had lived under a virtual "reign of terror" directed at anyone who might be suspected of not believing slavery the most admirable of institutions.[75] Slavery had become "a social passion" not merely of the slaveholding class but of the entire Southern white population, a population that included four million "mean whites" who were "too poor to keep slaves and too proud to work." This was a "degraded and dangerous" class necessary to the slave power, which might employ them to repress slave insurrections, since they hated the Negro, and to man "filibustering expeditions" such as those that had terrorized Kansas in the 1850s.[76] Cairnes noted that the Southern slaveholders had allies in the merchants and financiers of the seaboard towns of the Northeast, the very classes that had formerly carried on the slave trade, and now used their capital to carry on slave agriculture.[77] This part of the old mercantile system clearly survived.

The South's desire to create slave states to increase its representation in the Senate had produced a Southern "career of aggression" beyond the region's "mere industrial necessities." Since the annexation of Texas in 1847, the South had had more territory than slaves with which to cultivate it; this, indeed, generated a movement in the late 1850s to reopen the slave trade.[78] Men who had for decades possessed "paramount influence" in North America were now "meditating plans of annexation and conquest." Spurred by political ambition and by the need for fresh lands, an "absolute necessity," the South might well create "a great slaveholding confederacy" that would include "the whole tropical region of the New World."[79]

In the fall of 1862, Cairnes delivered an address entitled "The Revolution in America" in which he asserted that despite the insistence of the federal government that its aim was solely the preservation of the union, slavery was both the cause and the leading issue of the struggle. Noting the Seminole War, the annexation of Texas, the war with Mexico, the filibustering attempts on Cuba and Central America, he described the previous half-century of American history as one of Southern aggression. The Southern party since 1820 had had for "its leading idea, its paramount aim, almost its single purpose . . . to extend slavery, and to achieve power by extending it." The South had risen in revolt in 1861 because it understood that unless slavery could be extended to fresh soils, it must perish.[80] "I am convinced," Cairnes concluded, "that the slave system in America is the greatest curse which has yet darkened the earth, and I believe that the blow which effectually breaks it up must be a blessing."[81]

In early August 1861, Cairnes sent proofs of *The Slave Power* to John Stuart Mill, already an admirer of Cairnes's earlier work on political economy. Cairnes "powerfully" demonstrated, Mill wrote him after reading the proofs, that American slavery depended on "a perpetual extension of its field" and in consequence "must go on barbarizing the world more and more." When English journals called for recognition of the Confederacy and "for letting slavery alone," they did not understand that "slavery will not let freedom alone." It might be necessary to raise "a crusade of all civilized humanity" to crush the slave power.[82] A few months later, when Cairnes's book was ready for publication, its author asked permission of Mill to quote his letter in the volume. Mill now hesitated at calling for a crusade, for which he believed a wider public needed more preparation. On this occasion Mill was content to warn his fellow countrymen that a community that wished to spread "this scourge [of slavery] through the whole of the American continent" was not "a society just like any other." It constituted a serious danger to world peace and had to be "crushed in its commencement, before it has made itself such a pest to the world as to require and justify a general crusade of civilized nations for its suppression."[83]

In November 1862, Mill wrote an article, "The Contest in America," in an effort to counter the Southern sympathies of much of the British press. In this piece he presented a theory of the expansionism of the slave system which resembled that of Cairnes but featured an interesting amendment. For Mill, it was cotton cultivation in particular (and not the ineffectiveness of slave labor) that exhausted the soil, making it always necessary to find fresh fields to cultivate. After making this brief qualification, he nonetheless followed Cairnes in denouncing slavery and not cotton culture as the cause of Southern expansionism. After having exhausted the soil of the United States, Mill warned, slavery, if it were to survive, would be compelled to invade Spanish America. If the South succeeded in maintaining its independence, and took possession of half the federal territories, as it hoped to, Europe would be faced with a new power, men who "set themselves up, in defiance of the rest of the world, to do the devil's work." They were "enemies of mankind"—demons of empire that threatened the liberal ideal. Such a Confederacy would profess "the principles of Atilla and Genghis Khan as the foundation of its Constitution," and would let its victorious armies loose "to propagate their national faith at the rifle's mouth" in Mexico, Central America, Cuba, Puerto Rico, Haiti, and Liberia. In five years' time, Mill predicted, Britain would be at war with the Confederacy to put down a revival of the African slave trade.[84]

One may speculate that Mill, at this time when Great Britain was hesitating as to the role it should take in the American Civil War, was unwilling to dampen the efforts of Olmsted and Cairnes to depict slavery as the grand spur of Southern expansionism. Consequently, he somewhat blurred the lines of his economic analysis to further what he believed a moral struggle against slavery. Thus Mill appeared to accept the major thrust of the Olmsted-Cairnes economic thesis on the predominant role of slavery in Southern aggression. However, he clearly saw the exhaustion of the soil by cotton growing as a more substantial cause. (Both his father and Ricardo some decades earlier had written of the declining returns from agriculture as a chief reason for colonization.)

Beneath the surface of this evasion may have been Mill's recognition of the role the international division of labor played in perpetuating slavery. Even under a free-labor system, the two Southern monocultures (tobacco and cotton) would exhaust the soil without a proper rotation of crops. The South's role as Britain's chief (almost exclusive) supplier of cotton, one may argue, obliged the planters to overwork their acres and move on to fresh ones if they were to retain their privileged place in the free-trading economy of Britain's vision. When the Civil War cut off American cotton supplies, Britain turned to India and Egypt for its cotton and also tried to encourage cotton growing in other semitropical regions.

Of course, both Mill and Cairnes attacked the Southern landed class and restated the sociological theory condemning the militant, feudal ethos. The development of this school of analysis, from the eighteenth century onward, accompanied the more strictly economic case against mercantilism—sometimes explicitly, more often implicitly. The Southern planting class was an anomaly by the middle decades of the nineteenth century, an artificial aping (following the chivalric ideals in Scott's Waverley novels) of an outmoded class of British landed gentry. But though defeated after the 1846 repeal of the Corn Laws, even in comparatively advanced societies like Britain the landed order possessed considerable influence. In the more backward nations of the Continent the aristocratic and landed classes were even more powerful.

3 Liberal Social Theory and the Persistence

of the Feudal Ethos

Feudalism had largely disappeared from Western European life by the end of the eighteenth century. The French Revolution saw itself as waging battle against feudalism, but despite certain vestiges, the medieval system was already dead, for the landed nobility had long since yielded its authority to the monarch and the royal bureaucracy. The Revolution called a halt to such aristocratic perquisites as a relative freedom from taxation, and the armies of the Republic and of Napoleon did what they could to end both the forms and the realities of the seigneurial system (with varied success) wherever they established French authority.

With the defeat of Napoleon, the fortunes of the traditional landowning classes revived. In most of Europe, many of the older institutional forms maintained their vigor. Despite the abolition of serfdom and of feudal devices, the Revolution and capitalism had (outside France) failed to make important changes in land ownership or to alter the social structure of the countryside. In a victorious Britain the political and economic influence of the landed gentry and the aristocracy in both houses of Parliament remained considerable, and their social standing untarnished, but the new industrial society was bringing the middle classes into greater prominence. The formulators of classical political economy, drawing on the Ricardian theory of rent, saw the landed class as parasitically profiting from the success of the commercial and industrial order. Members of the House of Lords and their close relatives continued to dominate British cabinets even during the last third of the century—at a time when the working classes formed a majority of those eligible to vote. On parts of the Continent, the landed classes retained an even more pronounced political role than in Great Britain.

The quasi-feudal landed society possessed a stable ideology and a social prestige that the bourgeois could not claim and which he envied and admired. The scions of the landed classes, whether of feudal or more recent origin, maintained an allegiance to the traditional values of the old order, to loyalty, courage, honor, qualities characteristic of what liberal social theorists called a "militant society." The qualities of an "industrial society," those of rationality, industry, and frugality, were directed to peace, while those of a militant society, founded on passion, turned to conquest. This was the steady refrain of liberal theorists and Radical politicians. (Wars would, of course, produce places in the services and, in many cases, in the colonies for the younger sons of the gentry and aristocracy, as Radicals rarely failed to add.)

The liberal social theorists, while not entirely ceasing to dread their demons—the return of the landed classes to their former authority, and, with this, the revival of the feudal ethos—proclaimed the coming of a new stage in the history of the world. There would be a complete transformation of the values that had dominated the affairs of men for millennia. A peace-loving industrial bourgeoisie, the product of merit, not birth, would replace a bellicose landed order as the governing class. A new era in the history of humanity was dawning. Reason would put the passions under control, and men would at last follow their true interests, which were those of peace. Liberal social theory was not merely "scientific" analysis but a battle cry and a warning to the men of the old regime that Historical Providence had already pronounced its irrevocable doom against them.

In the first two-thirds of the nineteenth century, liberal social theorists were most confident of the ultimate victory of the industrial ethos. This was the period during which Saint-Simon, Comte, Buckle, and Lecky presented their optimistic analyses. The Cobdenites, less sanguinely, persisted in their old fears.

Henri Saint-Simon

Comte Henri de Saint-Simon, born in Paris in 1760, was the scion of a noble family that traced its descent from Charlemagne. As a young man, he had fought with the French forces supporting Washington's army at Yorktown, and during the French Revolution he accumulated a fortune by successful speculation in national lands. His aristocratic background, however, made him an inevitable target of the Jacobins, and he soon found himself dependent on the financial support of a former servant. From the turn of the century until his death in 1825, Saint-Simon was a writer on social and political questions and made repeated, and largely unsuccessful, efforts to attract attention to his plans for a society that he called, coining a new word, one of *industrialisme*.[1]

The term *industriel,* as Saint-Simon and other social theorists would employ it, meant the pacific ethos and activities of the new commercial society, that of the merchants and men of the professional classes as well as of the later factory owners, as opposed to the militant spirit and aggressive behavior of the earlier, quasi-feudal landed society. (A French historian would note a quasi-apostolic transmission of the term among succeeding generations of social theorists from Saint-Simon to Comte, from Comte to Buckle, and from Buckle to Herbert Spencer "who gave it world-wide popularity."[2]) Although usually seen as a "utopian socialist" and a predecessor of Marx, Saint-Simon was the prophet of a community ruled by an elite of capitalists, primarily bankers, and intellectuals, largely scientists and engineers. (The Pereires, later to found the Crédit Mobilier, were disciples of Saint-Simon, as were other French bankers such as the Eichthals; the engineer Ferdinand de Lesseps, who would supervise the building of the Suez Canal, was also a Saint-Simonian.[3])

For Saint-Simon, as it would later be for Marx, history was the story of class struggles. To know the character of a society, Saint-Simon wrote, it was necessary to know the basic drives of its ruling class. Europe was still in a transitional period in history, one in which class status was largely determined by birth or wealth. This would not be the case in the future, when status would be determined by innate capacity or aptitude. Saint-Simon dismissed the first two estates of the *ancien régime,* the clergy and the nobility, as dying classes, *fainéants,* "idlers" who had outlived their usefulness. The soon-to-be-victorious *industriels* would institute a new regime founded on the industrial virtues, on commerce and peace.[4]

Saint-Simon was an eloquent defender of the new bourgeois era, whose most conspicuous accomplishment, he declared, would be the end of war. In his *L'Industrie,* in 1817, he described the system of "commercial government," the pacific, liberal, constitutional regime that the British had already established and which the French had instituted in 1789. The law by which France at this time had renounced offensive war was proof that the attainment of a pacific commercial society had been an essential goal of the Revolution.[5] In the past, "Kill or be killed" had been the guiding principle of politics; now the nations of Europe were more interested in advancing the well-being of their peoples. (This was at least true of countries like Britain, France, and the Netherlands, which enjoyed "commercial government.") War put property at risk, for it "impedes production, interrupts commerce, blocks trade routes," making it impossible for neighboring nations "to live up to their commitments." Similarly, for a people "whose goal is liberty, war is the greatest scourge," since "liberty like industry, in the modern world, cannot exist without peace." Saint-Simon insisted on the inherently peaceful nature of the new capitalism and contemptuously dismissed the colonialist policies of the mercantilist era. "Some statesmen still spoke of waging war to promote commerce," he wrote; but this would be a "contradiction in objectives," for only industry, not arms, could further trade and national welfare.[6]

Saint-Simon called for a Confederation of Europe to maintain the peace but warned that old prejudices and outmoded traditions would hamper such a proposal. In the "shadows" of contemporary politics, an irrational, premodern national hatred, "the memory of old hostilities, originating in long-forgotten causes," continued to play a venomous role.[7] There were, moreover, "vestiges" of a more recent past that would prove an immediate obstacle. The wars of the French revolutionary armies and those of the European peoples against Napoleonic despotism had had the unfortunate result of preserving the habits and ethos of a warrior society. The nations of Europe, even the most free, had persuaded themselves of the need for large military establishments. Such bellicose habits would be overcome in time, but for the moment they remained to plague a continent that wanted and needed peace. In the new bourgeois society of the future, these vestiges would expire because "industrious, wise, and free nations" would reject war and a militarism that would "destroy liberty and drain off wealth" and "arm them, like barbarians, with instruments of destruction."[8]

In writing about war in these terms, Saint-Simon was in agreement with other contemporary writers, most notably Benjamin Constant, the outstanding French liberal theorist of the time, who had become well known as an articulate opponent of Napoleon's authoritarian rule and as the long time companion of the prominent writer on political subjects Mme de Staël. In his *L'Esprit de conquête* (1815), Constant wrote that although for certain epochs in world history, for example, among "the warrior peoples of antiquity," war had possessed many virtues, circumstances had changed profoundly. A new era was at hand. "The tradition of war, a survival of past times," might for a time retard efforts toward peace but could not halt them. The ruling classes might still render "homage to military glory" but would now avoid "openly avowing a love of conquest." "We have arrived," he declared, "at the epoch of commerce, a time which must inevitably supplant the epoch of war, just as that of war had inevitably preceded it." Modern nations wanted the security and prosperity that only industry could provide. "Among moderns a victorious war costs much more than it brings in," he argued, therefore concluding that war had become a "grotesque and funereal anachronism."[9] Another French liberal publicist of the time, Charles Comte, wrote along similar lines.[10]

The best known of Saint-Simon's successors was his one-time secretary and collaborator, the positivist philosopher Auguste Comte (not related to Charles). Comte would become a prime authority for advanced liberals. His "liberalism," it should be stressed, consisted primarily in his praise of the bourgeoisie and of what he, like Saint-Simon and the Saint-Simonians before him, called *l'esprit industriel*. There is some question as to who originated the essential ideas of positivist philosophy. Saint-Simon's disciples gave full credit to their master, whereas those of Comte were equally insistent on the claim of the younger man. While churlish in acknowledging any substantial contribution by Saint-Simon, Comte undoubtedly put forward in their fullest and most systematic form the positivist concepts earlier outlined *in nuce* by Saint-Simon.

Auguste Comte

Auguste Comte was born in 1798 of royalist and fervently Catholic parents in Montpellier, and in 1814 he was admitted to Napoleon's newly created Ecole Polytechnique, to be dismissed two years later for having taken part in a student revolt. In 1818, he met and became the secretary of Henri Saint-Simon, who helped to make the young man a sociologist, convinced that social phenomena no less than physical phenomena were the products of scientific law. In a number of tracts that appeared in the 1820s under Saint-Simon's direction and in Saint-Simon's name, the young secretary had set down virtually all the elements of the system he was later to elaborate in the six volumes of the *Cours de philosophie positive*, published between 1830 and 1842, and the *Système de politique positive*, whose four volumes appeared between 1851 and 1854. In the former, Comte produced a work that was praised by men of intellect throughout Europe. (In England, his best-known admirer was John Stuart Mill.) His later work, the *Système*, with its authoritarian politics and elaboration of a Religion of Humanity, repelled liberals like Mill but attracted a group of devoted followers in Britain, France, Brazil, Mexico, Russia, and India.[11]

For Comte, mankind proceeded through three principal stages: the theological, the metaphysical, and the positive or scientific. These were primarily mental or psychological stages. In the theological stage, people perceived external reality entirely in personal and subjective terms that bore little relationship to the actual world; during this period, they moved from a fetishistic religion to a polytheistic and finally a monotheistic religion. If, in the theological stage, human beings were concerned with deities, in the metaphysical stage they were taken up with entities, that is, abstractions which they saw as real. The metaphysical, in Comte's view, was less an independent period of development than a transitional one marking the beginning of the breakdown of the theological epoch. The final stage was that of a scientific positivism. For some centuries positive science had been undermining both theological and metaphysical thinking, and positive thinking had by Comte's time come to dominate almost all the abstract sciences. In the second quarter of the nineteenth century, Comte founded the positive science of society, calling it by a name he himself coined, sociology.[12]

Comte associated the three stages of intellectual development with the changing roles played by the military and industrial classes. A military social structure, for example, corresponded to the theological system. In the early, fetishistic phase of the theological stage, a savage brutality was the rule and wars frequently ended with the wholesale slaughter and sometimes the eating of the enemy. Primitive men had by nature been reluctant to undertake regular labor, and this military regime established order and discipline, making it possible for the industrial spirit to gain a foothold.[13] War and slavery at this time had exercised a progressive role, and the enslavement of the producers by the warrior class constituted a primitive division of labor.[14] Conquests of smaller and weaker populations, moreover, had enlarged organized society and repressed the military spirit among the conquered. The survival of the military system depended upon the support of the theological spirit, which bestowed a religious authority on the monarchs, who were the military chieftains of warrior armies.[15]

Comte was more vague concerning the metaphysical ethos of the intermediate stage, when spiritual power was in the hands of philosophers and political power was wielded by lawyers. But he noted that Protestantism, the characteristic religion of this period, had entered the political arena as an antimilitary force and as a supporter of the habit of free inquiry and discussion; indeed, the Protestants had "legalized spiritual anarchy" and admitted the consciences of the oppressors to be their only restraint. By the seventeenth century, standing armies of mercenaries had supplanted feudal military forces. The monarchs, then, after having achieved full political power, were compelled to allow others—ministers like Richelieu, men usually quite inexperienced in military affairs—to wield authority. In this, Comte saw the beginning of the decline of the military regime. The last wars that might be attributable to a "feudal exuberance," he wrote, had been those of the first half of the sixteenth century.[16]

By the eighteenth century, when mercantilism was in flower, industrial activity was becoming more and more important, and the military was put into the service of industrial interests.[17] The former predominance of monarchical and aristocratic policy gave way to the more pacific interests of the great commercial cities of Europe. In Protestant Holland and England, as early as the seventeenth century, there had taken place a union between feudal and industrial interests, and either directly or indirectly the aristocracy participated in commercial enterprises; in Catholic countries, on the other hand, it was the crown that associated itself with industry. If the Protestant spirit gave an impetus to personal exertion, giving the initial advantage in development to Holland and England, this superiority was a transient one because of a Protestant lack of capacity for the kind of regulation and organization that had characterized Colbert's administration in the France of Louis XIV.

The new organization of industry in the eighteenth century, Comte continued, was most evident in the colonial system. Certainly, the interest in colonies reinvigorated both the military and the religious spirits and hence appeared to extend the military and theological regime. But colonization so greatly stimulated commerce and industry as to make its real influence the progressive one of speeding the triumph of the industrial spirit, even in areas that did not directly participate in colonial activity. Protestant and aristocratic colonization, the Dutch being the leading example, was marked by individual enterprise and greed, while Catholic and monarchical colonial activity had a more political than industrial character. Frequently, therefore, as in Spain, colonization had the retrogressive consequence of increasing the opportunities of the priests and aristocrats, while offering a field of activity for rebellious spirits who might otherwise subvert the domestic regime.[18]

In the seventeenth century, military superiority remained the chief national objective, Comte observed; by the eighteenth, industrial advantages were the prime goals, and the military forces were valued insofar as they could help in obtaining them and undermining foreign competition. The subordination of the military to the industrial spirit might be seen in the commercial wars of the eighteenth century, which Comte perceived as having had overall a progressive character. But Britain's commercial lead erected on the basis of the close association of the aristocracy and the commercial classes had extended the life of the military and theological system by incorporating it into the industrial system. For this reason, he argued, nineteenth-century Britain found itself trapped in what ought to have been the purely transitional phase of the metaphysical period. By encouraging greed and repressing sympathy, moreover, Britain risked a future retribution.[19]

Comte saw the expansion of the system of public credit as having given rise to the formation of considerable financial companies, and, like Saint-Simon and his followers, Comte believed the interests of the more powerful bankers made them the natural leaders of the industrial class throughout Europe. Following Saint-Simon, Comte saw bankers as the most perfect embodiment of *l'esprit industriel,* the spirit of association, of production, and of peace which was everywhere replacing the feudal "spirit of conquest." In Comte's positivist utopia, bankers would be the chief wielders of temporal power. Bankers, the elite of the new class of *industriels,* were cosmopolitan by disposition and interests, dedicated to maintaining the peace, and to joining all Europe in a single economic system. Only bankers could have assembled the capital for the building of railways, both the symbol and the actuality of a new industrial system. Since war was the chief threat to the industrial society, another Saint-Simonian, Michel Chevalier—who, as a minister of Napoleon III, would negotiate a treaty in 1860 to establish a freer trade between Britain and France—wrote in 1832 that he looked forward to the time when bankers would form their "holy alliance" and transform their economic power into political power, thus assuring a universal peace. (This was at a time, as we shall see, when French and German writers, both socialist and conservative, were damning bankers as Jewish and British predators; a recent scholar has noted that, unlike almost all the leading nineteenth-century ideologies, Saint-Simonianism and Comtism were free of anti-Semitism, and many Jews were among the followers of Saint-Simon.)[20]

The decline of the military classes was temporarily halted during the years following the French Revolution, Comte noted. When the French wars against the European monarchs moved from defense to offense, the military authority of France, formerly under civil control, acquired a new independence: the rise of Napoleon Bonaparte and his establishment of a military dictatorship gave the situation an even more retrogressive tendency. Napoleon, raised in a backward Corsica, was an admirer of the traditional hierarchical system. Such a man could imagine no system other than that of the military and theological regime. He had restored the institutions of nobility and clergy, and, imitating the former monarchs, he successfully appealed to national vanity. Frenchmen indulged in the childlike satisfaction of glorying in the expansion of French empire and were further seduced by the prospect of plunder. Comte blamed the French people, and especially the literary class, which had been particularly enthusiastic about imperial conquests, for not having resisted Bonaparte, more than he blamed the emperor himself, caught in the grip of military instinct.[21]

The lesson that Comte drew from the Napoleonic episode was that "a retrograde system" required "active and permanent warfare" if it were to survive.[22]

In the end, however, the revolutionary crisis utterly destroyed the military and theological regime. The citizen armies of the republic and the empire discredited the aristocratic, military caste. The trade wars of the eighteenth century were brought to a close and the old colonial system went into decline. In the future, only wars of principle were possible, and governments would be afraid to wage even these for fear of provoking revolution at home. With conscription, the armies of Europe had been transformed from professional forces into a mass of citizens who would take up arms only with reluctance and as a temporary obligation. The time had come, Comte observed, when Europeans might congratulate themselves on the end of "serious and durable warfare."[23]

Yet Comte believed that war had served a useful social function in past times. All of men's faculties had been stimulated and developed by a warfare that had habituated them to collective action and hence to social solidarity and discipline.[24] Industry, on the other hand, from its earliest days did not have the moral and social character of war. It was an individual or family affair and bore the taint of selfishness. "The substitution of Labour for Conquest seems to be only replacing violence by fraud," he concluded.[25] For this reason, among others, the Comtian utopia envisioned a spiritual elite of scientists and intellectuals to exercise a moral supervision over the temporal ruling class of bankers.

H. T. Buckle

One of the outstanding figures associated with positivist (though not Comtian) thinking in mid-Victorian England was H. T. Buckle. Born into a well-to-do Calvinist evangelical family in 1821, the historian is regarded as a pioneer of British sociology. Buckle's once famous *History of Civilization in England,* the first volume of which was published to great acclaim in London in 1857, was written in the eighteenth-century French historiographical tradition. The historian saw the past as a battle between the forces of obscurantist religion and ignorance on the one hand and of tolerance, reason, and science on the other, much in the manner of Voltaire's *Essai sur les moeurs.* Like Montesquieu, Buckle attempted to ground his history upon the basis of geographical determinism, stressing the influence of climate, food, and soil in historical causation; and he added to these the concept of the progressive movement of mankind through successive epochs of development found in Turgot, elaborated by Turgot's disciple the marquis de Condorcet in his celebrated *Esquisse,* and reinforced by Saint-Simon and Auguste Comte. Though the direct influence of Comte on Buckle's thought may not have been great, his *History* was seen by contemporaries as quasi-Comtian. It was very well regarded in liberal and positivist circles in Britain, and on the Continent.[26] Up until the war of 1914, Buckle's work enjoyed a considerable reputation as a contribution to both sociology and history: Bertrand Russell, writing of the books with which he had become familiar as a young man, thought only Mill's *Logic* and Buckle's *History* possessed "intellectual integrity,"[27] and George Bernard Shaw saw Buckle and Marx as the only nineteenth-century thinkers likely to be remembered.[28]

Buckle had no doubt that, with the progress of European society, war, which along with religious intolerance he regarded as the two greatest evils besetting humanity, was declining. Was this a consequence of the improvement of moral feelings? Not at all: For centuries people had not been under any illusions concerning the moral evils of war; political philosophers had long argued that only defensive wars were just. Buckle saw the increasing authority of the intellectual classes, in which he included the men of commerce and industry as well as the professional classes, as the major factor making for change. The conflict between the military and the "intellectual and pacific classes" was a natural and inevitable one. It was one between "persuasion and force," and every improvement in the human intellect had been "a heavy blow to the warlike spirit." In the savage state, military glory was held in the greatest regard. From this stage onward, there had been a series of steps by which the preeminence of force gave way to that of thought. Buckle suggested that, while classes engaged in trade or manufactures might be less inclined to peaceful pursuits than those in literary, scientific, or philosophical callings, even the least pacific of the former were more devoted to peace than the older military class, which saw in war a means of increasing personal prestige and wealth.[29]

Buckle set down these views in 1855, when Britain and France were at war in the Crimea to rescue Turkey from Russian aggression. War had not broken out between civilized nations, he observed. France and Britain had put aside their own differences "to protect the civilized world against the incursions of a barbarous foe." The Russians were not warlike because they were immoral: they were no more vicious in their habits than the British and French and were undoubtedly more earnest in the performance of their religious duties. "The fault is in the head, not in the heart." The martial propensities of the Russians were embedded in the backward state of the national intellect. "The intellectual classes lack influence: the military class, therefore, is su-preme." Russia did not yet possess middle classes which were the seat of "thoughtful and pacific habits."[30]

In Britain, on the other hand, the middle classes had deprived the military class of all influence, and, indeed, because intellectual progress was so rapid, there was even the danger lest Britain neglect its military defenses against less advanced nations. "We may safely say, that, in our country, a love of war is, as a national taste, utterly extinct," Buckle declared. This had come about not because of the success of moral preaching but because with the advance of society, certain classes with an interest in keeping the peace had come to exercise authority over those with no such interest. Men of talent no longer entered the army or the Church as they had done in the past. Rather, they sought greater opportunities in commerce, in industry, and in advancing knowl-edge.[31]

Before gunpowder had come into common use at the beginning of the fifteenth century, Buckle continued, all men except ecclesiastics were regarded as soldiers, ready to be pressed into battle. With the invention of gunpowder, more expensive equipment than a sword or a bow was required for warfare, making necessary well-trained and well-equipped professional armies and establishing a division of labor between soldiers and civilians. Aided by a more and more complex division of labor, knowledge continued to move forward, increasing further the authority of the middle, intellectual class and further weakening that of the ecclesiastical and military classes. In the eigh-teenth and nineteenth centuries, the intellectual class subjected both constitutional monarchs and despots to regulation by public opinion.[32]

In the eighteenth century, Adam Smith's *Wealth of Nations*—whose great practical influence, Buckle believed, made it "probably the most important book that has ever been written"—destroyed the erroneous views associated with mercantilism and the old colonial system. Since the progress of knowledge had already proceeded sufficiently far, the opinions of Smith and his school were adopted by the leading men in the government. The new science of political economy had dis-proved the hoary belief at the heart of the mercantilist doctrines that whatever was gained by one country was lost by another, and it ex-ploded the view that the possession of colonies and of precious metals was desirable. Such opinions concerning the character of trade had been incitements to hatred and wars between nations. Statesmen now understood that if trade were free, its benefits would be reciprocal. No longer did men pursue policies that tended to promote hostility between nations. The "commercial spirit," formerly warlike, was now "invariably pacific." Few men fully understood the principles of political economy, but all were affected by "the spirit of the times," a product of "the extent and tendency of intellectual progress."[33]

The discovery of the steam engine, and its use in facilitating travel between different nations, also served to inhibit martial impulses. Greater ease in transportation was helping to destroy the ignorance and contempt that peoples frequently felt toward one another. Long-time national enmities, so frequently the cause of war, would soon vanish, and increased familiarity had resulted in the French and British people thinking more charitably of each other. These were additional guarantees of peace.[34]

Buckle, to conclude, saw in the rise of the intellectual classes the leading cause of the decline of war and colonial expansion. Though, generally, nations were under the control of either the military classes (as in Russia or Turkey) or the intellectual classes (as in Great Britain or France), he noted that even in Britain the military classes continued to possess considerable influence. The conflict, then, was intranational as well as international. The result, however, was sure. Through the uncertainties of history, "as the tide rolls on, now advancing, now receding," there was "a far higher movement." It was the ceaseless march of intellectual progress, which made the triumph of the pacific spirit over militarism a certainty.[35]

W. E. H. Lecky

In his *History of the Rise and Influence of the Spirit of Rationalism in Europe,* published in 1865, the Irish sociological historian W. E. H. Lecky, who in his early efforts described himself as a disciple of Buckle, continued Comte's and Buckle's lines of argument. Lecky, born in 1838 of gentry stock, was educated at Trinity College, Dublin, and his first ambition was to become a clergyman. Besides his sociological works—that on rationalism and another on the *History of European Morals*—he is best known for his history of eighteenth-century England.[36]

In his work on rationalism, Lecky observed that in the first stages of civilization, religious and military achievements were the primary sources of prestige, of dignity and respect; and consequently in medieval Europe, the warlike feudal nobility enjoyed the dominant position.[37] This remained the situation in the fifteenth century when the New World was discovered. At that time, it seemed as if Spain and Portugal, because of their overseas discoveries and colonies, would possess "the sceptre of industry." But Spain gave its energies not to manufacturing but to the mining of gold and silver, and its view that the precious metals were real wealth became the basis of the fallacious and warlike colonial and mercantile system. The restrictions of mercantilism ruined what might have proved a rich colonial empire.[38] Moreover, the Church and the aristocracy, neither of whose spirits were conducive to industry (both preferring the past to the present, distrusting innovation, and favoring birth over personal merit) were strengthened.[39] A "stigma was . . . attached to the laborer," and slavery was revived. Spain's fanaticism, its expulsion of the Jews, who were its leading financiers and merchants, further undermined the possibility that it would grasp the commercial supremacy soon to be achieved by the Protestant Dutch and English.[40]

In the late eighteenth century, the long-held conviction that wealth could only be attained by conquest was exploded by the political economists. The spread of free trade in the nineteenth century undermined "great heterogeneous empires" by obliterating the special advantages of colonies. With the advance of civilization, and the growth of the democratic spirit, moreover, "not only does [rational] interest as distinguished from passion, gain a greater empire," but "passion itself is mainly guided by its [interest's] power." The passion for war would diminish and then virtually disappear.[41]

Lecky touched on a number of issues that were to play important roles in future discussions of imperialism by social and economic theorists. One was the question of usury. During the Crusades, missionary and commercial enterprises had been allies in the dissemination of civilization, he observed, but there soon developed a great hostility between them over the lending of money at interest. Among people ignorant of political economy, the creditors were always a target of dislike as "oppressors of the poor,"[42] but the political economists had now presented a scientific justification for usury. Consequently, as soon as "rationalistic modes of thought" became prevalent over "dogmatic" ways, the true character of the taking of interest became evident, and the medieval *odium theologicum* against the sin of usury was dissipated. Lecky decried the Church's unjust persecution of the Jews, whom he praised for having long sustained Europe's spirit of learning and commercial enterprise against the attacks of the Church.[43] This spirit of enterprise had encouraged a taste for luxury, which stimulated human energies, and together with a delight in knowledge acted as principal "agents of human progress."[44]

Lecky invoked the "antagonism" between town and country, between manufacturing and agricultural interests, which produced "entirely different intellectual tendencies" in religion, politics, and political economy. The country, the landed interest, represented "stability, immobility, and reaction"; it was superstitious, held fast to the old religion, and was hostile to innovations. The towns, the commercial

---

Liberal Social Theory and the Persistence of the Feudal Ethos   51 interest, stood for "progress, innovation, and revolution"; they did not take the way of "reaction in politics, or of superstition in religion," and indeed, "the past rests lightly, often too lightly upon them." There were similarly an agricultural and a mercantile school of political economy. The first was concerned primarily with making a nation entirely self-supporting and was hostile to the expansion of manufacturing, and to the moneylending and the credit system upon which a considerable manufacturing establishment was necessarily based. This credit system, in Lecky's view, was "one of the great moralising influences of society" in its reliance upon "character," and "one of the great pledges of peace, by the union it has established between different nations." In the eighteenth century, the physiocrats, although free of the mercantilist superstition that gold was wealth, pursued the line of the agricultural economists that manufacturing and finance, unlike agriculture, did not create new wealth. Adam Smith saved mankind from both the superstitions of the mercantilists and the errors of the physiocrats, and following his prescriptions, contemporary Britain represented the new tendencies of commercial and industrial society to their greatest extent.[45]

Lecky explored what he called the "theological consequences" of the science of political economy. First of all, he argued, political economy, with its proof of the virtues of free trade, would contribute powerfully to the final achievement of the Christian goal of universal peace. The eighteenth-century French *philosophes* had attempted to make intellect prevail over the military spirit. But the martial impulse had been preserved by the wars of the French Revolution, and then by the "pernicious genius" of Napoleon. Political economy now proved that the prosperity of neighboring nations was an advantage and that the nations of the world were so closely connected by commercial ties that "war is usually an evil even to the victor."[46] Every new commercial enterprise was "an additional guarantee of peace." Economic science supplied a "strong and more permanent principle"—that of "an enlightened self interest," which was pacific.[47]

Such a view might appear "unreal and utopian" so long as dynastic monarchs sought to "arrest natural political development" by brute force. But such monarchies must soon disappear. Even the most optimistic economist could not absolutely predict the utter end of war, for "explosions of passion are not always restrained by the most evident ties of interest," and the commerce that linked civilized communities "has ever forced her way among barbarians by bloodshed and by tyranny." Yet Lecky had every reason to be hopeful. The industrial classes were destined to become dominant, and the principles of political economy would soon be accepted as "axioms by the masses." As

The Liberal Ideal and the Demons of Empire

a country advanced, peace would favor a nation's real interest, and its love of war would decline. In the past, war had depended on brute strength and courage, and a rich nation, while attracting the greed of its neighbors, became too soft to defend itself. But now, Lecky observed, the peace-loving industrial nations were already the wealthiest and consequently the most capable of waging war successfully. No doubt with a commercial Britain in mind, he did note the unhappy examples of the great commercial city-states of Carthage, Corinth, and Tyre, victims of the greed and military power of their rivals. He pointed out, however, that with "the elaboration of military machinery," war now depended to a greater extent on "mechanical genius" and "financial prosperity." Consequently power steadily inclined to the nations that most desired peace.[48] The only future source of war that Lecky could envision was that of subject nationalities striving for self-determination against the power of multinational dynastic states.[49]

The Radical Liberals

Buckle and Lecky shared the views of the most radical and articulate elements of the British middle classes. At this time, the leading political spokesmen for the liberal ideology were Richard Cobden, John Bright, and their followers on the extreme left of the Liberal party. It was these Radicals, or Cobdenites, who campaigned most strenuously against the landed interest and for free trade, and who inveighed most fervently against the bellicose and expansionist instincts of the aristocracy. What helped to make many Victorian Radicals antiexpansionist, and, indeed, quasi-pacifist, were the doctrines of Protestant Dissent, which had taken hold of a substantial portion of the new classes of professionals, merchants, and factory owners. Dissenters were persuaded that God intended a millennial reign of peace and that this era was at hand. War, even preparation for war, displayed an unredeemed nature. The true enemies of peace and progress were not France or Russia, they insisted, but the feudal classes, supported by such pernicious groups as armaments manufacturers and financiers, and frequently in alliance with the still unredeemed masses, psychologically dependent on the aristocracy. The Radicals condemned the politics of the past, which were based on aggression and irrational appeals. When war with Russia came in the Crimea in 1854, they, not surprisingly, denounced the conflict. Colonial and trade wars in India or China pleased them no better. (The bulk of the middle classes, in contrast, supported these conflicts with varying degrees of enthusiasm.)[50]

Even Radicals sympathetic to new ventures in the colonization of

---

relatively uninhabited regions lashed out at what the Radical *Spectator* in 1840 called the "unjust, unnecessary, and dishonorable" Opium War (aimed at forcing a trade in that drug)[51] which a Whig-Liberal government was waging against China at the instigation of "sinister interests." The *Spectator*'s description of these interests was much the same as that offered by Bentham. The aristocracy was described as "the predominant interest," which crowded "the Church and the Bar with younger sons" and found "a vent for family hangers-on in the augmented Army and Navy." Others supported the aristocracy: dealers in arms and provisions, shipowners, and "capitalists, who foresee the need of loans—all are ready to drive the country into war, by which they hope to gain at the public expense. And all these parties reckon, not without cause, on the easily-excited pugnacity of the multitude." These warlike interests were the same as those associated with the commercial and financial mercantilism of the past. The *Spectator* was gravely disappointed because it insisted that "the voice of the general mercantile community ought to be for peace."[52]

Radical politicians like Cobden and Bright understood contemporary politics as a struggle between the commercial middle classes and the aristocracy. For Cobden, a Manchester manufacturer, "the commercial interest" was the party of peace and "the territorial interest" that of war. "The middle and industrious classes of England can have no interest apart from the preservation of peace," Cobden declared in 1836; "the honours, the fame, the emoluments of war belong not to them; the battle-plain is the harvest field of the aristocracy, watered with the blood of the people."[53] Cobden's chief aide, the Quaker pacifist John Bright, observed in 1858 at a time of war with China concerning trade that "nothing could be so foolish, nothing so mad as a policy of war for a trading nation." "Any peace," he added, "was better than the most successful war." The aristocracy, no doubt, favored violent conflicts, though it usually disguised its selfish interest by a pretended principle such as liberty or the Protestant cause. Their real concern was jobs in the army and navy for their sons; the military and colonial system was "neither more nor less than a gigantic system of out-door relief for the aristocracy of Great Britain." This was why the governing aristocracy fostered the country's "perpetual delusion that it is about to be attacked."[54]

While looking to the capitalists as their principal constituency for these views, Cobden and Bright were often disappointed by the petty self-interest of this class. In their narrowness and selfishness, the commercial classes "may not be all that you & I wish," Cobden wrote his aide in 1861: still, they were the only effective "counterpoise to our ruling class." With this in mind, Cobden warned Bright (who was

The Liberal Ideal and the Demons of Empire

given to demagogic hyperbole) "not to encourage a feeling of alienation from the capitalist class." In time capitalists would be awakened to their true interest.[55] And perhaps this Radical faith was justified, since by the end of the century, much of the Cobdenite program became the official policy of the Liberal party and its leader W. E. Gladstone (though the actual policy of Liberal governments was at times rather different). By the last quarter of the century, many in the middle classes would desert the Liberals for a Tory party more friendly to imperial concerns.

Even before the coming of full-scale industrialism, liberal opinion in Britain and France had become convinced of a rational and pacific future. The spread of manufacturing to much of Europe and North America and the growth of the complex, highly differentiated society which accompanied the steam engine, only confirmed that view. As the century progressed, liberals increasingly saw the new age as qualitatively different from what had gone before. If peace and plenty had never previously been possible, they were now. In an age of industrial capitalism, where a free market and not a bureaucracy determined economic relations, and where a free trade flourished between nations (making possible a universally beneficial international division of labor), reason *must* triumph over the passions that led to war.

This idealization of free trade and an international division of labor provoked the anger of the German and American national economists. They saw this liberal ideal as a dystopia—a revival of colonialism in disguise. Britain, in their view, was determined to use free trade to impede the economic development of the rest of the world to its own advantage. Other nations would become mere "hewers of wood and drawers of water" for a British workshop of the world. The agricultural nations, they asserted, must ally themselves to resist the overwhelming power of British industrialists, traders, and financiers.

---

4   The National Economists against

Free-Trade Empire

In January 1846, the Tory prime minister, Sir Robert Peel, modestly observed in an address to the House of Commons that Britain had achieved a "manufacturing and commercial pre-eminence."[1] A month later, a future prime minister, Benjamin Disraeli, went somewhat further, seeing Great Britain's position as that of "the metropolis of the world," which received "the tribute of the world."[2] Their descriptions of the British workshop of the world—and not only the leading industrial but the chief commercial and financial power as well—were not far off the mark.

In the last quarter of the eighteenth century, Great Britain had experienced the first phase of an economic transformation that would make it the world's first industrialized nation. By 1801, about 30 percent of the British labor force was employed in manufacturing and mining; in 1841, at a time of rapid population increase, this had risen to 40 percent. By 1815, the value of exported cottons (produced by the power-driven mills that dotted the landscape of Lancashire and the north) amounted to 40 percent of the value of all British exports. Between 1832 and 1850, the weight of cotton consumed by British mills rose from 259 million pounds annually to 588 million pounds; British pit-iron production advanced from 700,000 to 2,250,000 tons, and coal from 26 million to 60 million tons. Iron and steel goods and coal added to the overall value of British exports, which quadrupled between 1800 and 1830.

By the early 1850s, Great Britain enjoyed a virtual monopoly position in the export trade in textiles, while its share of the world's export trade in manufactures generally was probably more than 40 percent. During the first half of the nineteenth century, moreover, Britain received dividends from overseas investments and fees for commercial and financial services (so-called invisible exports) constituting about 20–30 percent of overall receipts from the rest of the world; in later decades these invisible exports would increase, both absolutely and as a share of Britain's overall balance of payments. Free trade appeared successful in every particular, validating the analyses of the political economists.

The classical economists had argued, we have seen, that the mercantilist system had been directed toward an unnatural, inequitable, and antisocial appropriation of a large share of the national product to the benefit of a small part of the country. The mercantile and financial classes, in alliance with the governing aristocracy and gentry, had persuaded the state to fashion protective legislation and to employ its military and naval power to establish colonies and trading arrangements that would result in great profits for the commercial interests, to the disadvantage of all others. For over a century preceding the establishment of the new system, there had been almost continual wars for trade and overseas colonies among the mercantile powers, and it seemed as if trade, piracy, and war had become virtually synonymous.

But the new industry, according to the classical economists, now made possible an absolute increase in the world's wealth: a nation no longer needed to turn to war to steal its neighbor's trade. The British political economists and middle-class Radicals argued and campaigned for the end of mercantilist restrictions; and gradually, in the 1820s, 1830s, and 1840s, Parliament removed tariffs on imported raw materials (including food) and manufactures, and the middle classes secured for Great Britain a virtually free trade. The consummation of the liberal ideal seemed in sight.

On the European continent and in America, the so-called national economists—notably, the American Henry Carey and the German Friedrich List—produced full-scale indictments of British free trade. They charged that British financial, commercial, and industrial power, in the guise of free trade, sought to impede the natural economic development of less advanced agricultural countries and to make them forever the vassals of a demonic Great Britain. The national economists attacked with special fervor the grasping finance capital of the City of London, Great Britain's financial hub. Unlike a productive and progressive industrial capital, they asserted, finance capital was parasitic and regressive. Moreover, they contended, the resources of British finance capital were so immense that it could dictate to the governments of agricultural countries courses of action highly profitable to the bankers of the City though gravely injurious to the people of these less developed countries. This argument would become a leading theme of a number of nineteenth- and twentieth-century theories of imperialism.

The relationship between advanced and less developed nations in a relatively free international market had for some time been a subject of analysis. The mid-nineteenth-century discussion had been anticipated by a controversy in the 1750s regarding the economic relations of "rich" countries, understood to be commercially and industrially developed, and "poor" or entirely agricultural countries. The debate was between David Hume and Josiah Tucker.

The Hume-Tucker Debate

David Hume, philosopher, historian, and economist, the pride of the Scottish Enlightenment, had argued in a tract in 1752 that, under conditions of a free trade, wealth would inevitably be transferred from a richer to a poorer state until the riches of each country were equal. The theory of the automatic mechanism, which Hume himself had proposed earlier, asserted that since the precious metals distributed themselves in accordance with the requirements of trade, mercantilist restrictions on the movement of gold and silver were unavailing. Consequently, if the amount of the precious metals in Britain were halved overnight, the low wages and low prices that would result, in accordance with the quantity theory of money, would so promote British exports that the influx of precious metals paid by foreigners for these exports would replace the gold and silver lost, as well as restore former wage and price levels. Arguing less carefully, Hume proceeded to suggest that as a consequence of its low wage and price levels, a poor country might, in similar fashion, drain a richer country of its precious metals.[3]

Hume's analysis provoked Josiah Tucker, whom we have already encountered, to present a counterargument. Tucker, the son of a farmer and educated at Oxford, was in 1758 appointed to the deanery of Gloucester. The remainder of his life was devoted to superintending, rather well, the estates of the diocese and to his writings upon questions of trade (some of which were translated by Turgot into French and were highly regarded on the other side of the Channel). As an economist, he has proved difficult to classify: some authorities, remembering his views on the balance of trade, on population, and on the evils of forestalling, have called him a mercantilist, while others, thinking of his opinions on colonies and on trade, have set him down as a liberal.[4] In his argument with Hume he was both free trader and economic nationalist, a prophetic combination.

Taking England and Scotland as independent nations, Tucker suggested, in a reply to Hume in 1758 and in a fuller response of 1774, that if England were suddenly to become immensely richer than Scotland because of the discovery of gold and silver or because of privateering, then Hume's conclusions would undoubtedly be correct. However, they would just as surely be false if this increase of wealth were acquired "in the Way of general Industry." Tucker regarded the question as ultimately this: "Which of these two Nations can afford to raise Provisions, and sell their Manufactures on the cheapest Terms?" Tucker insisted that the richer country had all the advantages. First of all,

> As the richer Country hath acquired its superior Wealth by a general Application, and long Habits of Industry, it is therefore in actual Possession of an established Trade and Credit . . . a great Variety of the best Tools and Implements in the various Kinds of Manufactures . . . good Roads, Canals, and other artificial Communications: . . . good Pilots, and trained Sailors. . . . Whereas the poor Country has, for the most Part, all these Things to seek after and procure.

The richer country had "superior Skill and Knowledge"; it had the capital to make experiments and to embark upon "expensive and longwinded Undertakings"; it had a prosperous home market. In the richer country, because of the intensive division of labor, a workingman might become an expert artisan: "Is it not much cheaper," Tucker inquired, "to give 2s. 6d. a Day in the rich Country to the nimble and adroit Artist, than it is to give only 6d. in the poor one, to the tedious awkward Bungler?" In the richer country, goods were cheaper as a result of the competition of rival tradesmen. Finally, "in the richer Country, the Superiority of the Capital, and the low Interest of Money, will ensure the Vending of all Goods on the cheapest Terms" and would make possible the granting of longer credits.[5] (This was an elaboration of the argument, already discussed, that he would use again in 1776 to urge that no interference in British trade would result from the independence of the American colonies.)

Tucker proposed a "law," which would gain considerable support, in somewhat altered form, among the later classical economists: "That *operose*, or *complicated Manufactures* are cheapest in rich Countries; — and *raw Materials* in poor ones: And therefore in Proportion as any Commodity approaches to one, or other of these *Extremes*, in that Proportion it will be found to be cheaper, or dearer in a rich, or a poor Country." For example, timber was always cheaper in a poor country, but not cabinetry. Although Tucker was able to recognize the enormous advantages that rich nations possessed over poorer ones,

The Liberal Ideal and the Demons of Empire

he was not so illiberal, he observed, as to wish to keep backward nations from progressing. Since no nation could "ever be ruined but by itself," Tucker urged that the English, because of "the very Largeness of their Capitals, and their Vicinity to Scotland," might help the Scots by loans and technical assistance. The increasing prosperity of neighboring nations would make them better customers.[6] In this fashion, liberal trade principles would serve the national interest.

Hume was willing to admit all the advantages favoring the richer nation noted by Tucker, but he insisted that there would come a limit, a *"ne plus ultra."* At this point the rich nation would check itself "by begetting disadvantages, which at first retard, and at last finally stop their progress." Among these were "the dear price of provisions and labour, which enables the poorer country to rival them, first in the coarsest manufactures, and then in those which are more elaborate."[7]

Tucker made two rebuttals to this argument, the public one of 1758 and 1774, which we have noted, and another of a different character in a private letter of 1758. In his public reply, Tucker stated that such progress could be carried on so far that "no Man can positively define, *when,* or *where* it must *necessarily* stop." Although the poorer nation could not compete with the manufactures of the richer in the international market, it still might have certain local advantages. (Tucker noted particularly the superiority of Scotland and Ireland in linen manufacture.) However, Tucker cautioned Hume that in charting the progress of the poorer country, he had neglected to take into account that prices, wages, etc., would be rising along with this progress, thus depriving the poorer country of many former advantages.[8] In a private letter of 1758, Tucker described tariff protection as the best course for the poorer nation: "It is true likewise, that all of them [the poor countries] have it in their power to load the manufactures of the rich country upon entering their territories, with such high duties as shall turn the scale in favour of their own manufactures, or of the manufactures of some other nation, whose progress in trade they have less cause to fear, or envy." And, Tucker concluded, "thus it is, in my poor apprehension, that the rich may be prevented from swallowing up the poor; at the same time, and by the same methods, that the poor are stimulated and excited to emulate the rich."[9]

During the 1780s, two British prime ministers, Shelburne and Pitt, sought to apply to the imperial economy the lesson that a profitable trade did not depend upon the maintenance of a restrictive trading system; that the growing industry of Britain would prosper only if it had abundant foreign markets, both European and colonial; and that, as Tucker had understood, an advanced economy would not be injured but very much assisted by freedom of trade. Pitt's Irish and French

---

The National Economists against Free-Trade Empire

trade proposals in the eighties have long been regarded as prime examples of how Great Britain, in the decade before it was diverted from reform by the French Revolution, had been moving in the direction of free trade. Adam Smith is usually given the credit for having taught Pitt his free-trade principles, and there was certainly no way of avoiding Smith's influence during this period. But the influence of Tucker was also present during the French debate in 1787, and overwhelming in the earlier 1785 debate upon the Irish proposals.[10]

In the nineteenth century the British classical economists would manage to identify free trade with cosmopolitanism, despite the efforts of the American and German national economists to depict it as the necessary policy of British economic nationalism. The national economists would have found confirmation of their position in Tucker's views, had they known of them, and in the manner in which his arguments were employed in Parliament by Pitt and his supporters. Of course, Tucker had also anticipated the remedy that Hamilton, List, and Carey were to offer the agricultural nations—tariff protection for industry.

Alexander Hamilton

The earliest American national economist was the first secretary of the treasury, Alexander Hamilton. In 1790, Hamilton presented a "Report on Manufactures" to the U.S. Congress in which he attempted to convince his fellow countrymen, mostly believers in the superiority of agriculture over manufacturing, that the reverse was the case. Nearly four decades before the English economist Nassau Senior put forward the law of increasing returns from industry, Hamilton observed that "the labor of artificers being capable of greater subdivision and simplicity of operation than that of cultivators," it was therefore "susceptible in a proportionately greater degree, of improvement in its productive powers, whether to be derived from an accession of skill or from the application of ingenious machinery." Consequently, to allow foreign manufacturers to supply a nation with their products would transfer to their nations the advantages of employing machinery.[11]

The very nature of a trade between an agricultural country like America and a manufacturing country like Britain, Hamilton argued, placed the first at a great disadvantage. Foreign demand for agricultural products was "rather casual and occasional, than certain or constant," whereas the growth of domestic manufactures would provide an assured home market for the nation's farmers. A manufacturing nation could avail itself of the "more numerous attractions which a more diversified market offers to foreign customers and the greater scope which it affords to mercantile enterprise"; customers would always be most attracted to markets where commodities "while equally abundant, are most various." The terms of trade between an agricultural America and a manufacturing Europe were weighted in favor of the European importers by those factors and also because of the high transport costs caused by the "bulkiness" of raw produce. Indeed, the exchange of manufactures for agricultural products put agricultural nations at a permanent disadvantage. While the United States had a "constant and increasing necessity" for European manufactures, Europeans had "only a partial and occasional demand" for American agricultural exports. This "could not but expose" Americans "to a state of impoverishment, compared with the opulence to which their political and natural advantages authorize them to aspire."[12]

Hamilton consequently called upon Congress to establish a system of protection, the remedy Tucker had put forward in the 1750s. Not only protective tariffs to foster American industry but in some cases prohibitions, bounties, and drawbacks would prove useful to "the degree in which the nature of the manufacture admits of a substitute for manual labor in machinery." The United States, he added, ought to aim at possessing "all the essentials of national supply." Hamilton also wished to encourage inventions and to promote the building of canals and roads, and he argued for a tax policy that would encourage investment. Noting that certain European nations possessed more capital than could be profitably placed at home, he urged Americans to welcome such foreign investment as a "most valuable auxiliary," not a rival.[13]

Other American economists, among them a Baltimore lawyer, Daniel Raymond, subscribed to Hamilton's position and his remedies. In 1823, Raymond observed that individual interests were "perpetually at variance" with national interests. While it might be good for Southern planters to import cheap textiles from Britain, which was the prime market for their raw cotton, this was hardly a boon for the country. "Although it may be beneficial for the time being, for a nation to import, than to manufacture its own comforts of life," he observed, "how will it be fifty years hence?" Because of Britain's superior skill, it was impossible for Americans to compete with British manufacturers on equal terms. Raymond called for a tariff that would protect American industry.[14]

The German national economist Friedrich List would offer essentially the same analysis and prescribe the same remedy as Tucker and the American protectionists. List, however, presented these more systematically, invoking historical as well as economic arguments.

Friedrich List

The German economist Friedrich List was born in Württemberg in 1789, the son of a well-to-do tanner. In 1817, he was appointed professor of public administration at the University of Tübingen, and in 1819, he was elected a deputy to the Representative Assembly of Württemberg. As a deputy, his efforts to reform the administration of the state aroused the antagonism of the king, who saw him as a dangerous revolutionary, imprisoned him, and later expelled him from the kingdom. List went to America, where he became editor of a German-language newspaper in Pennsylvania. He read the works of Alexander Hamilton and under his influence wrote the protectionist *Outlines of American Political Economy* in 1827. In 1828, he became one of the founders of the Reading Railroad. Anthracite coal, discovered on land that the railroad owned, made him financially independent and prompted his return to Europe, where he became a strong advocate of the development of a German railway system.[15]

In 1819, in a petition he had formulated on behalf of merchants and manufacturers, List called on the German Federal Assembly to establish a federation free of all tariff barriers. "Not until universal, free, and unrestricted commercial intercourse is established among the nations of the world will they reach the highest degree of material well-being," he observed; this would be the "highest stage of civilization." Meanwhile, before such a universal free trade has come to pass, the states of Germany must not merely end all internal tariff barriers dividing their federation but must also erect an external tariff as a defense against foreign goods, which were "the canker worms which devour German prosperity." List's particular target was Britain's textile industry, which was successfully competing with that of the German states. "In our view," he concluded, "federal obligations include defence not merely through armies but through a tariff."[16]

When List came to the United States, he saw that country faced with a situation similar to that of the German states, and he again advocated tariff protection as a remedy. List wrote as a defender of the protectionist American system, which was very popular in Pennsylvania, where industry was attempting to establish itself. In the *Outlines,* in 1827, he attacked the "imaginary superiority in science and knowledge" of the disciples of Smith and Say and defended "common sense." The founders of the "dangerous doctrine" of the political economists were undoubtedly clever men "whose talents enabled them to give their castles in the air the appearance of strong, well-founded buildings." Their erroneous doctrine had consequently been taken up by the political and scientific leaders. List implored the American

The Liberal Ideal and the Demons of Empire

people "not to die of a *beau ideal*," to be ruined because they trusted in "the infallibility of two books," those of Smith and Say, the "general failure" of whose teachings would soon be acknowledged by all.[17]

Smith and Say had written as if all the nations of the world were as united as the states of the American union. If that were truly the case, List observed, "there would be no national interest, no national law contrary to the freedom of the whole race, no restrictions, no wars." But this was patently false. While such conditions might be desirable, while hope for them might "do honour to the heart of a philosopher," and while they might "even lie in the great plan of Providence to accomplish it for after ages," they were "not the state of the actual world." Smith's system was as chimerical as the abbé St. Pierre's plan for a universal peace, for nations were still prepared to go to war to defend their interests. And nations had better be prepared to defend such interests by economic as well as military means, List maintained.[18] The enemy of this program of national interest was a Britain determined to monopolize the industrial power of the world. The British support for a free international trade was "one of the most extraordinary of first-rate political manoeuvres that have ever been played upon the credulity of the world."[19]

List presented much the same analysis (though in more substantial form) in his *Natural System of Political Economy* of 1837. Again, he noted that "the fulfilment of the dreams of the free traders" had to await the establishment of "a world republic";[20] and once more he warned against the devices of an insidious Britain.[21] This tract was clearly a way station to the fully argued volume he would publish seven years later.

In 1844, after his return to Germany, List completed his principal work, *The National System of Political Economy,* a book that urged the German states to found a manufacturing industry behind the walls of their new Zollverein, or customs union. His book was again directed against what he termed the "cosmopolitical" economy of Adam Smith and the British classical economists, which was based on "a disorganizing individualism," one that thought only of momentary individual profits and took no account of the moral or political interests of the future. He urged Germany to adopt and maintain a protective system until it was in a position to compete on its own with the advanced productive capacities of Great Britain. The "power of creating wealth" (i.e., manufacturing and agriculture) was "vastly more important than wealth itself," List asserted, denouncing that "insane doctrine" of the classical political economists that sacrificed the claims of productive pursuits to the "pretensions of commerce—to the claims of absolute free trade," to the absurd doctrine that regarded the whole world as

---

"a republic of merchants, one and indivisible." While denying that he was a mercantilist, List sought to put the idea of "nationality" back into political economy. The British economists had ignored nationality and international politics and saw only private individuals; history, however, taught the necessity of state intervention to promote the national interest.[22]

List described Britain's free-trade empire in these terms:

In all ages there have been cities or countries which have been preeminent above all others in industry, commerce, and navigation; but a supremacy such as that which exists in our days, the world has never before witnessed. In all ages, nations and powers have striven to attain to the dominion of the world, but hitherto not one of them has erected its power on so broad a foundation. How vain do the efforts of these appear to us who have striven to found their universal dominion on military power, compared with the attempt of England to raise her entire territory into one immense manufacturing, commercial, and maritime city, and to become among the countries and kingdoms of the earth, that which a great city is in relation to its surrounding territory: to comprise within herself all industries, arts and sciences; all great commerce and wealth; all navigation and naval power—a world's metropolis which supplies all nations with manufactured goods, and supplies herself in exchange from every nation with those raw materials of a useful or acceptable kind, which each other nation is fitted by nature to yield to her.

List took particular note of Britain's financial hegemony. That nation was the "treasure house of all great capital—a banking establishment for all nations, which controls the circulating medium of the whole world, and by loans and the receipt of interest on them makes all the peoples of the earth her tributaries."[23]

Free trade was the means of endowing Great Britain with "a world-manufacturing monopoly" and would enable it to exploit the world at will.[24] Britain now perceived its error of 1815 in having installed a system of agricultural protectionism; had it freely admitted foreign grain, thus providing a market for agricultural nations and enabling them to buy British manufactures, its position in manufacturing would be all the more overwhelming. But even if, to secure the exchange between industrial and agricultural nations, the British should soon abolish their Corn Laws, why should second-rank manufacturing countries give up hard-won gains to become "dependent" agricultural nations?[25] With British free trade in operation, France, Spain, and Portugal would offer Britain their best wines (with France, perhaps, also exporting her millinery); Germany would supply "children's toys, wooden clocks, and philological writings," as well as mercenaries for

Britain's colonial armies, soldiers "who might sacrifice themselves to pine away in the deserts of Asia or Africa, for the sake of extending the manufacturing and commercial supremacy, the literature and language of England." Such a humiliating fate could be avoided only if the nations of the Continent and the United States turned to a policy of protection to build their own manufacturing enterprises.[26]

Like the mercantilists of the past, and like Hamilton, List was convinced that nations that exported manufactured goods and imported raw materials were wealthier and more powerful than exporters of agricultural products and importers of manufactures. Such states possessed the tremendous "power of machinery" which was "destined to exercise" an incalculable influence in world affairs, notably on the progress of civilization of barbarous countries and the colonization of uninhabited lands overseas. Manufacturing served to increase the material capital of a nation; the rate of interest in an industrial state was lower, prices were more stable, and more money was available for enterprise. The merely agricultural nation was subject to greater economic fluctuations in its markets abroad and was generally in debt to the manufacturing nation. In a country that enjoyed a "harmony of the productive powers" of industry and agriculture, land values, rents, and the profits of farming would increase, and the wages of farm labor improve. Even the merchant benefited by the establishment of manufactories, as a comparison of the commerce of Spain or Poland with that of Britain readily proved.[27]

But what could largely agricultural nations do to rectify their situation? While the United States and Germany could not compete with Britain " 'in the natural course of things,' " it would not prove useful for these nations "to resign themselves to a state of perpetual subordination to the English manufacturing supremacy." For Britain would not feel obliged to buy its cotton only from America or its wool only from Germany but would feel free to seek competing supplies elsewhere. Again like Tucker and Hamilton, List maintained that only tariff protection for American and German industry would prove useful. The difficulties of starting manufacturing enterprises and the national advantages of such enterprises justified the enactment of protective duties in nations whose territorial expanse, population, natural resources, and advanced agriculture, civilization, and political development qualified them to take their place among states preeminent in economic, military, and naval development.[28]

List's *National System* was a paean not only to manufacturing and protection but also to colonization as "the highest means" of developing manufacturing power: overseas colonies were valuable as markets, as sources of raw materials, and as sites for investment and the settlement of an overflowing population. List envisioned a relationship between metropolis and colony virtually identical to that conceived by the defenders of the old colonial system. Its "fundamental condition" was the exchange of the manufactured products of the mother country for the raw materials of the colonies. The American colonies had revolted against Britain once they felt able to manufacture for themselves. Canada would do likewise. But there were countries like India, and others of the torrid zone, which were colonies by nature. (Such a view, of course, resembled Aristotle's belief that certain men were slaves by nature.) "All Asiatic colonies of the torrid zone will pass gradually under the dominion of the manufacturing commercial nations of the temperate zone," he wrote, and even South America would remain "dependent to a certain degree."[29]

During the time when the great manufacturing nations of the future, which List saw as Germany and the United States, were still in their early protected growth, Britain could still find new, non-European markets for its surplus products and sites for the investment of its overabundant capital. The British, with the assistance of other powers, might bring civilized government to South America, Asia, and Africa, construct roads and canals, and promote education and morality on these continents—in a word, prepare these regions for the possibility of an increasing trade with Europe. In compensation, Great Britain, because of its present superiority in manufacturing, would secure the lion's share of these new markets. The nations of the temperate zone "specially fitted by nature for manufacturing" would exchange their manufactures for such products of the torrid zone as cotton, sugar, rice, and coffee. There was enough profit in such a trade for all nations, and Britain had nothing to gain by excluding others from it. Finally, List concluded ominously, should western European nations and the United States "be hindered in these endeavours by England's manufacturing, commercial, and naval supremacy," then they should seek "in the union of their powers" the "means of reducing such unreasonable pretensions to reasonable ones."[30]

With the United States as his prime example, List described the way in which the superiority, indeed supremacy, of Britain's finance capital had distorted less developed economies and impeded their progress. America's commercial crises were at root the consequence of that nation's adverse balance of trade with Britain, he asserted, a situation that the credit facilities and low rates of discount offered by the Bank of England to facilitate British exports to the United States helped to bring about. Britain, moreover, had invested considerable sums in the construction of canals and railways in the United States, and this capital had been made available to Britain by America's unfavorable trade balance. By its discount operations, the Bank of England could at will lower the prices of British products to the disadvantage of American manufactures and increase American consumption of these products; and Americans would be compelled to cover the purchase of increased imports by the export of stocks and government bonds, which left the American economy even more vulnerable to manipulation to suit British convenience. When bad harvests brought about a considerable export of British bullion to purchase from Russia or Germany crops in short supply, the Bank of England simply limited credit and increased the discount rate. When this occurred, the demand in Great Britain for American stocks and bonds declined, and the loans at the former rate already on the market were called in. The "cash circulation in America really belonged to the English," List wrote, and they "could dispose of that ready money on whose possession the whole bank and paper system of the United States was based, according to their inclination." An agricultural nation like the United States which permitted the British a predominant position in the supply of manufactures likewise became a vassal to the British people—"permanently indebted to them," "dependent on their many institutions, and drawn into the whirlpool of their agricultural, industrial, and commercial crises."[31]

List shared Adam Smith's doubts concerning the importance of the balance of trade between a mother country and its colonies. A colony was not endangered by hostile commercial or banking operations and was indeed under the financial and political wing of the metropolis. But once independence had been achieved, as in the United States, conditions changed decisively. He pointed to an America glutted with raw produce, the prices of which had been halved, yet continuing to contract huge debts by purchases of British manufactures.[32] List drew attention to what would later be called "dumping," when at times of production gluts, British manufacturers put their stocks of goods into steamers to sell in Germany or New York at half their value. The British manufacturers "suffer . . . but they are saved"; their foreign counterparts were ruined. The British compensated themselves later on by increasing prices. When such things happened, he inquired, should we not be skeptical concerning the regulation of economic life by cosmopolitan principles? Just as a wise father was ready to educate his sons, sacrificing present value to future productive capacity, so a nation must protect its infant industry by giving up the immediate but ultimately destructive advantage of cheaper British manufactures. In the long run, a nation that protected its manufacturers would obtain an even cheaper product than it at present enjoyed from the foreigner, and it would secure industrial independence if war came.[33]

Would it be to America's advantage, then, to regain her former status of British colony? There would then be no Corn Laws to inhibit its grain exports, nor tobacco duties limiting tobacco exports; American timber and cotton would be free from competition in the British market, and so on. List's answer to the question was a qualified yes, but only "if the United States do not manufacture, if they do not found a durable system of credit of their own; if they do not desire or are not able to develop a naval power." If this were, indeed, the case, all American talk of "future national greatness is in vain." List chastised the efforts of the cotton planters "to persuade the Congress that the prosperity of America depends on the industrial sovereignty of England over North America."[34]

As a political liberal, List observed that there was a difference between freedom of internal trade and freedom of trade between nations. Individual liberty might easily prosper under conditions of a strong state and a policy of protection in international commerce. Using Britain as his prime example, List stressed that the trade between nations was not regulated merely by "the natural course of things," as the classical economists and the German "popular school" maintained, but by the influence of the commercial and financial power of the nation. He reminded his readers that Britain had progressed to its preeminence in commerce, in industry, in navigation, and in colonies not by a system of free trade but by one of protection, a policy designed to increase its power. The British had protected their shipowners and manufacturers until they were capable of competing, and turned to a freer trade only when they could easily undersell the shipping services and manufactures of their neighbors. In the eighteenth century, Great Britain had imported from India and sold on the Continent fine Indian cottons and silk fabrics, while excluding them from the British home market in order to protect the inferior and more expensive goods of domestic silk and cotton factories. From the standpoint of the cosmopolitan theorists of value, this was foolishness. But the British ministers of the time sensibly preferred manufacturing power to low-priced goods.[35] When Britain subsidized foreign armies, notably that of Prussia during the Seven Years' War, these grants came in the form of British manufactures, which crushed foreign rivals.[36]

History had demonstrated, List argued, that nations passed through several stages, to each of which a different trade policy was appropriate. Free trade would best help to raise nations in the first stage such as Spain, Portugal, and Naples from "a state of barbarism." In

The Liberal Ideal and the Demons of Empire

nations in the second stage like Germany and the United States, only tariff protection could effectively promote manufacturing, foreign commerce, and navigation. For those in the last stage, at which Britain had certainly, and France almost certainly, arrived, a turn to a freer trade was useful so that their producers and merchants might be "preserved from indolence, and stimulated to retain the supremacy" achieved. Britain's urging that all nations adopt a cosmopolitan system was a subterfuge designed to conceal how its own greatness had really been reached so that others would not follow.[37]

The British, List continued, hoped to destroy the protective German customs union, the Zollverein, by a program of divide and rule. The maritime Hanse towns, with their free-trade proclivities, would have to understand that they had more to gain as the nucleus of a united German mercantile marine and navy than by their present commitment to a cosmopolitan trade. Two frigates from the British colony of Heligoland at the mouths of the Weser and Elbe, List warned the Hanse merchants, could in a day undermine the hard-won commercial positions of the German traders. On the other hand, a German union would protect the interests of German merchants with a fleet of its own and enrich them with its own colonial trade. List saw the return of the Netherlands to the new Germany as bringing about the revival of that declining power: Holland was at present "a satellite for the English fleet—unite it with Germany, she is the leader of the German naval power."[38] The British were attempting to seduce the Prussian landowners by offering a free trade for grain and timber, but the Prussians would be made to see that with the extension of manufacturing, Prussia would possess a greater and more secure home market for its agriculture than it could ever secure abroad. The British effort to persuade the Zollverein to reduce its protective duties was an effort "to reduce Germany to the position of an English agricultural colony." The "all-monopolising islanders" wished to restore Germany to its former condition, that "of hewers of wood and drawers of water for the Britons," despised by all, treated "worse than a subject people" like the Hindus.[39]

The Continental nations had so many common interests in opposition to the British financial, industrial, and maritime supremacy, List warned, that they must avoid internecine wars that served only to further British wealth and power. In constructing his Continental System, Napoleon had possessed a correct understanding of European interests. The idea of such a system would be revived as British "preponderance" increased. List suggested that France might lead a Continental alliance against Britain if it avoided the territorial ambitions of the Bourbons and Napoleon, and he foresaw the possibility that

Britain would yield to the just demands of such an alliance without resorting to war. An attitude of compromise on Britain's part would prove a useful hedge against the time when it would require Continental support against the rise of the United States, which in the following century would surpass Great Britain in wealth, in naval power, and in influence over the nations of the Western Hemisphere.[40]

But for the moment, Britain continued its demonic game. In his earlier efforts to convert Germans to a policy of protection, List had discovered that the "scientifically-educated" officials, newspaper editors, and economists were all advocates of free trade, as were German merchants who dealt in British goods. This was due to a carefully devised conspiracy. The British had not only managed to convince the educated classes of Germany that any system but that of free trade was a theoretical absurdity, but had also encouraged these German "advocates of the interests of England" by payments of British gold: "It is notorious what a powerful means of controlling public opinion abroad, is possessed by the English Ministry in their 'secret service money'; and they are not accustomed to be niggardly where it can be useful to their commercial interests."[41] (Napoleon had also seen his enemies at home and abroad as corrupted by British gold.)

The general positions of List and the national economists received apparent confirmation by statements made in the British parliament, particularly by those campaigning for the repeal of the Corn Laws. As early as 1829, Joseph Hume, a leader of the small Radical group in the House of Commons, urged that a free trade in corn would "render all the world tributary to us."[42] In a debate in 1842, the Whig-Liberal historian T. B. Macaulay argued that once the Corn Laws were repealed, "we might supply the whole world with manufactures, and have almost a monopoly of the trade of the world," while "other nations were raising abundant provisions for us on the banks of the Mississippi and the Vistula."[43] When a liberal-Tory prime minister, Robert Peel, proposed the completion of free trade by the repeal of the Corn Laws in early 1846, he argued that cheap and abundant food could maintain Britain's economic "pre-eminence."[44] German and American national economists might find solid ground for their views in such parliamentary pronouncements. In 1838, a protectionist Tory, Disraeli, saw it as a delusion that the Continent "would suffer England to be the workshop of the world"[45] and, two years later, decried such "arrogant aspirations" as founded on a "profound ignorance of human nature."[46]

An American, Henry Carey, who believed himself undeluded—whose most important writings appeared after the repeal of the Corn Laws—was to take a position much like that maintained by Hamilton,

Raymond, and List, adding to it his own special theory of British exploitation.

Henry Carey

Henry Carey, born in Philadelphia in 1793, was the son of Matthew Carey, a prominent Irish-born publisher of that city who had come to America as a political refugee. The elder Carey had adopted the protectionist economics of Alexander Hamilton, which he saw as the young republic's only defense against the British industrial and commercial monopoly. Henry Carey would become the leading American economist—both Mill and Marx would engage him in debate—as well as the principal exponent of his father's economic program, and a leading critic of the classical economists.[47] Carey was a prolific writer on economic issues. Between 1837 and 1840, he produced his protectionist *Principles of Political Economy,* in which he argued the harmony of interests between capitalist and worker, not the antagonism depicted by Malthus, Ricardo, and their followers. The French political economist Frederic Bastiat in his *Harmonies Economiques* in 1850 would make this optimistic vision known among European economists. In this early work, Carey presented this happy interplay of interests as a consequence of a providential benevolence.[48] Carey's three-volume *Principles of Social Science,* published in 1858 and 1859, was a synthesis of the many smaller works he had published in the 1840s and 1850s and fully outlined his advocacy of a protective system. List clearly played a substantial role in shaping Carey's ideas, but Carey's own law of rent assumed a dominant position in his argument.

In 1848, Carey first offered this new economic principle as a basis for much of his analysis. He rejected Ricardo's law of rent, which held that men first cultivated the best soils and, as the population increased, moved on to inferior soils, a law that described the landlord as the noncontributing beneficiary of economic growth. The true law of rent, Carey asserted, was invariably the opposite: inferior soils were cultivated first, and after the growth of wealth and population, richer soils were brought into production. The American frontier provided many examples of this phenomenon. Furthermore, he disputed Malthus's law of population, contending that an increased population was necessary to achieve any considerable growth in the food supply.[49]

Carey explained the inefficient dispersion of the American population in part by this law of rent, and in part by the continued exhaustion of the soil arising from a defective manufacturing sector and a dependence on foreign markets for the sale of agricultural produce. (This, not the slave system as Cairnes would argue, was responsible for Southern expansionism, as it was for the persistence of slavery itself.) In the early days of civilization, a cultivator, weak and without tools, could till only the higher and poorer soils, which yielded so little that he lived a solitary and brutish existence. As population and wealth progressed, a better-equipped farmer could cultivate the lower and richer soils, "the dense forests and dreary swamps" that had discouraged the earlier efforts of "poor and scattered men." With protection and the growth of manufacturing, Carey argued, it would no longer be necessary to find distant markets for what farmers grew; there could be a concentration instead of dispersion of population and a diversity in employments that would bring producers and consumers together in a mutually beneficial *commerce*. A farmer could then return to the soil the nutriments in the manure, produced by the consumers of his harvests, that would restore the fertility of his land.[50]

Instead of such a healthy commerce, however, a free-trade Britain fostered a pernicious *trade* where a middleman exploited both producer and consumer. Carey maintained that the British political economists had invented and disseminated the Ricardian and Malthusian doctrines of rent and population so as to relieve the feelings of guilt of the "class that lives by appropriation and directs the affairs of nation." The classical economists thought particularly well of the trader, the middleman, and the others who lived by appropriation, such as the broker, the slaveowner, the wagoner, and the shipowner. Justifying itself by false economic doctrines, Britain sought its treasure in the unproductive manipulations of foreign trade rather than by a fruitful domestic commerce.[51] Protection, then, was "a measure of resistance to that oppressive system [of free trade] under which manufacturing industry tends to become more and more centralized in a single little island," Carey declared. Like List, the American economist praised a universal free trade as a distant goal, but only after all nations had developed a manufacturing power equal to that of Britain.[52]

Carey amalgamated liberal social theory with the economic arguments of the national economists. Under primitive conditions, he observed, the soldier and the trader joined together to oppress the people. The soldier sought plunder and slave-worked estates; the trader profited by buying commodities or men where they were cheap and selling them where they were dear. The intimate connection between war and trade, which favored appropriation over production, was everywhere apparent in the past as in the present. In the Homeric world, or that of the Vikings or the Elizabethans, traders and pirates were indistinguishable, as they also were in Britain's Opium War of 1839,

The Liberal Ideal and the Demons of Empire

or in the use of an American naval force in 1853 to compel the Japanese to trade. In a good society, one characterized by a developed individualism, soldiers and traders would merely be instruments. Where war and trade predominated over a peaceful commerce—in Ireland, for example, or in Italy, India, Turkey, or Carolina—there was a tendency toward centralization, the growth of great cities, and "a constantly increasing inequality," with "the few accumulating fortunes most rapidly as the chances of war and trade tend to deprive the poorer classes of bread." As ever more persons and resources were devoted to war and to trade, such a society ended in ruin.[53]

Carey drew on history to prove his thesis. In ancient Athens, for example, before the sixth century B.C., there had been peace, individual freedom, democracy, and decentralization. The wholesale destruction caused by the Persian Wars, however, transformed this stable and pacific society. The aristocracy, whose interests had turned to war and plunder, now acted to destroy the power of association and to enrich itself. As mistress of the seas, Athens controlled the export of the surplus production of all states and established an empire of tributary dependencies. The wealth and splendor of the city grew, but at the same time, the wages of labor declined and the poverty of the people, more and more dependent on the state for employment, increased, and there arose the need to export people to distant colonies. Class struggles between rich and poor exhausted the people and left them "mere instruments," first of Philip, and then of Alexander of Macedon. Carey saw Britain and its trade empire as a modern Athens.[54] Other states (Carthage, Venice, and Holland among them) had followed similar paths and met similar fates, Carey declared; in each case, the villains were the soldiers and the "trading aristocracy."[55]

From 1688 onward, the history of Great Britain was one of almost continuous trade wars, but the system that Britain established was at core different from those of earlier trade empires. Previous empires had sought only to regulate the relations of their subordinate states with one another and with foreigners; Britain alone worked also to control the internal structure of its colonial dependents. Carey proceeded to attribute exclusively to Great Britain, no doubt the most successful of the empires of mercantilism, what was common in the relationships of colonies and their metropolises in other empires of the old colonial system.[56] More recent British policy compelled other peoples to "continue mere tillers of the earth" and become Britain's "economic dependents." Thus it perpetuated, albeit under the auspices of free trade, the goals of the mercantilist colonial system. The constant object of the British trading system was to secure terms of trade favorable to the producer of manufactured goods, that is, to obtain the greatest amount of sugar or rice with the smallest quantity of cloth or iron manufactures. The trader and transporter were to be enriched at the expense of the consumer and producer. Adam Smith had denounced these wasteful tendencies of mercantilism and had written in praise of the home trade. Nevertheless, "from that hour to the present . . . the system he denounced has been pursued."[57]

Carey then considered the situation of a number of the British colonies, formal and informal, which suffered as a result of the trading system. In Great Britain's West Indian colonies, particularly Jamaica, the planter, before emancipation, had been a mere "superintendent of slaves" for British merchants, to whom he was usually in debt.[58] A supposedly independent Portugal was ruined by the Methuen Treaty of 1703, which had offered a British market for Portuguese wines in exchange for British woolens, and had thereby undermined Portugal's efforts to establish its own woolen industry.[59] After a virtually free trade between Turkey and Britain was established in the eighteenth century, Turkey's industries declined, so that after the 1780s, Turkey sold only raw cotton abroad instead of its former exports of cotton cloth.[60] After the American Revolution, Ireland had managed to free itself from many of the mercantile restrictions of the old colonial system and, in the interests of promoting its linen and wool industries, even levied taxes on foreign manufactures. Commerce progressed in consequence. With the Act of Union in 1801 came centralization, and a crippling blow to Irish industry. Manchester and Birmingham now supplied Ireland with textiles, and poverty drove tens of thousands of Irishmen from their country.[61] In India, the native cotton industry had been undermined first by heavy British duties on imported Indian cotton goods and then by the lower price of the machine-produced cotton goods of Lancashire. The result was a system that destroyed commerce and turned an entire nation into "a mass of wretched cultivators on the one hand, and grasping money-lenders on the other." In their insatiable quest for new markets and revenues, the British merchants became traders in Indian-grown opium, "levying upon the Chinese a tribute of some 20 million pounds annually for its purchase, and making war in support of this trade."[62]

The British trading system made "the agriculturists of the world mere slaves, dependent for food and clothing upon the will of a few people, proprietors of a small amount of machinery." As was frequently the case in exclusively agricultural countries, the cultivators were perpetually in debt, "and the money-lender fleeces all." Great Britain represented in the modern world what history had displayed so often in the past: the determination of the wicked alliance of the military classes and the traders to destroy commerce. Again pointing

The Liberal Ideal and the Demons of Empire

to the exhaustion of the soil as the great defect in an agricultural nation, Carey declared, in perhaps an anticipation of more abstract descriptions of capitalist anality, that in this way, Britain had become "a grand reservoir" of the manure of virtually half the world. That Britain was a free country, far from alleviating the evil, increased it, Carey observed, and he reminded his readers that the democratic Athenians were "the most oppressive of taskmasters." This British system, moreover, carried with it the necessity of wars, as had occurred in India, Afghanistan, China, and Turkey—wars that always aimed at producing cheaper raw materials and lowering the price of labor of their tillers.[63]

Carey devoted much of his attention to a discussion of money and banking and to the role played by finance in subjecting the agricultural nations of the world to Britain's trading interest. He took issue with the views of the mainstream of British political economy and with the practical application of much of their doctrine in Peel's restrictionist Bank Act of 1844. (Though he did not name them, his sympathies were clearly with the monetary heretics, the men of Thomas Attwood's inflationist Birmingham Currency School, who were regarded as cranks in their day.) Money was not merely a neutral instrument; it had a considerable power of its own. When the money supply was large, as the inflationists desired, the circulation of money was rapid and the producing classes (though not the appropriating ones) greatly benefited.[64] The greater the supply of money and the precious metals, the lower was the interest rate. With the lowering of interest, the prices of raw materials tended to rise and those of manufactured goods to fall to an ever nearer equality, to the advantage of the agriculturist. This was why, according to Carey, the orthodox political economists and the Bank of England favored currency restriction and the free-trade policies designed to keep interest rates high.[65]

Carey's chief villain was the Bank of England, whose tight-money policies had an undue influence on the international monetary system. The Bank's directors promoted the interests of the pernicious British trading system, as well as their private fortunes. It was "the most influential moneyed institution the world has yet seen." The British government had granted this private bank a monopoly control and management of the circulation of money, and its misuse of this authority had brought about a dangerous instability, one that resulted not from the overuse of banknotes (as the orthodox believed) but from the effort to restrict them. Through raising and lowering the rate of interest, the Bank of England had so altered the value of labor and property, both at home and abroad, that "the poor were made poorer, while the rich were being still further enriched." The Bank's support for the return to the gold standard in 1819 had protected the capitalist against the laborer and confiscated the properties of the producing classes to the profit of those who received fixed incomes. Land and labor fell in price, and only the moneylender, along with the annuitant and the officeholder, prospered. These were the classes who "lived by the exercise of their power of appropriation."[66]

The British financial system sought to secure cheap raw materials, cheap land, and cheap labor, while keeping the costs of manufactured cloth and iron as high as possible. A policy that aimed at an approximate equalization of the price of raw material and manufactured goods—a just term of trade between the two, in present-day usage—was one that promoted progress and civilization; the British system's attempt to enlarge the difference between them was simply barbarism. Great Britain's single-minded effort to extend trade (as opposed to commerce) produced everywhere a stagnation in the circulation of capital. The more cotton that was stocked in American warehouses, the more the trader in cotton could dictate prices to the disadvantage of the grower. At home, the more unsteady the prices of cloth or iron goods, the less demand for labor and the greater the advantage of those who had large capital. The small capitalist was being forced out of contention. As commerce gave way to trade, the two hundred thousand landowners of the time of Adam Smith had given way to a system of hired laborers and absentee landlords. Savings were formerly amassed in small savings banks. Now, in 1858, Carey noted, "the enormous mass of capital invested in life insurance offices, savings funds, &c. &c.," while little profiting the owners of these accumulations, enabled "the few who control their movements to accumulate fortunes for themselves."[67]

Carey's indictment, like Wakefield's earlier analysis, had a proto-Marxist ring. The middle class tended "gradually to pass away." In factory towns, an ever wealthier elite presided over an increasingly impoverished mass, the two linked merely by a cash nexus and animated by class hostility. The "successful bankers and traders" were alone in the "immensity of fortune" which the system enabled them to acquire. The view that economic welfare depended on a cheap and abundant labor supply made it necessary that capital keep labor in subordination; men were being everywhere reduced to slavery by a system in which land and capital become more and more strengthened, consolidated, and centralized. Clearly, when the small landed proprietor had vanished, and the small capitalist had become an annuitant since economic conditions made it too perilous for him to risk an entrepreneurial undertaking, there would be less possibility for self-government. "The atmosphere of England is one of gloom," Carey warned; "everyone is anxious for the future, for himself or his children."[68]

Slavery was the "ultimate tendency" of the classical political economy that had deserted Adam Smith's view of the superiority of domestic commerce to favor foreign trade. A system based upon the Ricardian theory of rent and the theory of diminishing returns from agriculture was one that inescapably led to people becoming slaves and civilization giving way to barbarism. Malthusian and Ricardian theory, indeed, was designed to permit those who profited by it "to account for the diseases of which it was itself the cause." God never intended "the division of nations into agricultural and manufacturing ones—the single workshop being thousands of miles distant from the places at which the materials are produced." Nor could the Deity regard labor as a commodity. For the British classical school, man was "only an animal that *will* procreate, that *must* be fed, and that *can be made* to work." The Malthusian-Ricardian doctrine "repudiates all the distinctive qualities of man, and limits itself to the consideration of those he holds in common with the beast of burden or of prey." The classical economists had denied that God intended that "every man should find a place at his table." Adam Smith, Carey concluded, "knew nothing of any such 'dismal science.' "[69]

"Two systems are before the world," he maintained, the British system of trade and the French system of commerce. These systems were engaged in a contest for leadership. The French system sought to make more equal the prices of manufactures and raw produce, the British to widen the difference. Now fewer than a half-million British workers produced the manufactured goods that purchased very large amounts of raw produce from abroad. Soon the agricultural communities of the world would understand how little was given in exchange for their efforts. They would then decide to mine and manufacture for themselves. The countries of Europe and North America were becoming convinced that their only hope lay in the adoption of the French system of protection. When this happened, Britain would suffer severely and would be compelled to give up the trading system. All the world, Carey declared, had a stake in the defeat of this wicked system. It was now better understood that there was a "solidarity of interest—of prosperity, or of adversity" among the agriculturists and laborers of the world against the trader.[70] Carey lauded "Professor List, the man to whose patriotic labors, the existence of the Zoll-Verein is due," for promoting this better understanding of the two opposing systems.[71]

The United States had heretofore moved from one system to the

---

other, seeking protection when an increase in treasury revenues was needed and free trade when it was not; but a more sympathetic view of a policy of protection for industry was emerging. Its prime opponent was the social system of the South, and Carey observed (as had Olmsted and as Cairnes would) that it was in the South that "all the warlike disposition" of the country was to be found, with the slaveowner performing the role of a trader who regulated the exchange between the slaves, who grew cotton and tobacco, and those who consumed cloth.[72] Yet America, with an almost unlimited quantity of fuel to power its industry in the coal deposits of the Appalachians and with boundless quantities of iron ore, did not need to suffer the disadvantageous terms of trade endured by agricultural nations.[73]

In the strain of a later American populism, Carey regretted that the financier and the railroad promoter, with their "almost irresistible" influence in the legislatures of the nation, had become the masters of American society, impoverishing the farmer and the laborer. A trading society fell more and more "under the control of gamblers in stocks, in cotton, and in flour," of men whose "rule of life" was " 'Get money honestly, if you can, but get money.' " While commerce created "self-governing and responsible" beings, trade divided society into "a responsible and irresistible class—the master of slaves on one side, and the slaves themselves on the other." Political and judicial corruption had become "almost universal," with "crime and corruption becoming hourly more common, and anarchy becoming from year to year more near at hand." "Wall Street governs New York," Carey declared, "and that city directs the legislation of the Union."[74]

Carey observed that the circumstances and ethos of this system necessarily accompanied, indeed promoted, both British and American expansion at the expense of the "weaker communities" of the globe. As a result, "the world has been belted round with colonies—alliances have been made and broken—thousands of millions of pounds have been spent on ruinous wars—millions upon millions of lives had been sacrificed." British policy has "impoverished and exhausted" Portugal, Turkey, Ireland, India, and, most recently, China. There had been wars in the Sindh, Afghanistan, Punjab, and Burma. "Trade and war thus travel always in company with each other—always exhausting the earlier fields of action, and always compelled to seek for new ones."[75] In the United States as well, trade had been responsible for wars, that of 1812 for instance, and a desire for new lands because of soil exhaustion was the motive for the seizure of Texas, the Mexican War, and the occupation of California, as well as the interest in appropriating Cuba, Dominica, and Central America. Trade was "always dispersive and warlike," Carey asserted; "it sends fleets to Japan, and expeditions to Africa and the Amazon—seeking outlets for population abroad, while closing its markets for its labor at home." Commerce on the other hand was pacific. While commerce would increase the value of land at home, trade sought new lands to conquer, sending expeditions to other continents while, in the case of the United States, neglecting the impediments to the navigation of the Mississippi.[76] The tendency to colonial expansion that past and future liberal social theorists assigned to mercantilism was attributed by Carey to the free-trade system of Britain and its political economists.

Carey's later writings continued in the same vein, only in perhaps more polemical form. In 1858, for example, he again wrote of free-trade policy as designed to perpetuate the economic subservience of the world to Great Britain, and he appealed to "all the agriculturists of the world" to recognize their "solidarity of interest" against the British traders.[77] "The system which looks forward toward making Britain 'the workshop of the world,'" he observed in 1867, "is, of all the forms of tyranny ever devised, the one that, *par excellence,* tends to the establishment of slavery as the normal condition of the man who needs work."[78] Carey saw a Britain that had foolishly neglected the home for the foreign market as having "passed her zenith."[79] The future belonged to Germany, Russia, and the United States.[80]

John Austin, a Benthamite and a friend of J. S. Mill, wrote an article for the *Edinburgh Review* in 1842 on List's *National System.* For Austin, as for British political economists more generally, List's treatise was a reversion to a prescientific mercantilism. The book was the "work of a zealous and unscrupulous advocate," and therefore "unworthy of notice."[81] Mill wrote to Austin, in praising this article, that "List seems to have as much confusion in his head as the advocates of prohibition [tariffs] generally have, but the state of public feeling to which the book recommends itself is a very serious consideration."[82] (In his *Principles* [1848], Mill would concede the usefulness for a country to protect its infant industries for a short period;[83] in later years he would regret having written in a fashion that many took as justifying tariffs.[84]) The prevailing view in Britain was probably that of the *Times,* which in 1847 denounced List and his followers for propagating "the most erroneous and absurd notions of the policy of this country" and described the ideas of the national economists as "extravagant fictions."[85]

It is particularly interesting to note Mill's reaction to Carey's economics. The British economist regarded Carey with a certain respect but believed him wrong-headed and attributed his failure to see economic questions properly to the limitations of his American background. Mill took special issue with the American economist's dismissal of the law of rent. In a letter to Carey in 1845, Mill argued that only in a new country did there appear to be no limit to the increasing returns from agriculture, but such a limit would soon be reached even in America.[86] Mill believed, furthermore, that the protectionism so popular among the French and German publics derived from "a strenuous desire to bring down the wealth and power" of Britain.[87] In the 1860s, Mill saw protectionism in America as having become the "creed" of the majority, and even of the educated classes, and saw Carey as having played an important role in converting Americans to this doctrine.[88] Carey's writings were, unfortunately, "untrustworthy—perverse and absurd," although Mill thought the American economist's "feelings . . . are usually right."[89] A year later, Mill described Carey's tome, which gave "the prestige of scientific authority" to protectionism in the United States, as "about the worst book on political economy I ever read."[90]

In 1853, Karl Marx saw Carey, the "only important North American economist," as the misguided exponent of class harmony; Carey's fault was his having taken " 'undeveloped' conditions" in the United States for " 'normal conditions.' "[91] While Carey condemned the destruction of India's cotton industry by Lancashire, Marx viewed it with approval as progressive and "*revolutionary.*"[92] In the *Grundrisse,* Marx again dismissed Carey's belief that Britain, in its quest for industrial monopoly, had disrupted what would otherwise have been a "fundamental harmony" between a domestic industry, labor, and agriculture. Carey had not understood that "world-market disharmonies" which he saw as produced by the predominance of Britain's "large-scale" industry, were "merely the ultimate adequate expression" of internal, domestic disharmonies. In this, Carey was typically American. The special character of Carey's analysis, Marx concluded, was in his belonging to a country "where bourgeois society did not develop on the foundation of the feudal system, but developed rather from itself."[93]

Carey's view of the financial and trading class was much like that which Marxists would later put forward. Indeed, Carey's description of the trading system, particularly its British variant, where finance capital played an especially malevolent role, was quasi-socialist, and his writings were welcomed by Horace Greeley's *New York Tribune,* which also modishly flirted with Fourier's socialism. Fourier and his disciples also depicted Britain and the finance capitalists as villains. For the Fourierists, as we shall see, the usurious Jew joined a perfidious England in the dock. In a Catholic France, in the nineteenth century—where so many of the bankers were indeed Jewish—this was perhaps a natural

The Liberal Ideal and the Demons of Empire

association. For an Irish-American like Carey, the Jewish banker (virtually nonexistent in the United States of his time) was unnecessary to his argument. Britain's imperial sins might stand on their own, particularly given the memories of two American wars against the repressive policies of the British trading colossus. By the end of the century, however, the Fourierist portrayal of both a British and Jewish finance capital would be common even in America.

The French critics of finance capital may be seen as a variant of the tradition of the national economists. In their first phase, these writers reflected opinion in a society that was backward in its economic development and consequently saw merchants and bankers, not industrialists, as typical capitalists. Moreover, after over a century of war with France's longtime rival, many French writers had come to see Britain's victory over Napoleon as due to commercial and financial skulduggery, not military prowess. British gold had supported the dynasts of the Continent and corrupted Continental (including French) statesmen and journalists. The victorious British aristocracy had preserved its feudal privileges, they further argued, and, in alliance with British monied interests and Jewish bankers, was attempting to impose a new and diabolical feudalism of finance on the world. We shall see that the coming of the great depression of the 1870s, which seemed to accompany the widespread adoption of the gold standard in the third quarter of the century (by France, the United States and Germany, among others) gave the French attack on British and Jewish usury a wider appeal—not only to those most committed to the vanishing traditional society, but even to liberals and Marxists, who welcomed industrialism but dreaded a usurious finance capitalism.

5 The International Usury of

Finance Capital

Not too far beneath the surface of the attacks of the national economists on finance capital, and on Britain as the most successful wielder
of its power, was the traditional revulsion at usury. The moneylender
abused industry, the child of nature, and disobeyed the biblical injunction that man must gain his bread by the sweat of his brow. The
prejudice against usury—the unnatural spectacle, in Aristotle's phrase,
of money making money—was deep and far-reaching in agrarian
societies, where bad harvests could prove calamitous without relief
from those with stores of capital; persons who withheld such resources
or charged interest for their use were enemies of mankind. The medieval Catholic Church had banned usury, making an exception for
the Jews, whose lending of money at interest to non-Jews was not
forbidden by their faith. Medieval and early modern princes, to whom
Jewish moneylenders had made loans, at times directed the hostility
of their subjects against these creditors. Since Jews were traditionally
held to be an accursed people beloved of Satan, their association with
moneylending served to bring both them and usury into even greater
disrepute.

For centuries, Europe was caught between the ethos and needs of
an agrarian society and those of a commercial society requiring speculative investment and accepting the legitimacy of the payment of
interest (and when the risks were great, a high interest). In the sixteenth century, a time of economic transition, Martin Luther mounted
one of the fiercest attacks on usury, though some of the Reformation's
leaders, notably Calvin, did accept the taking of interest, while insisting
that it not be excessive and making a distinction between loans made
to secure commercial advantage and those made to the needy in severe

straits. Lecky had written of this change of attitude as one of the characteristics of the rise of rationalism.

In the seventeenth, eighteenth, and nineteenth centuries, economic thinkers in Britain (among them John Locke, Jeremy Bentham, and David Ricardo) and on the Continent argued the futility of trying to regulate the price of the rent of money. They held this practice would be destructive of trade and useful only to bankers who had the skill to evade the legal rate—yet even Adam Smith, despite his brief for the free market, had sought to fix the rate of interest by law. The later classical economists viewed interest fixed at market rates as legitimate and finance capital as productive; their successors of the neoclassical school saw finance and industry as equally productive at the margin. Though this was the consensus of what called itself economic "science" and might be provable by the criteria of that science, such arguments did not disturb the widespread intuitive opinion to the contrary.[1]

The portrait of the usurer as an insatiable bloodsucker, enriching himself by exploiting the needs of the poor and desperate, survived these economic defenses of moneylending and interest taking. In all parts of the European continent, there were still peasants, often heavily in debt, prepared to find in Satanic Jewish moneylenders the prime cause of their distress. Despite the Catholic Church's gradual abandonment of the prohibition on usury, the nineteenth century saw many priests make the battle against moneylenders an underground cause in the Church. The theme was also taken up by populist and socialist critics of the new commercial and industrial society. Karl Marx argued in this mode in one of his early writings, making Judaism (and its greedy and usurious, and therefore quintessentially capitalistic, outlook) a prime target. The "worldly cult of the Jew," Marx wrote in 1843, was "huckstering," his "worldly god" was "money." In Judaism there was "a universal *anti-social* element" which had now attained its full realization in Christian bourgeois society. Marx concluded by calling for "the emancipation of mankind from Judaism."[2]

Those who saw a communal agricultural society exposed to atomization and alienation by modern commercial and industrial society often blamed the lending of money at interest. More rural nations, where industry had not yet become the prevailing mode, witnessed the most fervent denunciations of cosmopolitan bankers, who arranged for money to be either plentiful to encourage borrowers to overextend their commitments, or tight so that creditors could foreclose on the disappointed hopes of the debtors. (List and especially Carey, we have seen, argued along these lines.) Even in early nineteenth-century Britain, where the new society was most deeply entrenched, the populist

The Liberal Ideal and the Demons of Empire

William Cobbett saw the Jewish bankers of the London Exchange as the principal enemies of a benevolent and caring society. By the end of the nineteenth century, such arguments were to be found among French and German socialists and American populists.

A number of writers—Continental and American; liberal, socialist, Marxist, and national economist—would link colonialism and imperialism with the manipulation and speculation of bankers. These villains, they declared, plotted to make all nations subservient to Britain and to the international financiers housed in the City of London. By the end of the nineteenth century, many liberals and socialists would see what they had once regarded as useful industrial capital as having become the puppet of a parasitic finance capital. The special preserve of international finance was understood to be the high returns available overseas, and it would become common to depict financial interests as the power behind the scenes in promoting or dooming risky colonial ventures, and profiting grandly from them. The all-powerful financiers even determined which country won in controversies over colonies. Such writers often invoked the demon of usury as the force behind all the unpleasant aspects of capitalism and colonialism.

One of the earliest writers in this vein was the socialist Charles Fourier, who had a wide influence in France and abroad. French industrial development lagged behind that of Great Britain and, in later decades, that of Germany and the United States as well. French banking houses, in what appeared a continuing association with exploitative mercantilism, were the leading representatives of economic modernity, and Jewish banking houses, in good part because of their readiness to assume government loans believed risky by others, were prominent among large-scale bankers. These circumstances reinforced and perpetuated the long-held horror of usury. The association of this dread with the hatred of the feudalism of the old regime, over which the Revolution had triumphed, was a stroke of genius on the part of Fourier and his disciples. The Fourierists had little sympathy with liberalism or the capitalist system and felt a strong antipathy toward a demonic Britain. Like List and Carey, they saw the new system as an instrument for establishing an imperial hegemony that would exploit the labor and resources of the world in British interests.

Charles Fourier

Fourier was born at Besançon in 1772, the son of a well-to-do draper, and he himself worked as a textile broker, one of the middlemen of commerce he so detested, for much of his life. A bachelor, Fourier spent his leisure hours developing his sometimes fantastic, sometimes illuminating theories. Fourier's utopia included both sexual and economic prescriptions: he called for a free gratification of libidinal desires that would satisfy the many varieties of sexual temperament; in place of an "unnatural" individualism and competition he called for "association" of men and women in phalansteries in which all would cooperate to perform the necessary work of the world. These settlements would devote themselves primarily to agriculture, which he believed the most productive pursuit, or, rather, primarily to horticulture and arboriculture, since the cultivation of grains was a more laborious and dreary undertaking. Though his plan for communal living and cooperative labor placed him among the socialists, Fourier was also a defender of inheritance and private property, and of harmony between classes. An optimist, he was convinced that if only society adapted itself to humanity's true nature, instead of attempting to force it into the unnatural mold that it called "civilization," virtue and happiness would triumph.[3]

The system of laissez-faire and commerce, so praised by the political economists, Fourier declared, was the enemy of humanity. Commerce subordinated society to "a class of parasitic and unproductive agents, the merchants."[4] It despoiled industry by dishonest devices (false bankruptcies, forestalling, stock market manipulation) that he labeled the "parasitism" of superfluous agents.[5] Far from being of use to industry, which was genuinely productive, an unproductive commerce was "the natural enemy of factories," on which it levied tribute: "In the majority of manufacturing cities," he observed, "the small, not very prosperous, manufacturer works for the dealer in materials; just as it often happens that the small cultivator works only for the usurer."[6] The trader was "an industrial corsair." Free competition resulted in a system in which large capitals enabled monopolists to reduce to "industrial slavery" all lesser proprietors. Merchants and bankers daily hatched plots to cause artificial rises and falls of prices ("agiotage"), "gorging themselves with gold, at the expense of general industry." Governments were in thrall to traders and financiers, monopolists, stockjobbers, and forestallers of vital commodities.[7]

In 1808, in his first work (in which virtually all the ideas of his system appeared), Fourier began his assault on what were to be his principal villains—the Freemasons, Britain, and the Jews. Fourier saw a conspiratorial Freemasonry as having engineered the French Revolution. The Masons were rich men who wished to increase their riches still further; they had given up revealed religion in favor of the Enlightenment's new religion of reason, which in their hands had become a corrupting "culte de la volupté." They were moreover the willing allies of a perfidious England. A more religious age, Fourier wrote, would have seen Britain's "debasement and persecution" of humanity as a "scourge" wielded by God, a divine chastisement. The British trade monopoly had destroyed the industry of all nations, incited wars that impelled nations to tear each other apart, rendered the European monarchs subservient to British financial subsidies, and, finally, outraged the honor of mankind by subordinating all of society to "vils calculs mercantiles." This was "the abyss to which economic science had led."[8] At this time, Fourier still hoped that Napoleon's Continental System might defeat Britain's goal.[9] Along with the Freemasons and Britain, Fourier placed the Jews.

The Jews personified all the worst features of the commercial system. Fourier's emblematic figure of false bankruptcy was "the Jew Iscariot," who ruined his creditors while making huge profits. Jews were the "secret enemies of all nations."[10] Fourier denounced ancient Carthage—like Britain the seat of a trade empire—as having been debased by the commercial spirit; the British were the "modern Carthaginians," and the fellow Semites of the Carthaginians, the Jews, were likewise a people "addicted to traffic, to usury, and to mercantile depravity." The Jews were "a nation of usurers." Liberal prejudices had led to such "shocking actions" as the granting of citizenship to the Jews, opening the door to a parasitic people whom an "enlightened policy would have excluded as a social contagion."[11]

The Jews and the Freemasons were determined to assist Britain, favored by geographical position and a powerful navy, in its effort to subject the entire world to a new "mercantile feudalism." Fourier noted that Britain would enforce this system less by an exercise of direct political authority than by "the tyranny of a handful of merchants." The new commercial world order would be an easy one to organize. All the British politicians, regardless of party, pursued the same program (a secret one like that of the Freemasons) of bringing all nations, both barbarous and civilized (Persia, India, China, and Siam as well as Continental Europe) into Britain's commercial orbit.[12] The tyranny of Great Britain was driving the great Indian empire to its ruin.[13] Fourier foresaw a complete conquest of the world by a maritime Britain, an empire holding hundreds of kingdoms in vassalage.[14] The final consequence of the "mercantile spirit of the noble science of political economy," the system of the British, the Freemasons, and the Jews, would be to transform civilization into an "industrial feudalism." This system, by establishing trading empires on the model of the British East India Company throughout the world, would "reduce to bondage the masses and the small proprietors." Such a condition would constitute the last phase of civilization, conforming to "the law of the meeting of extremes," and it would end as it began, in "a feudalism reproduced in the direction opposite to the first."[15]

Thus twice within a generation, Fourier concluded, philosophers would have brought about social retrogression: "first by an excess of political liberty in 1793, which led Europe swiftly to barbarism; and secondly, by an excess of commercial liberty which, today, is pushing us rapidly downward towards the feudal order." These philosophers, "scientific charlatans" hoping to sell their books, were prepared to give credence to "any chimaera which might replace the theological discussions" they displaced. Commerce was the "golden calf" of this social cult, replacing "wisdom, virtue, and morality." The "true greatness of a nation, its true glory, according to the economists, was to sell neighboring empires more pairs of trousers than one buys from them."[16] The embodiment of this commerce was an insular Britain, enriched by "monopoly and piracy," where merchants had become "pillars of society"—a Britain, finally, before which all the cabinets of Europe were prepared to "debase themselves" in return for "a tenth of the industrial tribute" that Britain derived from them.[17]

Fourier's immediate influence was felt not only in France but throughout Europe, even in Russia, where Alexander Herzen was for a time a disciple, and in America as well. Among his several thousand French followers was the future Emperor Napoleon III. We must note, however, that Fourier's view of Britain, the Freemasons, and the Jews did not always accompany the acceptance of his sexual opinions or of his views on cooperation. This was certainly the case with respect to Fourierists in the United States, although we may see elements of Fourier's positions on Britain and finance capital, along with his belief in the harmony of the classes, in the opinions of Henry Carey. Among several dozen Fourierist communities established in America (after the master's death in 1837), Brook Farm attracted many of the principal figures of the so-called New England Renaissance, including R. W. Emerson, Henry Thoreau, and Nathaniel Hawthorne. Prominent journalists like Albert Brisbane, Horace Greeley, and Charles Dana came under Fourier's influence. In the 1830s and 1840s, a number of Fourierist newspapers appeared in France, disseminating the various aspects of the doctrine. One of the most popular of these journals was edited by Alphonse Toussenel.

Alphonse Toussenel

Toussenel, editor of two Fourierist journals in mid-nineteenth-century Paris, was principally known for his *Les Juifs, rois de l'époque* of 1845. The book mounted a violent attack on Jews, Britain, and finance capital. Subtitled "Histoire de la féodalité financière," the history of financial feudalism, Toussenel's tract denounced the new feudalism of finance as even more oppressive and insatiable than the old feudalism of the nobility. Both Fourier and Saint-Simon had described its founding, Toussenel wrote, but Saint-Simon and his followers, allies of the Jewish bankers, had actually set about to establish it.[18] In the past, the old nobility had charged the traveler and the merchant tolls for crossing its property; today, all the canals, railways, and other transport enterprises belonged to the "high and powerful lords of the bank," the Jews. The industrial magnates even exacted "les droits du seigneur" from their female workers, not waiting until they were about to be married, but as soon as they were nubile.[19] The "misery" of the "Manchester *mechanic*" and the Irish peasant was equally "horrifying." But medieval or Russian serfs at least enjoyed the protection of their masters, whereas the nineteenth-century manufacturer disclaimed any responsibility for the well-being of his workers. The new feudalists would be obliged to alter their behavior once they understood that such neglect of their industrial serfs would incite revolutions.[20] Although wars of conquest were no more, Toussenel added, there were two exceptions to the rule: a Britain under the influence of the new feudalism and a Russia still in the grip of the old.[21]

Jewish bankers had taken possession of the "hereditary privileges of the *ancien régime* abolished by our fathers."[22] When he wrote *Jew,* Toussenel observed, he meant the term "in the power sense of Jew: banker, usurer." *Jew* stood for every "unproductive parasite living upon the work of others." But for Toussenel, the Jew as Jew was sufficiently reprehensible: masters of fraud and treason, they had crucified the Savior, were undoubtedly the "people of Satan," and lived "by exploitation, by parasitism and usury." Voltaire, the Encyclopedists, and Charles Fourier, the most powerful minds of the century, had warned the nations against the Jew, whom Frenchmen had too hastily accepted as fellow citizens. Fourier, particularly, had observed and described the beginnings of "la féodalité mercantile et le règne de Juda." The Jews in France—"cosmopolitan bankers," not true Frenchmen—were a nation within a nation, who dominated parliamentary government by their wealth. Toussenel blessed the providential circumstance that "la féodalité mercantile" in France saw the hated Jews as its first representatives, so that Christians could recognize the squalor by "the filth of its name!"[23]

Toussenel declared a "remorseless war against the parasites of all religions and flags, war on cosmopolitan bankers" who were making France their prey. The British, Dutch, and Swiss merchants and bankers—because of their Protestant absorption with the vengeful Jewish Bible rather than the loving Christian Gospels—were Jews in spirit and deed. A Protestantism that substituted freedom of the individual conscience for papal infallibility was a retrogressive movement designed to favor the power of princes, "an insurrection of commercial peoples ['races de trafiquants']" who, finding themselves cramped by the ethos of the Gospels, had turned to a testament that permitted them to rob with impunity. The British headed these Protestant robbers, and France was their chief victim, Toussenel observed.[24] The pillagers of the public treasury (the bankers of Judah, London, and Geneva) had secured the monopoly of credit and controlled the building and management of the railways. In the world as a whole, France, now a second-rank power, had humbly yielded a monopolistic police of the seas to the British navy. Toussenel called on the king and the people to join in defeating the aristocracy of money just as they had in an earlier time united to defeat that of caste.[25]

The Fourierist journalist saw the Jews as managers of a conspiracy to maintain peace in the interest of Britain and international finance, to the detriment of French interests. This explained why war between France and Britain had not erupted over Tahiti and Morocco, and why France permitted Britain, always seeking control of the Suez peninsula, to throttle Mehomet Ali in Egypt. Since the majority of the British House of Commons and of the French Chamber of Deputies owned shares in both British and French railways, war would not suit their pocketbooks and hence would not take place. Unlike the France of the Restoration, Louis Philippe's France played the game of the Jews and of Britain and was disposed to concede Britain's control of Suez rather than "break the peace dear to the heart of Israel."[26]

Great Britain was the shop in which "pernicious drugs and doctrines" were distilled and marketed: the whiskey that consumed the American Indians and the opium that poisoned the Chinese, as well as "the principles that set citizen against citizen, people against people, race against race." By disseminating the slogan of "independence," the British had deprived Spain, an ally of France and ruled by Bourbons, of its empire, so that the Iberian Peninsula itself could become, as had South America, a market for Britain. The "false science" of the political economists advanced the "absurd doctrine" of laissez-faire, which worked toward the "annihilation of authority." In the hope of ruining its rivals, Britain had raised the cry of free trade.[27] Great Britain had long prospered under protection and understood that other states adopting such a system would lead to their being able to compete with it; yet it wished other countries to give up their tariffs against imported manufactures, so that it might benefit.[28] "When the English say the words *liberty* or *competition,* our ears should always hear *monopoly* and *forestalling.*" The French liberal economists were secret allies of Britain, ready to support the interests of the British monopoly, as were French Protestants like Guizot.[29]

Britain, "once again, lives by mercantilism and the commercial exploitation of all peoples," Toussenel declared. The so-called commercial liberty of the British was "a war waged by machines and by capital" which insured Britain's victory since it had immensely more machinery and capital than the French.[30] Since Britain manufactured enough to supply the entire world twice over, every foreign manufacturer was its enemy. Its policy was to engross trade everywhere. It possessed the narrow seas commanding the main trade routes and from these bases flooded neighboring continents with British goods. Britain worked to prolong "the industrial infancy" of other nations. War—not peace, as Toussenel had suggested earlier in connection with Morocco, Tahiti, and Suez—was Britain's prime interest. "War nourishes monopoly, monopoly feeds war," and when either ceased, English power immediately collapsed. "The Englishman belonged to a predatory people . . . compelled to kill in order to live."[31]

Toussenel urged the mounting of a crusade, a holy war of vengeance against a perfidious and hypocritical Britain, whose parasitism would lead inevitably to its own destruction. All the ancient world had cheered the fall of *its* mistress of the seas, Carthage, "the Albion of yesterday." The time was now ripe for the destruction of the modern Carthage and the rescue of the battered Irish millions and millions of English proletarians, "our suffering brothers who await with us the day of deliverance."[32] In its efforts to kill off "productive work" abroad and make all foreigners consumers of its goods and "tributaries of [its] industry," Britain had impoverished the world. Other nations would no longer be able to purchase British goods, with the result that sooner or later Great Britain would die of hunger, surrounded by its mountains of manufactures. "And that day is not far off," Toussenel exulted, "for all mechanical progress, and all tariff unions, like the Zollverein, bring it closer."[33]

In the 1880s the French anti-Semitic journalist Edouard Drumont praised Toussenel's work, which had served as a model for his own. Drumont's *La France juive,* published in 1886, wrote of "l'exploitation juive" and "la nouvelle féodalité juive."[34] The new feudalism had its base in an oppressive and anarchic commercial monopoly characterized by insatiable greed and bad faith, he asserted; this "despotism of the strong-box" was personified by "le Juif cosmopolite." Europe was in feudal bondage to Israel, and "the product of labor and of all the workers poured into the coffers of the Jews in the form of the bonds of the national debt." The establishment of the Third French Republic had seen the complete triumph of Israel.[35]

Drumont compared the victory of the Jewish minority in France to the conquest of England in the eleventh century by the Normans, when a cohesive minority of sixty thousand soldiers led by William the Conqueror was able to seize the lands of the Saxons and to institute the feudal system. Both the old feudalism and the new compelled one people to labor for the benefit of another. Productive work was not responsible for the fortunes of either the Norman or the Jewish feudal masters. These were due simply to the expropriation and exploitation of a servile by a dominant race. The Rothschilds had "made no invention, discovered no mine, cleared no land"; "they had lifted three milliards from the French people without giving anything in exchange."[36]

In the past, France had waged war for honor: now its soldiers died in distant lands to profit Jewish financiers. Under the Third Republic, Drumont charged, the Jew Gambetta began a war in Tunisia for the sake of the international bankers; and to enrich this same class, French ministries supported British rather than French interests in Egypt.[37] Jewish bankers slaughtered ten thousand French soldiers in Tonkin so as to profit by financing the enterprise. A future historian, Drumont predicted, would tell the story of how the Jews attracted money for a loan to Honduras with splendid promises and then profited by cheating both the Hondurans and the bondholders.[38] Drumont contrasted these colonial ventures of Jewish finance capital with the straightforward and relatively benign Russian conquests in Asia, where the czars did not deliver the conquered populations to either "publicans or Jews."[39]

Drumont's assaults on international Jewry would not be without apparent confirmation from other, quite respectable sources elsewhere at the time, particularly in the United States and Germany. One may ask why it was that an argument more suited to the lagging industrialism of nineteenth-century France (as well as pre-1870 Germany)— more suited to regimes of petit bourgeois accumulation than to an advanced capitalism—appeared with such force by the end of the century in, by then, advanced industrial powers like Germany and the United States. The answer seems to lie in the changing character of industrial development. In Britain, entrepreneurs in the eighteenth and early nineteenth centuries had established their factories and mills on a small scale and had employed gains derived from hard work and frugality to expand their undertakings. By the 1870s and 1880s, German and American industrialists had to turn to the banks and to rely on stock-floating financial houses for the capital to establish the large-scale enterprises that the prevailing technology and competition made essential. The result was the control of the new industries by finance capital, with its long association in the public mind with an exploitative mercantilist finance and medieval usury. Confirming this association with mercantilism, the banks and their industrial subordinates in both Germany and the United States sought tariff protection for their manufacturing companies and organized monopolies and trusts to heighten their profits at the expense of the domestic consumer. Such a situation brought many journalists and intellectuals who admired the accomplishments of creative industrial capitalists to denounce what they believed to be the purely exploitative role of the finance capitalists.

British banks during this period concentrated on their usual commercial functions, not the ownership and control of industry, and Britain continued under a regime of free trade that was not conducive to the organization of monopolies. Yet the Bank of England would be as much a target for the later national economists, particularly those who concentrated on the evils of usury, as they had been for List and Carey. The chief reason for this was probably the acceptance of Britain's gold standard by the leading financial powers in the 1870s; by the end of the century many less advanced countries had followed this lead. The gold standard, aimed as it was at monetary stability, appeared to be primarily in the interest of creditor nations and classes, and, its opponents argued, exploited the industrial and agricultural classes. The worldwide depression that began in 1873, like the British difficulties between 1819 and 1850, may have been triggered by the need for an increased currency when there were limited new gold supplies to back such an expansion. The American populists of the 1890s—to cite one among many examples of the opposition to the gold standard—denounced the bankers of Wall Street and their British and Jewish masters in the City of London as crucifying mankind on a cross of gold. (With the discovery of new gold mines in South Africa and Alaska at the close of the 1890s, the depressed conditions of nearly a quarter of a century began to improve, although other forces were also at work in bettering economic conditions.)

Both the new role of finance in industry, almost everywhere but in Britain, and the belief that the gold standard was unnecessarily

---

prolonging the depression, led to a wholesale attack on finance capital, on bankers everywhere and the Bank of England in particular. Allegations made by the American historian Brooks Adams and the German economist and historian Werner Sombart, for example, though somewhat less frantic than those of Drumont and Toussenel, were equally severe. For Adams, Britain was the primary villain, but the Jews were Britain's willing accomplices.

Brooks Adams

In the course of a broad historical survey, published in 1896 as *The Law of Civilization and Decay,* Brooks Adams, grandson and great-grandson of American presidents, described several different human types, each of which embodied instinctual responses that were passed on to progeny; such "controlling instincts" were "involuntary" and virtually divided men into distinct species. In the more barbaric stages of development, the imagination had produced religious, military, and artistic types. As civilization moved from the barbaric conditions of physical dispersion to a situation of concentration, the types produced by imagination were overwhelmed by one dominated by greed.[40] The imperial Spaniards, founders of the greatest empire of the sixteenth and seventeenth centuries, had been children of the imagination, priests and soldiers. They were replaced by the English economic type, "mercantile and sceptical." After the ruin of Spain's "great imaginative empires" in the seventeenth century, England established its own, based on "purely economic centralization."[41]

Having first grounded their nation's prosperity on "piracy and slavery," British commercial adventurers moved to conquer India and to seize its enormous treasures of gold and silver. It was from this mid-eighteenth-century plunder of Clive and his soldiers that Britain procured the capital that made possible the industrial revolution, enabling Great Britain to establish its economic and political hegemony.[42] (The English economist J. M. Keynes was to put forward much the same suggestion over thirty years later, noting that Queen Elizabeth's share of Drake's pirate booty in 1580, if invested at 3.25 percent, would in 1930 be equal to Britain's entire foreign investment;[43] such speculation was to become a staple among Third World writers by the middle decades of the twentieth century.) Britain's accumulations of capital, when they had become great enough, Adams continued, tended "to preponderate over productive energy"; this capital became "autocratic" and "the controlling social force." In the modern world, he observed, the power of accumulated capital was best personified in the usurer.[44]

The Liberal Ideal and the Demons of Empire

Adams's analysis of British usury appears to owe something to Henry Carey, although Adams made no specific reference to the Pennsylvania economist. In the half-century since Carey had begun writing, of course, the industrial development of the United States had proceeded so successfully that, unlike Carey, Adams could not regard America as entirely subservient to British finance. Yet the City of London remained the world's leading banking center. In the 1890s, American radicals and populists attributed the hard times that had beset the world since the 1870s to the machinations of the Bank of England and its allies, the bankers of New York and Boston, and to the rigid adherence by international finance to a monometallic gold standard; these bankers had constricted credit and depressed prices and thereby caused the failure of tens of thousands of farmers and small businessmen. Adams shared these opinions. By the end of the century, the Fourierist view that high finance was under the control not merely of the British but also of the Jewish bankers—for both of which groups the Rothschilds stood as symbol—had become as common in America as on the European continent.

Like List, Carey, and Fourier, Adams distinguished between a class of genuine producers (agriculturists and industrialists) and unproductive moneylenders. The story of modern usury, for Adams, was that of Mayer Amschel Rothschild and the five sons who had founded their banking houses in the chief cities of Europe. Nathan had settled in London and become "the despot of the Stock Exchange" before whom peers and princes bowed. From 1810 onward, economic conditions favored the "usurious mind" of the Rothschilds, and the reestablishment of the gold standard in 1819 confirmed their predominance. Under the previous "reign of the producers," it had been possible to cheapen the currency when prices were depressed; but after 1819 international financiers could control the economy by decisions to discount or not discount commercial paper. The gold standard, by fixing the quantity of money, made it impossible for currency expansion to meet growing demands. "Powerful usurers, like Rothschild," had in gold a "circulating medium sufficiently compact to be controlled by a comparatively small number of capitalists" who might then "hold the whole debtor community at their mercy."[45]

Like Carey, Adams denounced the restrictive British Bank Act of 1844, shaped in part by the Unitarian banker Samuel Loyd, an act that made even more certain manipulative control by the financial interests.[46] Loyd's usurious policy had "not only forced prices down throughout the West, but had changed the aspect of civilization," Adams declared. It had doomed the Irish peasantry and the British farmers and landowners, all debtors, and even a considerable number of manufacturers who now found themselves in the hands of the "creditor class." The financiers first squeezed the economy, depressing prices, and then gave relief when it proved to their advantage. Pauperism increased, revenues fell, Chartist discontent emerged, and revolution threatened. "Nor was it Great Britain only which was convulsed: all Europe was shakened to its centre."[47]

What prevented a "dire convulsion" was the discovery of California gold in 1849, temporarily making possible an expansion of the currency and the raising of farm prices, an increasing demand for manufactured goods, the raising of wages, and the consequent dissipation of discontent. As the effects of this infusion of gold wore off (because of the need of a growing trade for still more currency), the international bankers continued to press for contraction. The enormous reparations stemming from the Prussian victory over France in 1871 had confirmed the domination of financial interests in France, Adams observed, and had also placed the new German empire in the hands of its bankers. Germany, following the interests of international finance, adopted the gold standard in 1873; France, Italy, and the United States soon followed suit. The price of gold with respect to other commodities increased, and manufacturers and agriculturists once again suffered as the usurers waxed rich.[48]

The old feudal landed aristocracy of Britain, after nearly four centuries of wealth and power, became victims of "a new race," of "men like Nathan Rothschild and Samuel Loyd, probably endowed with a subtler intellect and a keener vision" than the usurers of previous epochs. (Samuel Loyd, it should be noted, was not Jewish, but his first name may have left Adams, and very likely his readers, under a misconception.) These financiers had formulated "a policy unrivalled in brilliancy," one that "made them masters of all commerce, industry, and trade": "they engrossed the gold of the world, and then, by legislation, made it the sole measure of values." Thus it was that "the human race became the subjects of the new aristocracy": this was "the climax of consolidation" and "centralization." And even among the new aristocracy, there emerged "the craftiest and subtlest types": in Byzantium, it was the Armenian, in India the Marwari, "and the Jew in London."[49]

We may briefly note that Brooks Adams's better-known brother Henry largely agreed with this analysis. At the end of the century, Henry supported the bimetalism of the populists rather than the gold standard defended by his own Republican party; the Republican Senator J. D. Cameron of Pennsylvania, a very close friend of Henry and a son of an old leader of the Pennsylvania industrial block (for which Carey had spoken), also went against his party on this question. Writing about the congressional confirmation of a rigid gold standard in 1893, Henry Adams noted that "the banks alone, and the dealers in exchange insisted upon it; the political parties divided according to capitalistic geographical lines, Senator Cameron offering almost the only exception." Adams observed that he himself had "hugged his antiquated dislike of bankers and capitalistic society until he had become little better than a crank." But in the 1890s the majority had turned away from a "simply industrial system" and turned toward the gold standard and the "capitalistic, centralizing, and mechanical system." Henry particularly resented that the elite of society had "joined the banks to force submission to capitalism."[50] In his private correspondence of the period, Henry Adams unleashed a torrent of abuse against England, the "British trader," Wall Street, and (while not entirely accepting "Drumont's anti-semitic ravings") the Jews, for whom, as for the serpent, he had "an instinctive fascination and terror."[51]

By this time, such opinions were already common currency on all the levels of discourse. Certainly the economist and historian Werner Sombart was not the first German to expound these views, although he was among the more academically respectable.

Werner Sombart

Sombart was a professor of economics, first at the University of Breslau from 1890 to 1906, and then at the Handelshochschule at Berlin until 1917, when he was appointed to the chair of economics at the University of Berlin. His more important scholarly works focused on the development of capitalism and modern social movements. Sombart was regarded as a socialist critic of the capitalist system, but his position was not so much socialist as it was one of sympathy for a "natural" precapitalist order rather than the "artificial" contemporary system of industry and finance. In 1911, he published a book in which, as in earlier works, he described the development of the capitalist ethos and institutions in invidious terms, this time finding them the product of Judaism and the Jews. After World War I, it is useful to note, he would become a fervent opponent of Marxist socialism, which he would also see as the product of Jewish thought. Thus, when a socialist, he condemned capitalism as Jewish; when an opponent of socialism, he denounced socialism as Jewish. We may assume that Sombart's view of the Jews was not impartial. In his *Deutscher Sozialismus,* published in 1934 after the rise of Hitler, Sombart declared himself a supporter of Nazism.[52]

In his work on capitalism and the Jews, Sombart associated Judaism with all aspects of the growth of commerce in the medieval and early modern period. The wanderings of the nomadic Jews, he asserted, produced the movement of economic centers from Venice to Antwerp to Amsterdam to London. It was through the agency of the Jews that the newly discovered gold and silver of Spanish America made their way to Europe, and, contrary to the false doctrines of Adam Smith, this bullion was the source of all capitalist growth. (Brooks Adams, we recall, saw subsequent capitalist development as the product of Britain's looting of India's precious metals.) Colonial expansion thus secured and fortified the new system, Sombart continued, and Jews played "a most prominent" role in the colonial process through many centuries, from the seventeenth-century Dutch colonization of Brazil and the West Indies to the nineteenth-century development of British South Africa that had led to the Boer War. The sugar trade, "the backbone" of the old colonial system that became the basis for early modern capitalism and imperialism, had been virtually a Jewish monopoly.[53]

Jewish *haute finance,* he observed, had played a critical role in the founding of the modern European states. The great army purveyors and contractors of the Continent during the seventeenth and eighteenth centuries were Jewish. As early as the Middle Ages, monarchs had farmed out taxes and salt mines to the Jews, and Jews were also the chief moneylenders to the Crown. In the seventeenth century, English finance fell under Jewish control, and by the time of the great colonial swindle, the South Sea Bubble, the Jews were "the greatest financial power in the country."[54] (Sombart's proof of Jewish involvement in the South Sea affair was what he characterized as "the Jewish appearance" of portraits of the Bubble's Scottish promoter, John Law.)[55] To the Jews were due the arbitrage business of the London Exchange and the eighteenth-century speculations in government debts. "If to-day London is the chief financial centre of the world, it owes this position in large measure to the Jews." The Rothschilds had made the London stock market an international one, and their tactics of creating a demand for stock by "systematic buying and selling" had "artificially" enabled the successful placing of both government and other securities.[56]

What was true of the earlier capitalism was as true of the later, not least of all in the United States and Germany. Despite the general view that there was no considerable Jewish economic influence in America, Sombart saw Jews heavily involved in the consolidation of American industry and the formation of large trusts: he took special note of the mining activities of the Guggenheims and of Jewish investment bankers like Kuhn, Loeb. At one time or another, Sombart asserted, the Jews monopolized the American wheat, tobacco, and cotton trades. Jews established general stores to distribute the goods of industry to rural Americans and used their profits to set up banks for agricultural loans, amalgamating the farmer into "the money and credit system of the Old World."[57] In Germany, Sombart observed, the stock exchange was no longer an open market but was "dominated by *la haute finance*," and therefore by the Jews. He called this development "the commercialization of industry." Finance now determined which industries were to be established or enlarged and how commodities were to be distributed; it determined the prices of both manufactured and raw materials. Jews, though more attracted to commerce, were also industrial entrepreneurs, but their influence in industry had been small until industry was commercialized.[58]

Sombart described "two radically differing—nay, opposite—views on economic life," the Jewish and the Christian. The Christian outlook was akin to that which had prevailed in medieval Europe, when profit was seen as "improper" and competition frowned upon. It was the Jews who altered these conceptions. In disregard of the traditional view that one must not praise one's own goods, they began to advertise, founding the modern press to carry their advertisements. Jews actively searched for customers, stealing them from competitors when they could do so, and they were prepared to cheat and to falsify to make sales. In early nineteenth-century Germany, the Jews had undermined German industry by importing cheap British goods and monopolizing their sale. In all these matters, Sombart argued, the "Jewish outlook was the 'modern' outlook," and their ethos was accepted by traders everywhere. The modern commercial code was one of pushing "at the expense of others," in which "cleverness, astuteness, artfulness" were valued. This was the ethos of "free trade," "free competition," and "economic rationalism." Price was to be determined not by ideas of a just price but by "the higgling of the market." To those who, like Max Weber, suggested that the Protestant ethic represented the spirit of capitalism, Sombart, no less than Toussenel, replied that Judaism and Protestantism were identical.[59]

The wealth of the Jews was employed in moneylending, and "modern capitalism is the child of money-lending," Sombart continued. The Jew is naturally a trader, and even more naturally a moneylender. This was not an occupation forced upon them in medieval times (as had been argued), but one that they performed throughout their history. Only when slaves in Egypt were Jews debtors; and they left Egypt without meeting their obligations to their creditors. At all other times they were creditors preying on peasant proprietors. "In moneylending . . . you can earn without sweating; [and] . . . get others to work for you without recourse to force." "In fine, the characteristics of money-lending are the characteristics of all modern capitalistic economic organizations." There was "nothing organic or natural" in capitalism, only what was "mechanical or artificial" and "abstract," and hence it did not matter that the Jew had no understanding of the natural. They became "lords of money," Sombart concluded, and, through these devices, "lords of the world," founders and pushers of imperial enterprises like the South African ventures, and manipulators of the money and credit mechanism that put the world at the mercy of the City of London.[60]

Sombart's views, little different from those of Toussenel and Drumont, and very similar to those of the Adamses, were to underlie much of the twentieth-century German National Socialist vision of modern economic life. Sombart, like his predecessors, saw colonialism as a necessary companion of both early and late capitalism, with the Jews as leading actors in the exploitative process abroad as at home. For him usury was the essence of a wicked capitalism, and of its accompanying colonialism and imperialism; and, like the national economists as well as the Fourierists, Sombart saw Judaism as the instrument for establishing and maintaining British domination of the globe. Needless to say, Sombart's opinions on the Jews and modern capitalism have been the subject of considerable scholarly controversy.[61]

A quite different view of colonialism and imperialism was to dominate the thinking of later liberal social theorists such as Herbert Spencer. By the last quarter of the century, Spencer saw the "State socialism" of the emerging welfare states of Western Europe as well as the revival of universal military service (except in Britain) as marking the return of the militant ethos that earlier sociological theorists believed on its way to extinction. Spencer's disciple Hobson saw protectionism (entrenched almost everywhere except, once more, in Britain) as a threat to the liberal ideal. And even in Britain, a campaign to erect an imperial tariff was emerging. Hobson, like Brooks Adams, whom he admired, took the new role of finance into account and described the international financiers as villainous promoters of imperialism. Veblen's attack on pecuniary society, we shall see, resembled that of both Hobson and Adams, though he reserved his chief fire—along the lines of the earlier school of sociological theorists—for the feudal Junker leaders of the German empire.

6 The Later Liberal Sociologists and the New Imperialism

The liberal faith of the early sociological theorists was that of enlightened opinion generally. Theirs was a lofty confidence in an inevitable progress. Saint-Simon, Comte, Buckle, and Lecky never doubted the ultimate victory of the pacific and industrial over the feudalistic, mercantilist, and militant ethos. The liberal political and economic ideal was rational and scientifically true and its triumph certain. In 1861, an Irish liberal journalist and historian, Justin McCarthy, reviewing Buckle's *History of Civilization,* sanguinely asserted that an educated people could not relapse into ignorance. He added, with what would turn out to be hubristic overconfidence, that "there can no more be a reaction from free-trade back again into protection in such a country as England, than there could be a reaction from railways back to mail-coaches."[1]

In the years following, in the 1860s, 1870s, and 1880s, the United States, Germany, and France, among others, would adopt ever higher tariffs, principally to protect their industries against British competition. There were still other signs of a retreat from liberal individualism to the collectivism and militarism of the past. A renewed interest in colonial expansionism emerged as France and the new German empire struggled to achieve in Africa and Asia the place in the sun that they believed the longer-established British empire wished to deny them.

Three social theorists writing at the end of the nineteenth and the beginning of the twentieth century—the British philosopher and sociologist Herbert Spencer, his fellow countryman, the publicist and economist J. A. Hobson, and the American economist Thorstein Veblen—revived the essential elements of the earlier sociological theory to account for the "new imperialism" of the period. All saw the potent survival of a primitive barbarism, a resurrected mercantilism, and the bellicose ethos of the traditional, quasi-feudal, landed classes as impeding the triumph of the liberal ideal. The militant governing classes not only acted to restrict the liberties of the peoples of Europe, they argued, but also impelled their nations to move aggressively against neighboring countries and into overseas regions.

These later social theorists preached a somewhat different message than their predecessors. While Spencer, whose sociology strongly influenced the thinking of Hobson and Veblen, belonged almost equally to the time and the spirit of the earlier generation, the two younger writers would add a critical modern element to the earlier synthesis. Observing the great change in capitalist development, particularly in Germany and the United States, where the bankers supplied much of the capital for and exercised substantial control over industry, Hobson and Veblen saw finance capital, and (in the case of Hobson) Jewish financiers, as heavily involved, along with the landed aristocracy, in *fin-de-siècle* imperialism. Hobson and Veblen viewed this new configuration not in terms of an inevitable capitalist development, as would some Marxists, but as a regrettable and unnecessary reversion from a progressive industrial capitalism to a reactionary neomercantilism, in the case of Hobson, or a barbaric pecuniary society, in Veblen's view. Such explanations of imperialism justify our calling them, although they are perhaps better known as economists, primarily sociological theorists. For Spencer, as we shall see, this renewed interest in empire was a move to a new feudalism, as well as a new barbarism, not the *néo-féodalité* of finance of the anticapitalist Fourierists but a feudalism born of the collectivist and statist politics of social reform and militarism.

Herbert Spencer

Herbert Spencer, born in Derby in 1820, would become the leading philosopher of the Anglo-American world, regarded by many as the Aristotle of the nineteenth century. Beginning his career at seventeen as a civil engineer for a railway company, he turned to journalism three years later, preaching the laissez-faire individualism with which he is identified. In the 1850s, he began work on his monumental *System of Philosophy*, whose installments appeared regularly over the next four decades. This series included the three volumes of *The Principles of Sociology*, in which he systematically pursued the subject of war and colonial expansion.[2] It was Spencer, years before the publication of Darwin's *Origin of Species*, who coined the phrase *survival of the fittest*: Spencer approved of the social Darwinist competitive economic struggle within a nation as the sole guarantor of progress, while rejecting that variety of social Darwinism that saw nations and races making war against one another in a battle for supremacy. Any war of aggression, indeed, he found both immoral and potentially subversive of modern society, raising the specter of barbarism.[3]

For Spencer—the immediate heir of Saint-Simon, Comte, and Buckle—there were two fundamentally different types of political and social structure: one he called the militant type, the other the industrial. History had never known a purely militant or a purely industrial society; the characteristic traits of each were always mingled, and one could only describe societies as primarily militant or primarily industrial according to whether the ethos of one or the other predominated. A militant society was one so organized as to be most effective in war, while an industrial society was designed to be most effective when hostile foreign enemies had been replaced by other peaceful societies. In a condition of "chronic militancy," government tended to become a despotism and, in more advanced states, a highly centralized one. Such a society had little room for individual action, for liberty, or for private property, all characteristics of an industrial society.[4] In an industrial society, corporate action would give way to individual action, spurred by individual motives and only minimally restrained so as to contain the "aggressive traits of human nature which chronic warfare has fostered." The free market, which rewarded services precisely in accordance with the demands for these services, would serve as the instrument of a just distribution, and, no longer surrounded by hostile societies, nations would not need to seek self-sufficiency. In Spencer's view (as late as 1882) only Britain and the United States might be regarded as predominantly industrial societies.[5]

At this time, Spencer saw Russia and Germany as the modern states mostly clearly falling into the militant type. In Russia, all men, even the nobility, were servants hierarchically organized as in an army regiment, with the obligations of every subject defined in detail; even the proper method of harnessing horses was precisely prescribed. No one might leave the country without the czar's consent, and state permission was required even to move from one part of Russia to another.[6] Spencer spoke of a rapidly industrializing Germany as a nation of an essentially different order from an industrial Britain. He pointed to the growth and centralization of Germany's standing army and its system of reserves as evidence of its militancy. He noted as well that, since the forming of the empire in 1871, military supplies had been granted for three-year and then seven-year periods instead of annually (as in Britain), which in effect surrendered "popular checks on Imperial power." Bismarck's *Kulturkampf* had subordinated the

Catholic Church to state control. The state had intervened increasingly in economic life: usury laws had been revived, protectionist tariffs imposed, and the railways were coming under state ownership. Bismarck had acted to reestablish guilds, with their close regulation of members, and had set up a system of state insurance, which restrained the freedom of the working classes. This state socialism was a particularly dangerous form of the militant society, Spencer maintained.[7]

Spencer contrasted France, a nation still trammeled by militant traits, with Britain. Private warfare among the feudal nobility had been halted more effectively and more rapidly in Britain than in France, and as a result, industrial institutions were able to achieve a more solid foothold. Property in Britain came under the protection of the law, and representative institutions were firmly established. In prerevolutionary France, on the other hand, the older forms persisted, though somewhat amended, and the much greater involvement of France in foreign wars had helped to solidify military traits.[8] War was the great demoralizer. During the years of warfare between 1775 and 1815, Britain had partially reverted to a number of the older, militant traits but had saved itself in time. Spencer detailed the repression of liberties, the heavy taxation of property, the increase of crime, and the perversion of justice which had taken place during this war period. After 1815, Britain returned to the industrial characteristics that had earlier established themselves.[9] Individual initiative and enterprise, prime characteristics of an industrial society, were everywhere apparent in Britain (as in the United States); this was much less the case in France. Spencer observed that private British companies supplied towns in France and Germany with water, proving that among "the more industrially modified English, individual initiative is more decided."[10]

From the 1850s onward, however, war and the preparation for war once again beset Great Britain. After the coming to power of Louis Napoleon in 1851, Britain had felt the need to arm against a French challenge; it made war against Russia in the Crimea from 1853 to 1855; and it waged colonial wars to maintain or to expand its overgrown empire. In 1857, Britain suppressed a mutiny in its Indian army; and in the late 1850s, after the Arrow incident, there had come a second war against China. Conflicts arose in Africa, Abyssinia, and Ashanti; and there were the Afghan War in the late seventies, the campaign against the Zulus, and Gladstone's takeover in Egypt in 1882.[11]

As early as 1876, Spencer saw Great Britain in the midst of a full-blooded colonial expansion, one that he believed originated not so much in response to the activities of other nations—the competitive struggle to divide Africa was several years off—but because Britain, fearful of the growing forces of the Continental powers, had strengthened its own army and navy. This increase in forces had stimulated aggressive action, he declared, and each colonial acquisition had encouraged another. As in the classic militant type, any injury to British pride became the occasion for vengeance and, frequently enough, for further expansion.

Although this increased attention to enlarging the army and navy might originally have been intended for defense, Spencer argued, there was an almost inevitable revival of the "predatory spirit," threatening a reversion to the militant society. Ancient Athens had employed the army and navy it had raised to defend itself against the Persians to create an Athenian empire, and France during the Revolution had turned its forces from defense against the armies of the dynasts to aggression. So Britain employed its defensive forces as a predator in China, India, Polynesia, Africa, and the East Indian archipelago. "Reasons—never wanting to the aggressor—are given for widening our empire: without force if it may be, and with force if needful."[12]

Spencer saw further evidence of a British return to a militant order in "the extension of centralized administration and of compulsory regulation," and in a state seemingly determined on redistribution and social reform. Among the objects of his ire were the municipalization of gas and water companies, municipal programs of public housing, "schemes of coercive philanthropy" that aimed at keeping individuals from consuming alcohol, and legislation minutely regulating mines, factories, lodging houses, and even private homes—and, most glaringly, the penalties that such legislation dictated for any infractions discovered by official inspectors. People now received benefits, such as free access to museums and public libraries, not purchased by the fruits of their own labor. This, too, was "a socialist principle of the militant type." The Liberal party, which had once stood for individual liberty in opposition to the state, had now joined Toryism in increasing the power of the state administration.[13]

In the 1892 edition of *Social Statics*, Spencer condemned "Government Colonization," very much as Hobson ten years later would denounce "Imperialism." If emigrants, in voluntary association, unassisted by the actual or probable protection of the state, attempted to form a colony in a strange land amid an alien people in the mode of William Penn and the Quakers in America, they would behave well, Spencer declared. But if the colonists were accompanied by soldiers and protected by forts, they would become brutes and bullies. The whole history of state colonization was one of greedy and unscrupulous buccaneers. Thievery had been their universal motive, though they always sailed under some other standard: like John Bright, he noted that whereas earlier pirates had spoken of spreading the true faith, the new ones talked of extending commerce. Most of the colonies established by the state had no genuine commercial possibilities; moreover, they were costly to govern and to defend and were a frequent cause of quarrel and war. A malarial jungle or a desert island was hardly worth such sacrifices. Elaborate and expensive efforts were not necessary to the creation of trade, for if opportunities for a useful and profitable commerce truly existed, they would present themselves without the governmental machinery of colonization, and without the cruelties and bloodshed that accompanied expansion.[14] Nor was the excuse of the white man's burden a valid one: "Ask how the members of an aboriginal tribe regard that tide of civilization which sweeps them away," Spencer wrote in 1886.[15]

When Britain began its war with the Boer farmers of South Africa in 1899, Spencer again proclaimed his profound antipathy for the country's imperial expansion. The Boers were certainly in the right since "self-defense . . . is a duty." Patriotism was all very well, but "contemplation of the acts by which England has acquired over eighty possessions—settlements, colonies, protectorates &c.—does not arouse feelings of satisfaction." Spencer noted the sometimes subtle though more often brutal "transitions" that marked the British colonial empire: "from missionaries to resident agents, then to officials having armed forces, then to punishments of those who resist their rule, ending in so-called 'pacification.'" And all "with no more regard for the wills of the inhabiting people than for those of the inhabiting beasts." Such conduct did not "excite sympathy with their perpetrators."[16]

During the Boer War, employing the term *imperialism* in its present meaning, Spencer sharpened his argument that nations that chose imperialist politics would necessarily become slaves of the state. In proof he invoked the examples of ancient Egypt, Sparta, and Rome, the kingdoms of medieval Franks and of Louis XIV, the Japan of the Mikado, and the Russia of the czars. Russia was a prime instance: together with "that unceasing subjugation of minor nationalities by which its imperialism is displayed," Spencer again pointed to "its vast army, to service in which everyone is . . . liable," and to its "enormous bureaucracy ramifying everywhere and rigidly controlling individual lives." And in consequence of "the pressure felt personally and pecuniarily," Russia had become a land of "secret revolutionary societies, perpetual plots, chronic dread of social explosions." All were "in danger of Siberia," and the czar was "in constant fear for his life." But "so long as the passion for mastery over-rides all others the slavery that goes along with Imperialism will be tolerated."[17]

In Britain, Spencer found evidence of a "re-barbarization" of the nation. He warned that "the slumbering militant ideas and sentiments which have come down to us from early ages of perpetual warfare," and the "partially dormant instincts of the savage" were "readily aroused." Religious organizations like the Salvation Army, with its cry of "Blood and Fire," and the Church Army, by arousing a militant hatred of the devil, made it easier to incite militant hatred of foreign nations and awaken "those slumbering passions which are ready enough to burst out even in the intercourse of ordinary life." Spencer pointed to the military drills in the public (i.e., certain private) schools and universities, rifle competitions, and tournaments. He noted the wide and increasingly respectable interest in activities such as cricket, rowing, and "the most brutalizing" game of football; the revival of cockfighting and boxing; the growth of horse racing and the gambling with which it was associated; the increase of papers devoted to sports. Other evidences of rebarbarization were the books of adventure designed for boys, the stories of crime, the writings on military history. The "utter change of social sentiment" was revealed when it was decided to celebrate in 1901 the golden jubilee of the Great Exhibition of 1851: an event that a half-century earlier had been "expected to inaugurate universal peace" was now marked by a naval and military exhibition.[18]

Spencer presented the most thoroughgoing exposition of a purely sociological theory of imperialism. There was no hint of any economic need for war or for colonial territories; the science of political economy had exploded any such notion. Capitalists *qua* capitalists, representing industrial values, must oppose imperial ventures and state colonization as not merely unproductive but as subversive of the ethos of a society upon which their economic and political welfare depended. A desire to exercise power over others, a desire supported by instincts instilled by the long period of mankind's savagery, promoted aggression and imperial activity. Spencer suggested that the public school education of the members of Parliament and shapers of opinion, with its praise of the militant values of classical Greece and Rome, played a role in preserving the ethos of a military society. While the aristocracy and the gentry were the social base for the values of such a society, Spencer did not see the landed classes or the officers of the army and navy as the exclusive bearers of the outmoded military ethic. In his eyes, the social reform policies of the Liberal party, in their preference for state

---

rather than voluntary methods, were as much or perhaps more to blame for the revival of the barbarous society of the past. Militarism and socialism were but two aspects of the same polity, each stimulating, confirming, and reinforcing the growth of the other.

A clear disciple of Spencer (and of Cobden), the economist and sociologist J. A. Hobson, would accept and extend Spencer's analysis of imperialism, but, unlike Spencer, Hobson was an advocate of the "new liberalism," which looked forward to a welfare state. Hobson is perhaps best known as the expositor of an *economic* theory of imperialism; yet we shall see that Spencerian sociological theory formed the primary bases of his analysis.

J. A. Hobson

The journalist J. A. Hobson, as noted earlier, wrote the first systematic analysis of the new "imperialism" in 1902. Born in the English Midlands in 1858 and living until 1940, this self-styled "economic heretic" was a disciple of the liberal social and political theory of Richard Cobden (of whom he wrote an admiring biography) and Herbert Spencer, as well as of the free-trade economic views of Adam Smith and the classical mainstream. His principal economic heresy first revealed itself in an early work, *The Physiology of Industry*, written with A. F. Mummery in 1889. In this book, the two authors adopted the heterodox, Malthusian view of glut, and an underconsumptionist position was to remain an important aspect of Hobson's economic writings.[19] (J. M. Keynes in 1936 was to describe Hobson as having anticipated much of his own thought.[20]) Hobson's analysis of *fin-de-siècle* industry and finance would lead V. I. Lenin to write of him and the neo-Marxist Hilferding as the prime sources for Lenin's own theory of imperialism.

Britain's special circumstances when Hobson wrote his book on imperialism helped to define his position. Of course, most immediately, there was the Boer War, but perhaps as important was an impending political battle concerning protection. By 1846, we know, with the repeal of the Corn Laws, Britain had turned to free trade. By the 1890s, it was experiencing the intense competition of a protectionist United States and Germany in a number of fields, notably in iron and steel production.

The German tariff, to enlarge upon this example, became openly protectionist by 1879, and even more so by 1885; behind tariff walls, and taking advantage of the most modern technology (unimpeded, unlike Britain, by large investments in outmoded machinery and techniques), German industry was growing at a rapid rate. As late as 1890,

Britain was still the largest steel producer in Europe, but by 1900, despite some increase in British production, the widespread adoption by German industry of the new Bessemer process had nearly tripled that country's steel production, enabling Germany to take over the European lead. Germany's iron and steel combines were soon dumping cheap steel onto unprotected British markets. Operating similarly, American steelmakers dumped their iron goods onto such formerly British colonial preserves as Canada.

For a number of years, Joseph Chamberlain, the Tory colonial secretary, who represented Birmingham (and its metals industries) in Parliament, had hinted at the usefulness of tariff protection for industry and imperial tariff preferences that would bind the colonies more closely to Britain. Hard-pressed Midlands industrialists (in metals, chemicals, glassmaking, etc.) had, indeed, been pressing for protection years before Chamberlain presented his tariff proposals in 1903. For a Cobdenite like Hobson, a reversion to protectionism would be the basis for a return to an exploitative mercantilist colonialism, under the direction of sinister financial interests. (It is interesting to note that the bankers and merchants of the City of London would remain loyal to free trade, believing in Great Britain's future role as a center of finance and commerce, a brain in the body of a cosmopolitan international economy.)

Hobson's first contribution to the study of imperialism were his articles on the Boer War for the Radical *Manchester Guardian,* collected in 1900 under the title of *The War in South Africa.* His journalistic account of the war asked, "For whom are we fighting?" and while disavowing "the ignominious passion of Judenhetze," Hobson reported that the villains of the piece were "a small group of international financiers, chiefly German in origin and Jewish in race." Virtually playing the part of a national economist unhappy that his country's policies were in the hands of a more advanced nation, a fantastic conceit for an Englishman in Victoria's reign, Hobson described these Jewish financiers as possessing an "ability, enterprise, and organisation" "superior" to "the slower-witted Briton." Carefully excluding the small Jewish shopkeepers of Johannesburg from his attack ("a rude and ignorant people, mostly fled from despotic European rule"), Hobson aimed his guns at "the class of financial capitalists." They owned the gold mines, possessed the dynamite monopoly, controlled the liquor trade; "the Stock Exchange is, needless to say, mostly Jewish," as was the trade in horses. They also controlled the press and practiced their traditional trade of usury. The Jew had not "been backward in developing those forms of loan and mortgage business which have made his fame the world over," he noted. "I am informed that a very large proportion of the Transvaal farmers are as entirely in the hands of Jewish money-lenders as is the Russian moujik or the Austrian peasant." Although Jewish financiers had abstained from active politics elsewhere, in South Africa they aimed at establishing "a tolerably complete form of boss-rule." Their interests were not British interests, Hobson warned his countrymen; Britain was fighting the war in South Africa "in order to place a small international oligarchy of mine-owners and speculators in power at Pretoria."[21]

In 1902, in his study *Imperialism,* he attempted a deeper analysis, one that, despite certain small contradictions and ambiguities (which deserve and have received considerable recent attention), is still widely regarded as a classic work on the subject. Hobson wrote of *imperialism* as a catchall term "on everybody's lips" and determined to give it a more precise meaning. Imperialism was a "disease," he declared; the role he assigned himself was that of a social pathologist, confident that the disease could be cured, though he knew he could not hope to persuade those who saw imperialism as "the shove of some blind 'destiny,'" the fulfillment of an inevitable capitalist fate that made empire building a necessity, as the neo-Marxists and Lenin would argue.[22] In much of his analysis, Hobson may thus be seen less an anticipator of Lenin, despite his stress on the role of finance capital, than a successor of Cobden, Buckle, and Spencer.

Hobson distinguished between nationalism, which he, like other liberals, found admirable, and imperialism. The nationalist strivings of Poles, Hungarians, and Italians, trying to free themselves from the control of dynastic empires, might be seen as a way station to internationalism. At times, this nationalism tended to overflow and absorb alien territories. When such territories were vacant or sparsely populated, their settlement might be called colonialism, as in the case of the British migration to Canada and Australasia. Colonies of this kind were genuine expressions of the nationalism of the mother country and soon developed separate nationalities of their own. But in cases where the territory absorbed by the metropolis was held by "reluctant and unassimilable peoples," there developed that "debasement" of nationalism—imperialism.[23] From a political standpoint, this was "an expansion of autocracy," of the rule of a small white minority over "great hordes" regarded as "inferior" and incapable of self-rule.[24]

Nor did imperialism offer real economic benefits to Great Britain, as some had argued. He noted that Britain was enjoying the greatest increase in its exchanges with its closest foreign rivals, France, Germany, and the United States, while its trade with its colonies was relatively declining. The chief source of absolute growth in Britain's

The Liberal Ideal and the Demons of Empire

colonial trade was that with white, self-governing dominions, not with the tropical and subtropical colonies that had been more recently acquired. Nor was imperialism necessary as an outlet for surplus population. Hobson saw other areas of the world as much more thickly populated than Britain. In the past, furthermore, most emigrants had preferred to settle outside British possessions. That part of the population, the merchants, managers, engineers, or skilled workingmen (the "outlanders" as they were called in the Boer Republics), that accompanied the investment of British capital in commerce and industry in foreign countries certainly had no right to call upon the homeland for protection.[25]

If the colonies of the new imperialism were not a significant factor in increasing the field of employment generally, they did contribute to the employment of the highly influential, aristocratic upper classes. These Hobson characterized as among "the economic parasites of imperialism" (once again, Bentham's "sinister interests"). The services (the army and navy) were "imperialist by conviction and by professional interest." This professional interest of the services and of imperial officials received the "powerful sympathetic support" of the aristocracy and the rich, who sought careers for their sons in the army and navy, in the Indian Civil Service, or in the increasing number of colonial posts. Imperial expansion would also provide livelihoods as planters, ranchers, or missionaries for sons of the aristocratic and wealthy classes. Although, realistically speaking, comparatively few such jobs were at stake, still the professions in Britain were sufficiently overcrowded for there to be considerable interest in such possibilities. Hobson quoted James Mill, inaccurately crediting him rather than Bright, as having described the colonies as "a vast system of outdoor relief for the upper classes." Hobson was, however, prepared to accept the importance of certain "sentimental motives" (the "itch for glory and adventure") as well.[26]

There were other parasites of imperialism for whom economic considerations overwhelmed mere sentiment. There were the firms that built warships or freighters, or manufactured guns, ammunition and motor vehicles, or supplied food, horses, or clothing to the armed services. "These men are Imperialists by conviction," Hobson observed; "a pushful policy is good for them." In addition, there were manufacturers who produced goods substantially for the export market—some of the textile men of Manchester, the hardware, engine, and machinery manufacturers of Sheffield and Birmingham, and so on—and who prospered "by supplying the real or artificial wants" of the regions Britain annexed or opened to trade. Such interests produced "a very firm imperialist faith." The shipping trade, benefiting from state subsidies designed to prop up an industry essential to imperial defense, also had an interest in imperialism. While imperialism was "bad business" for the nation, Hobson declared, it had been "good business" for those classes and trades that, though but a small part of the British economy, had managed to gain command of national power in behalf of their private interests, usually by draping them in the colors of patriotic wars of defense.[27]

Imperialism, then, was not the necessary product of capitalist development: the economic parasites of imperial policy were on the whole the scions of the precapitalist, aristocratic, military society who sought positions of profit and professional advancement in a policy of expansion; they were also the manufacturers and suppliers of war goods who supported aggression (much as had their counterparts in mercantilist society), and, finally, the manufacturers of goods produced primarily for the export trade. These last were undeniably capitalists, but Hobson argued that they unnecessarily distorted the workings of a free-market capitalism in order to heighten a profit that would still have been theirs without colonial expansion.

There was another class, clearly capitalist, to which Hobson assigned a critical portion of the onus of modern imperialism—the finance capitalist. But this class of capitalists was also rooted in a preindustrial mercantilist class long known for its parasitism, particularly in colonial areas. These modern usurers (the *rentiers,* who in search of a higher return than was possible at home, invested their capital abroad) had revived the exploitative finance capitalism of earlier times. The *rentier*'s return was "tribute" and not properly capitalist profit, but unfortunately Great Britain had become "a nation living upon tribute from abroad," and the classes enjoying this tribute employed, when they could, "the public policy, the public purse, and the public force to extend the field of their private investments, and to safeguard and improve their existing investments." Recent British foreign policy was, first of all, a "struggle" to secure profitable regions for capital investment, and this was true also of Britain's chief rivals, France, Germany, and the United States. In all these countries, "modern capitalism had placed large surplus savings in the hands of a plutocracy or of a thrifty middle class" that could not find "at home the profitable use" they sought for savings and who therefore demanded that their government secure from risks the profits of overseas investments.[28]

The ordinary middle-class investors were merely "the cat's paws of the great financial houses," international bankers like the Rothschilds or J. P. Morgan. These banking houses formed "the central ganglion of international capitalism" and constituted the ultimate authority on issues of war and peace. The tight organization of this financial cap-

The Liberal Ideal and the Demons of Empire

italism was promoted by its control, "so far as Europe is concerned, chiefly by men of a single and peculiar race, who have behind them many centuries of financial experience," placing them "in a unique position to manipulate the policy of nations." It was hardly necessary to be more explicit; Hobson's readers would know he spoke of the Jews. "There is not a war, a revolution, an anarchist assassination, or any other public shock, which is not gainful to these men," Hobson continued, in the manner of Toussenel and Drumont. These bankers had profited by the South African war while private investors and the public exchequer suffered. The international financial houses, moreover, controlled the press of all the Western countries, and consequently public opinion, and used this control to protect their stake in imperialism. These economic "parasites" might mouth "noble phrases" about extending civilization, but their principal motive was securing their profits. Hobson was prepared to grant, as Toussenel had granted over a half-century earlier, that, where there was a threat of a war that might seriously damage "the substantial fabric of industry" and the profits of the bankers—as, for example, in the 1896 quarrel over Venezuela between Great Britain and the United States—the great financiers strove for peace.[29]

At this point, Hobson may have felt he had gone too far, that "to impute to financiers so much power" was "to take a too narrowly economic view of history." He was quite prepared to grant the importance of noneconomic factors in imperialism, among them "patriotism, adventure, military enterprise, political ambition, and philanthropy." While finance was undoubtedly "the governor of the imperial engine," its fuel and the generator of its power were elsewhere. Still, "finance manipulates the patriotic forces which politicians, soldiers, philanthropists, and traders generate"; it set to work "the enthusiasm for expansion" which stemmed from "an ambitious statesman, a frontier soldier, an over-zealous missionary, a pushing trader." But though such persons might even initiate an imperialist move, "the final determination rests with the financial power."[30]

Adopting the free-trade arguments that Adam Smith and the mainstream of the classical economists had mounted against the mercantilist system, Hobson suggested that if the colonies Britain had acquired at great cost since the 1880s had instead been absorbed by its imperial rivals, not only would these other countries have borne the expense of governing, developing, and protecting them, but Britain's trade with them might very well be the same. It was a delusion to think, as did mercantilists past and present, that there was "only a given quantity of trade, and that if one nation gets any portion of it another nation loses just so much." Only those afflicted by "a blind ignorance" of the principles of an interdependent, international commerce could believe that a nation could maintain the entire advantage of colonial markets. "These were the commonplaces of the economics of Free Trade," Hobson observed, "the plainest lessons of enlightened common sense," but "imperialism repudiates Free Trade."[31]

Great Britain remained, uniquely among the great nations, a free-trading power, and Hobson consequently turned to the protectionist example of the United States to demonstrate how economic pressures were forcing modern industrial nations to an expansionist policy. With the help of high protective tariffs, the United States had developed an enormously productive manufacturing power. After some decades of intense domestic competition marked by overproduction and price cutting, the "great trust-makers," making use of this tariff protection, had consolidated industries (forming combines, monopolies, trusts) and raised prices while reducing costs by more efficient production. This process of amalgamation placed a great quantity of wealth into the hands of a small number of capitalists. Luxurious living, investments in other industries, and the growth of the American standard of living no doubt absorbed a considerable amount of this savings, but consumption still could not keep up with the vastly increasing productive powers of industry. America had reached a level of "saturation": its manufacturing capacity was greater than the effective demand of the home market, and there seemed no outlet for accumulating capital. Blocked from European markets by tariffs, American financiers and manufacturers looked to South America and across the Pacific to China. With "a stronger and more direct control" over their government than that possessed by their British counterparts, the Rockefeller and Morgan interests had adopted a policy of imperialism so as to find and maintain profitable employment for their surplus capital. This, Hobson declared, was "the economic taproot of Imperialism."[32]

A contemporary reader of Hobson's study might have wondered at his use of America, and not Britain or Germany, as his prime example of an imperialist power. After all, imperialism after the 1880s centered on Africa, firstly, and then on the Asian mainland, where Britain, France, and Germany, not America, had the most active interests. But a free-trade country like Britain was by definition, in Hobson's view, not an imperialist one, unless led astray by marginal though powerful parasitic forces. The neomercantilist protectionists of the United States and Germany, on the other hand, were *necessarily* drawn to colonial expansion. Because of free trade, moreover, Britain's economy was not marked by that concentration of industry that characterized both Germany and America. If, then, Britain was not a suitable model, why not a protectionist, cartelized, and militarized Germany, under the management of the bankers and the Junkers? As a liberal and a Spencerian, Hobson may have understood that it would be difficult to separate neomercantilist from neodynastic (or neofeudal) elements in Germany's polity. The American example would certainly serve as a more useful warning to Hobson's fellow countrymen against taking the neomercantilist road that one architect of the South African war, the Tory colonial secretary, Joseph Chamberlain, would soon advocate, than would the example of Germany, whose political and social structure was widely perceived as archaic, preindustrial, and bellicose.

The Cobdenite Hobson believed protection to be "the natural ally of Imperialism" and worried because the propertied and professional classes, the investing classes, even those in the Liberal party, were turning against free trade. These groups were now persuaded that in a hostile world, a nation must become self-sufficient. They were reverting, he feared, to the mercantilist goal that sought an export surplus and seemed determined to make their nation an international usurer, "a creditor or parasitic nation to an indefinite extent." The tariffs that these neomercantilists favored would provide for the increasing needs of the Treasury by placing the financial burden of imperialism on the general public rather than on the propertied and "money lending classes." These classes also favored the creation of public debts as a useful investment for idle funds, as a means of avoiding further taxation, and also because the flotation of these public loans created a profitable business for financiers, dressed up "as Imperialists and patriots." Such a trade and fiscal program, of course, would compound the problem, placing even more of the nation's capital in the hands of wealthy savers. This would lead the nation ever more deeply into a policy of expansion.[33]

The choice, in Hobson's terms, was between "quantitative *versus* qualitative growth." Should a nation concentrate on the intensive cultivation of its own lands, after the model of Denmark or Switzerland, or, like Britain, spread its energies extensively, neglecting its agriculture and the education and welfare of its own people, in the interests of the speculative "profits of some new market," or "greed of territorial acquisition"?[34] Adam Smith had described these alternatives in much the same way in his analysis of the old colonial system. For Hobson, the option was Britain's: this decision was a matter of choice.[35]

Again and again—and this should be stressed because it differs from a frequently encountered view of Hobson's analysis of imperialism—Hobson asserted that imperialism was not a necessity for a free-trade capitalist country. The mere investment of capital abroad did not constitute imperialism for the Cobdenite economist unless it was accompanied by the demand and expectation of political control, as had been the case in South Africa. (In 1904, and again in 1911, several years after the publication of his work on imperialism, Hobson recommended an increase in capital export, in investment, without political expectations, as being of considerable benefit to the host nation as well as to the investor.) In future years, Hobson's opinions on the subject underwent repeated changes.[36] But in 1902, he was certain that it was "not inherent in the nature of things that we should spend our natural resources on militarism, war, and risky unscrupulous diplomacy, in order to find markets for our goods and surplus capital."[37] He made the point many times: "there is no necessity to open up new foreign markets"; it was a "delusion that expansion of foreign trade, and therefore of empire, is a necessity of national life";[38] the "supposed inevitability of imperial expansion as a necessary outlet for progressive industry" was "a fallacy."[39] Although "we may be told" that the process was "inevitable," this was merely the way in which it appeared "upon a superficial inspection."[40]

Hobson did not doubt the reality of glut in the modern industrial system; the book he had coauthored a decade earlier had surveyed the inadequacies of Say's Law under then prevailing conditions. Yet in the best tradition of the classical school, Hobson saw home markets as "capable of indefinite expansion."[41] Say's Law required an important amendment: "provided the effective demand for the goods that are produced is so distributed that every increase of production stimulates a corresponding increase of consumption." This was why consumption failed "to keep pace automatically," as Say's Law would have it, "with the power of production": the inefficient distribution of wealth which placed large sums in the hands of the wealthier classes, who would not spend them, rather than in those of the poorer, who could and would. If the state intervened so that the profits of production were more widely and equitably distributed, there would be "no natural and necessary limit to the proportion of the national product which can be sold and consumed at home."[42] If consumers raised their standards of consumption, there would be no glut and no economic pressures for imperial expansion.[43]

The fault was to be found in the recipients of unearned income, the landlords and the receivers of monopoly profits. The industrial revolution had unfortunately taken place in Great Britain, a country where a landed aristocracy possessed a virtual monopoly of the "land, education, and legislation."[44] Even on this economic matter, we see Hobson as a sociological theorist pointing to the harmful consequences of feudal survivals. The solution for Hobson, one based on Ricardo's analysis and the remedy then being advocated by British disciples of the American land reformer Henry George, was to remove these unearned increments of income derived from the great rise in land values brought about not through exertion on the landlord's part but because of the progress of society generally. The "oversaving" of which Hobson complained consisted not only of rents of the landlords, but also of "monopoly profits, and other unearned or excessive elements of income," income "not being earned by labour of head or hand," and therefore possessing "no legitimate *raison d'être*."[45] Such a view would have satisfied Ricardo, Cobden, and Mill, none of whom had much use for either rents or monopolies. Many Radicals of the time were urging heavy taxes on such unearned incomes, and in 1909 the Liberal government would formulate a budget to incorporate these views, thereby expanding government revenues while maintaining free trade.

Hobson was not prepared, however, to go along with the classical school on the question of a free market for labor. A number of political economists had seen subsistence wages, wages based on the cost of living, as necessary for the accumulation of capital. By the end of the nineteenth century, Hobson argued, not the scarcity of capital but its overabundance constituted the problem. What he wished was a system that permitted wages to rise "*pro rata* with increased efficiency." In practical politics, Hobson was ready to support "any turn in the tide of politico-economic forces" which would restore unearned surplus income "to the workers in higher wages, or to the community in taxes." Imperialism was the product of a false system, and " 'social reform' is its remedy." "Trade Unionism and Socialism" were "the natural enemies of Imperialism, for they take away from the imperialist classes the surplus incomes which form the economic stimulus of Imperialism." Of course, if the working class saved rather than spent its wage increases, the pressures to expansion would not be stemmed, but Hobson believed "powerful stimuli" would lead the workers to consumption rather than accumulation. This was "the economic theory for which we claim acceptance," Hobson declared, "a theory which, if accurate, dispels the delusion that expansion of foreign trade, and therefore of empire, is a necessity of national life."[46]

But if imperialism were not inevitable, neither was its demise. In the concluding chapter of his work, Hobson raised the specter of a pernicious international imperialism—an "inter-imperialism"—an association of the advanced European states organized by their upper classes to draw "vast tribute" from Asia and Africa, posing "the gigantic peril of a Western parasitism." Events appeared to be moving in this direction, one not unlike that taken by the imperialism of ancient Rome. Hobson turned to Brooks Adams's *Law of Civilization and Decay* and its description of Rome and its adventurers, "money-loaning aristocracy," and officeholders who drew their spoils from the "private official plunder, public tribute, usury and official income" of the provinces. This was the "plainest instance" in history, Hobson observed, of the "social parasitic process by which a moneyed interest" possessed itself of state power to promote "imperial expansion" and "to fasten economic suckers into foreign bodies so as to drain them of their wealth." (We may note the image of vampirism.) The "new Imperialism," he added, "differs in no vital point from this old example." Quoting Adams once more, Hobson warned against the "overcentralization" that he agreed with the American writer to have been responsible for Rome's decline and fall.[47] It may well have been Adams's book that helped form Hobson's view of international Jewish finance.

In Hobson's study of imperialism, we see a joining of the sociological theory of imperialism and the mainstream classical economic theory, modified by the heterodox view of glut, an insightful synthesis of key elements of earlier theories of empire building. But the "taproot" of imperialism for Hobson, though undeniably economic, was not a legitimate characteristic of true capitalism: instead it was a residue, a distortion resulting from the birth of industrialism in an environment in which the land and the legislature were under the control of the landowning classes. Rent, primarily a function of the growth in population and community progress, was an illegitimate survival of the profits of conquest and feudal rapacity. The persistence on the Continent of a precapitalist mercantilism—a protectionism and monopolistic consolidation that produced "surplus" or "excessive" industrial profits, also unearned—had resulted in an unnatural and unnecessary direction of industry. It had led to a reliance upon production for export (a mercantilist obsession) and to the failure to pay workers on the arguably capitalist basis of labor efficiency rather than the pre- and early-industrial standard of subsistence. But now it was for the state and the trade unions to counter the effects of these distortions so as to correct "the fallacy of the supposed inevitability of imperial expansion."[48]

In the last two-thirds of his work, which deals with the politics (rather than the economics) of imperialism, Hobson's debt to Spencer's sociology emerged even more clearly. Hobson complained that Britain's despotic rule of her empire had brought about a "reversion from industrial to military ethics";[49] imperialism fostered a "snobbish sub-

The Liberal Ideal and the Demons of Empire

servience and an admiration of wealth and rank," both being "corrupt survivals of the inequalities of feudalism" that undermined liberty at home and turned Britain toward aggression against both "lower races" and rival imperial powers.[50] Specifically referring to Spencer, Hobson noted how a bellicose outlook had taken over British life: "the animal lust of struggle, once a necessity, survives in the blood" and was evident in such sports as hunting and boxing, as well as in the continuance of the "humbler sports of feudal country life," among which, he noted somewhat mysteriously, was "man-hunting."[51] Hobson concluded, turning again to his economic theme, that certain "vested interests" had resolved to incite and direct these "brute lusts of human domination . . . everywhere latent in civilized humanity."[52]

The American Thorstein Veblen would pursue such themes more thoroughly. We have seen that Hobson had chosen America over a quasi-feudal Germany as an example of the cartelized neomercantilism against which he was warning his countrymen. Veblen took up the analysis of the German condition and its meaning to Americans in the early months of World War I. Veblen, also an admirer and disciple of Herbert Spencer, would combine the Spencerian model of a militant society with what he called the "pecuniary" society.

Thorstein Veblen

Born in 1857 of Norwegian immigrant parents, Thorstein Veblen was raised in a farm community in Minnesota. He pursued graduate work in philosophy and economics at Yale, where he received a doctorate in philosophy and studied with William Graham Sumner, Spencer's leading American disciple. After years of trying to find an academic position, he set off to Cornell for work in economics with J. Laurence Laughlin, an admirer of the economics of John Stuart Mill, whose abridgement of Mill's *Principles* became a leading textbook in the United States. When Laughlin went to the new University of Chicago in 1892, Veblen accompanied him as a teaching fellow. At Chicago in 1899, Veblen produced his classic *Theory of the Leisure Class*, in which he traced the persistence of the manners and ideals of primitive society into the feudal period and displayed how they had established themselves even in bourgeois capitalism; this directly foreshadowed the major themes of his later books. His biographer Joseph Dorfman has shown how much Veblen owed in this and subsequent works to the writings of Herbert Spencer. In 1904, Veblen published his *Theory of Business Enterprise* and in 1914 his *Instinct of Workmanship*, both of which distinguished between the creative character of early industrial society and the "pecuniary" economy and society of the later period. This pecuniary society retained the quasi-barbaric traits of a primitive society based on force and fraud, on manipulation and savage emulation, traits that sometimes prevailed over the outlook and characteristics of an authentic industrial civilization. The survival of these characteristics served to distort what might otherwise have been a laudable industrial capitalism.[53]

Exactly what Veblen meant by a pecuniary economy is often vague, and his use of the term sometimes shifted. Veblen, raised on a farm in the years of the nineteenth century's great depression, was a man of abstemious and puritanical bent who valued the virtues of thrift and workmanship: for him, a pecuniary economy was one of "wasteful expenditure" and "conspicuous consumption," the employment of economic resources to supply needs beyond the essentials of food, clothing, or shelter—what was "euphemistically spoken of as a rising standard of living." Such waste was characteristic of an economy associated with "businessmen" (the capitalists and bankers) who were at this time consolidating American industry into gigantic trusts. These businessmen were primarily interested in profits, while the earnest and hard-working earlier generations of industrial capitalists had been first of all concerned with production.[54] In Veblen's dichotomy, there was more than a hint of the distinction made by the national economists between productive industrial interests and those of a parasitic finance. The turn-of-the-century protest of the populist farmers in the United States against the financial interests of the Northeast was a further influence. For Veblen, only those interested in workmanship, in improvement for its own sake, could successfully direct an economy so as to free it from the bias for profits which inhibited improvement in advanced states.

Veblen's *Imperial Germany and the Industrial Revolution* was in progress in 1914, and the outbreak of war intensified Veblen's efforts to complete it. Published in 1915, the book was a comparative study of the British "industrial society," with its increasingly pecuniary tendencies, and the feudal "militant society" of Wilhelmine Germany. Veblen had foreseen the war, which he believed to have been produced by the retention of feudal institutions by a bellicose Germany that had adopted a modern technology without absorbing the modern ethos. Graham Wallas, a Fabian socialist and a professor of politics at the London School of Economics, would complain that Veblen had been too critical of Britain; others found him unwilling to see anything favorable in Germany. When America entered the war in 1917, Veblen's seeming ambiguities led the American government's wartime office of information to urge newspapers to publish parts of the work as a contribution to its anti-German propaganda, even as the Post

Office banned the book from the mails under the Espionage Act.[55]

Veblen traced Britain's economic and, as important for him, spiritual development as it became the world's first industrial society. During the centuries separating Elizabeth from Napoleon, he observed, the English had devoted themselves both to assimilating a new technology and to developing its cultural concomitants, even as the Continent was absorbed with wars from which Britain's insular position shielded it. England's industrial ethos was one of "democratic equality and non-interference, self-help and local autonomy," a spirit that had inspired the Glorious Revolution of 1688. Like Buckle over sixty years earlier, Veblen stressed the English transformation of the feudal spirit of loyalty to a loyalty grounded entirely on utilitarian considerations, a loyalty "far short of the feudalistic idea." The British had a materialist and mechanistic bias, a product of the new technology, and British society was more accepting of "insubordination and individual self-assertion" than was that of the Continent. Given these factors, it was not surprising that Great Britain had led the movement from handicraft "workmanship to engineering," the movement to the machine technology of the eighteenth-century industrial revolution.[56]

Unfortunately, Veblen continued, the increasingly rapid takeover of British industry by pecuniary interests (businessmen interested in profits, not workmanship) had in recent years altered the individualist basis of political and industrial life that had long prevailed. The conflict between workers and owners had become more severe, and the working class had organized itself for this conflict, becoming more disciplined and thus, paradoxically, "more amenable to control in the mass" by a ruling class interested in its own "aggrandisement." In Britain, he added, "the sense of national solidarity, and the support of national policies" that were irrational—possessing no "material value" to the ordinary citizen—were stronger than they had been a generation earlier. This had been Spencer's complaint at the time of the Boer War. The British economy, furthermore, was now marked by wasteful competition in production and consumption, by the pauperization of the workingman and the luxury of the rich, and by the wasteful devotion of energies and resources to salesmanship and advertising, all of which were "the essence of the business management of industry."[57] While the community might gain in efficiency by an industrial innovation, the businessmen in charge preferred to retain obsolescent equipment so long as it produced a profit; Veblen cited as examples the narrow-gauged British railways and the "diminutive blast furnaces" that wasted both energy and labor.[58] In these matters, the British were suffering from "the penalty of the lead," while the Germans, free of "the restraining dead hand" of "past achievement," were able to gain a competitive advantage through a greater readiness to make use of technological innovations.[59]

Germany's situation differed from Britain's in other matters as well. When the anarchy of German pagan culture broke down, Veblen observed, their polity became "a predatory organization" of the feudal type. Germany retained its primitive "warlike animus." While the ordinary person in such a nation might be pacific, "temperamentally erratic individuals," and others "schooled by special class traditions or predisposed by special class interest," would see the uses of "warlike enterprise and keep alive the tradition of national animosity."[60] As late as the mid-nineteenth century, Germany had still been in the handicraft stage, and its political framework still remained one of an autocratic state, one in which "subordination, personal allegiance" was the "prime virtue." The policy of such a state was to further both the power to make war and industrial progress. Elsewhere in Europe, Veblen noted, one might see the growth of the nonservile spirit, but in Germany the nation's strength had been erected upon the feudal ethos, an "anachronistic remnant of medievalism."[61] Since the foundation of the empire in 1871, the outlying kingdoms and principalities had been "Prussianized." The Hohenzollerns had mobilized the predatory animus and "servile allegiance" of feudalism to create "a highly efficient engine of dynastic aggression," one, moreover, "commanding sufficient material resources to make them formidable in international politics." While Britain had been erecting a commonwealth of pacifically inclined citizens, Prussia had created a "centralised and irresponsible" state in which the Junkers ("a feudalistic body of agrarian squires") had the decisive voice, a state whose continued existence in the modern world depended upon a regime of war.[62]

Given this militarist political structure, Veblen argued, it was almost inevitable that Germany's economic policy would be mercantilist, employing the nation's resources to advance dynastic purposes.[63] Modern conditions favored large-scale economic units, and the Zollverein, in removing tariff obstacles between the German principalities, had helped to make German industry more efficient. Once political union was obtained, the dynastic state moved to a tariff policy designed to further the interests of the state, to promote self-sufficiency and make Germany less vulnerable in wartime. A free-trade policy might be superior in furthering material prosperity: Germans could get food at less cost abroad than by growing it at home, for example. But such a policy would enmesh Germany in international trading networks that would have made war virtually impossible.[64] In these circumstances, there would have been no "plausible grounds for an exorbitant

The Liberal Ideal and the Demons of Empire

military and naval establishment," much desired by Germany's feudal Junker classes.[65]

The political and economic structure of imperial Germany, Veblen observed, was the result of the efforts of the traditional, feudal political authorities to gain mastery over the new industrial forces for their own purposes. The Hohenzollerns had shrewdly employed the new technology to improve state efficiency, and this in good part accounted for their ability to triumph over the other German dynasties in the creation of a unified Germany. A policy of aggression, marked by "the disciplinary effects of warlike preparation and indoctrination" as well as "a system of bureaucratic surveillance and unremitting interference in the private life of subjects," had secured the subservience of the individual to the state; such a system of repression maintained the allegiance of subjects against "the disintegrating discipline" of modern industrial life. Despite the supposed restraints of the new imperial constitution, Germany remained "a quasi-manorial demesne or domaine, to be administered for dynastic ends." Its government was one of "constitutionally mitigated absolutism." Veblen found the policies, objectives, and methods of the imperial Germany of Wilhelm II to be much the same as those of Prussia under Frederick the Great.[66]

Imperial Germany was driven by a powerful impulse to war and expansion, Veblen argued. It had reached that stage of economic development when a shortage of markets led officials to consider the acquisition of colonies. The rising demands of the working classes for an improved standard of living and for a greater share in the government worried the governing classes since such demands posed the possibility that the "disposable margin" might not be sufficient to support the "warlike establishment" of the state.[67] An imperialist program might resolve such difficulties.

An "adventure of imperialism," Veblen observed, was not in the interests of the common man. The dynasty and its civil servants merely exploited the habitual loyalty of the empire's subjects for their own interests. There had been a consistent policy of police and judicial repression of popular sentiment hostile to imperialism; the press had been organized as a vehicle of propaganda. With a more favorable view of sports than Spencer, Veblen noted that, instead of addicting its youth to athletics in the British manner, Germany had trained its young men as soldiers, thus contributing to the growth of "an aggressive war spirit" and producing a more docile working class. Like Spencer, on the other hand, Veblen saw the "policy of tutelage" that had produced old-age pensions and national insurance as making the ordinary German dependent on the state, sapping his initiative and "spirit of autonomy," while reinforcing his loyalty to the dynasty.[68]

The Later Liberal Sociologists and the New Imperialism

Veblen saw the core motive of German imperialism as "a profitless self-aggrandizement of the dynasty," an irrational concern with power.[69] The ruling class claimed that its aggressive behavior was motivated by a worthy concern for the preservation of a German *Kultur,* which Veblen described as a product of preindustrial romanticism more suited to "the medieval and feudalistic scheme of life." In all areas, in fact, "the feudalising Prussian State" strove to hold on to "atavistic" and "anachronistic remnants of the ancient regime."[70] Imperial Germany was consequently battling against the entire modern world, a world characterized by a coherent mechanistic and matter-of-fact philosophy and a belief in free, popular institutions. Germany's romantic ideal of barbaric and profitless war, then, depended on the modern science and technology to which its underlying bias was unremittingly hostile. "The Imperial State," Veblen concluded, "may be said to be unable to get along without the machine industry, and also, in the long run, unable to get along with it." What it was seeking through war was "in the nature of a reprieve for personal government." But such a reprieve could not last much longer.[71]

In an article written in mid-1915, "The Opportunity of Japan," Veblen discussed the Asian island nation, recently emerged from feudalism to take a place among the world's industrial states, in terms similar to those of his analysis of Germany. Veblen wrote of a "dynastic aggrandizement" based upon the feudal loyalty of the common people of Japan to the governing class. Japan's government was marked by the "absolute and irresponsible mastery" typical of feudal regimes and of such early modern states as that of Louis XIV, as well as of Kaiser Wilhelm's imperial Germany. For the ruling classes of Japan, the country and people were "an estate to be husbanded and exploited for the state's ends." Stressing the issue more strongly than in his study of Germany, Veblen followed Hobson in noticing among the beneficiaries of this imperial aggrandizement certain "enterprising business men" prepared "to profit by that trade that is said to 'follow the flag.' "[72]

For Veblen, the basis of Japan's strength was her ability "anachronistically to combine the use of modern technical ways and means with the medieval spirit of servile solidarity." Yet, given the nature of the Japanese people, the advance of civilization would compel Japan to take over the spiritual aspects that were the necessary companions of the new industrialism. Life under the price system—that is, the market system—was "incompatible with the prepossessions of medievalism." As soon as Japan had "digested" Western science and technology, it would assimilate its "spiritual contents." Then the "Spirit of

Old Japan" would no longer be available to the dynasty in its aggressive activities.[73]

Japan's "opportunity" as an aggressive power would consequently be found only within the "historical interval" between its acquisition of Western technology and the "consequent, slower but inevitable" accommodation to the industrial ethos. Industrialism required literate workingmen; the industrial "routine of life" inculcated "a matter-of-fact" and "materialistic habit of mind." The new mechanistic conceptions would dissipate belief in the *"opéra bouffe* mythology" of Shinto, on which the rule of the Mikado rested. The system of business enterprise was oriented toward gaining an individual profit through competition; it had no interest in "national, dynastic, or collective ends." The relationships of feudal fealty would be replaced by those of interest. The higher standard of living that would necessarily emerge would cut into the disposable surplus for imperial politics. Veblen concluded that Japan, if it were to be successful as an expansionist state, had to strike out for empire within the coming generation, before the complete deterioration of the old dynastic spirit.[74]

In 1917, Veblen saw Japan and a defeated imperial Germany, if it were to emerge from the war relatively intact, as likely to ally.[75] In the mid-thirties, of course, imperial Japan proceeded to form an alliance with Nazi Germany, and in 1941—even earlier in China—Japan began her great bid for empire as Veblen had foreseen. In the post-1945 period, Veblen's prediction of the effective disintegration of the feudal spirits of Prussia and the old Japan appeared finally to have been realized, although the neighbors of the two powers continue to experience twinges of concern.

After the war of 1914–18, Veblen described the society he believed should and would replace a pecuniary capitalism. Instead of wasteful competition and business for profit, a technocratic economy under the leadership of the engineers would be instituted. Industrial efficiency, not only for its utility but for its own sake, would be the standard of such a society. Wasteful production and consumption would be eliminated. In this way, Veblen believed, one might secure all the advantages of industrialism and the modern ideas and institutions associated with it without the atavistic remnants of barbarism which a pecuniary society retained. The survival of traits of primitive emulation and aggressiveness had distorted modern capitalism, and they would in the future be replaced by the true industrial spirit, by a return to the pleasures of workmanship and the puritanical values of the first phase of the industrial revolution.

Great Britain heeded Hobson's warnings against a protectionist imperialism and remained faithful to free trade until the 1930s, justifying Veblen's view of the country as a predominantly industrial society. In three general elections, one in 1906 and two in 1910, the voters rejected neomercantilist Joseph Chamberlain's program of tariffs and imperial preference, despite his grim warnings of the dangers of German and American competition. The greater part of the working classes depended on the health of industries like coal and textiles, which, unlike the hard-pressed metals industries of the Midlands, were doing relatively well. Moreover, the free-trade agitators of the previous century had convinced workers that tariffs, particularly the tariffs on food that imperial preference would bring, were both injurious and immoral. The financial classes of the City also opted for the continuance of free trade; unlike their Continental and American counterparts with their considerable industrial interests, British banks continued to specialize in commercial banking and believed a free-trade regime essential to maintaining what was a virtual international predominance in these fields.

For British financial interests, one may argue, the issue was not so much one between a neomercantile imperialism and free trade as between a dying industrial and a still vibrant financial superiority. The national economists, a half-century earlier, had already taken note of the advantages enjoyed by the Bank of England and British banks as a whole; yet they had seen this superiority as a consequence of the dominant British industry. What was new was the expectation that British financial control would survive the decline of British industry. Such a prospect, however, was in line with the calculations of the free traders: under free trade, Cobden had observed, as a nation succumbed to the competition of rivals in one area, it would turn its attention to other fields; he himself had foreseen the end of Britain's industrial monopoly accompanied by the extension of its commercial and financial influence.

In an address to the Institute of Bankers in London in 1899, the geopolitician and free trader, H. J. Mackinder, carefully distinguishing between the interests of industry and of finance, had even been prepared to concede Britain's predominance in international commerce because of the tendency "towards the dispersion and equalisation of industrial and commercial activity throughout the world." But, he maintained, these changes would make even more necessary the existence of "a controlling centre." "It appears, therefore, quite possible," he concluded, "that the financial importance of the City of London may continue to increase" even as the importance of British industry and commerce "becomes *relatively* less." (Mackinder, we may note, would soon be converted to the Chamberlain protectionist program.)[76]

Given his ties with populist thinking, it is surprising that Veblen had not explored the subject of British financial predominance in his early writings, as had his compatriot Brooks Adams. After the publication of his work on Germany and article on Japan, he wrote more on "the captains of finance" as the instruments of imperialism. In 1917, he wondered if there was much to choose "between the warlike aggrandisement of an imperial dynasty, and the unearned increase of pecuniary benefit that accrues to a ruling class of gentlemen-investors." He granted that an important difference was that the British gentlemen-investors "who rule the commonwealth under parliamentary auspices" were more "accountable to their underlying community."[77] In the mid-twenties, his biographer has told us, he regarded Britain, as he did both the United States and Germany, as predatory, but he saw the British as being both more restrained and more efficient than their rivals; they would therefore be likely to continue to exercise world financial control. All his previous writings, he felt at this time, were leading him to an investigation of British imperialism, and, we may speculate, to focusing more on economic than on sociological questions.[78]

In 1937, nearly a decade after Veblen's death, Hobson wrote a study of the American theorist in which he described him as "one of the great sociologists of our time." Veblen had seen the opposition between industrial and "pecuniary" capital and had properly condemned finance as "responsible for all modern economic maladies."[79] A year later, in his memoirs, Hobson noted that four decades earlier his views on oversavings and unjust distribution had "led me for a time to an excessive and too simple advocacy of the economic determination of history." "When I wrote my volume on *Imperialism*," he continued, "I had not gathered into clear perspective the nature of the interaction between economics, politics, and ethics, needed for anyone who might wish to claim the title of Sociologist."[80] We have seen that even in his 1902 study, Hobson had merited this title. (We may note, however, that, even as Veblen appeared to be moving to a greater emphasis on economic issues, Hobson was retreating from such a view.)

It is interesting, although perhaps not surprising, that Marx and Engels failed to develop a consistent, monocausal theory of their own and intermittently availed themselves of the decidedly non-Marxist theories of their contemporaries, including the dominant sociological one. This often noted "failure" on their part might be thought only good sense insofar as it implied that so complex a problem required

---

more than a simplistic solution. In their later years, however, as we shall see, Marx, and more especially Engels, explored the role of finance capital in the new imperialism. Neo-Marxists like Rudolf Hilferding, particularly conscious of the economic and ideological developments in German capitalism, would carry this analysis even further. Perhaps surprisingly, we may find an essentially sociological explanation implicit in Hilferding's later formulation of the problem, and this was even more pronounced in Karl Kautsky's numerous writings on imperialism.

7 The Formulation of a Marxist and Neo-Marxist Theory

Karl Marx and Friedrich Engels never developed a systematic theory of imperial expansion as twentieth-century Marxists would. They put forward, on a number of occasions, variations of the theories we have examined so far, finding little contradiction among them. They were clearly prepared to see colonialism as the product of several factors. In their later years, they did lay the basis for what our century would regard as *the* Marxist theory of imperialism, the only Marxist theory that a wide range of non-Marxist economists have taken seriously, in part, perhaps, because it appeared to flow so naturally from earlier discussions of the phenomenon. But the founders of Marxism merely sketched the outline of this theory; it would remain for such followers as Hilferding, Luxemburg, Bukharin, and Lenin to fill in the argument.

Some of the ambiguities in the writings of Marx and Engels may be explained, at least partially, by the special doctrinal position of the communist theorists. Seeing the market system as an inevitable stage of historical development, they felt obliged, especially in their earlier years, to praise the overseas expansion of a progressive industrial capitalism at the expense of a native feudalism. As the century advanced, the problems of capitalism became more sharp; the depression of the 1870s dissipated the optimism of the previous two decades; and the new model of a usurious finance capitalism took hold. Marx and Engels increasingly stressed the role of capitalism as a system of colonial as well as domestic exploitation and saw in this the seeds of the self-destruction of the liberal ideal.

131

Marx and Engels

Karl Marx was born in Trier in Rhenish Prussia in 1818. He attended the universities of Bonn and Berlin, where he studied history and philosophy, and as a student was attracted to the ideas of the left-Hegelians, who were a potent presence in intellectual circles. He became a journalist and the editor of the *Rheinische Zeitung* in Cologne during the 1840s, during which time he met and formed a close friendship with Friedrich Engels, two years his junior and also a Rhinelander. In 1848, when in flight from the repression of the revolutionary actions of that year, the two men coauthored *The Communist Manifesto*, a tract that described a class struggle between the industrial working class and the capitalist bourgeoisie and prophesied the inevitable revolutionary triumph of the proletariat. Marx's radical politics compelled him to leave Germany for a London exile in 1849; Engels was already in England, having served intermittently for some years as manager of the Manchester branch of his family's textile firm. In 1844, the young Engels had written a moving book, *The Condition of the English Working Class,* in which he detailed the misery of the English proletariat. In the 1850s, Marx and his family were relieved from considerable economic distress by Engels's generosity and by Marx's earnings as a free-lance London correspondent for the *New York Tribune,* whose managing editor, the Fourierist C. A. Dana, had encountered Marx in Europe and been much impressed. (Engels prided himself on his knowledge of military strategy, yet he gave a good deal of attention to economic questions. It seems likely that most of the *Tribune* articles on military and a number on political and economic issues, although appearing under Marx's name, were written by Engels, who wished to spare Marx the time and pain of journalism in the interest of Marx's completing *Capital,* the first volume of which would appear in 1867. The precise authorship of these articles is not always certain, but there seems to have been general agreement between the two colleagues, with one or the other at times stressing a particular aspect or argument.[1])

Perhaps we should begin by sketching a general outline of nineteenth-century economic development as seen by Engels (with Marx apparently concurring). In 1859, Marx described this outline, written by Engels in 1844, as "a brilliant essay on the critique of economic categories." Engels's essay began with a detailed overview of the interaction of power and economics through the centuries, written largely, if not exclusively, along the lines charted by List and the national economists, though without specifically advocating their mercantilist

The Liberal Ideal and the Demons of Empire

solutions. The young Engels sketched three periods of economic development, finding in the core of each a human greed and avarice that remained essentially the same even if rationalized by increasingly sophisticated, and increasingly hypocritical, analyses.

Engels's three stages, somewhat resembling Saint-Simon's and Comte's, moved from the most primitive to the mercantilist to the capitalist. In the first, primitive stage, the nations confronted one another "like misers, each clasping" his "precious money-bag" and "eyeing his neighbours with envy and distrust"—the original sin of what we may call the theological stage. Engels regarded the second stage, that of mercantilism, as merely a cosmetic alteration: the "avaricious character of trade" was "already beginning to be hidden"; the fig leaf was in place. However, the "old avarice and selfishness" survived and intermittently "erupted in wars" originating in "trade jealousy." These conflicts revealed that trade, like robbery, was "based on the law of the strong hand." The third stage was the free-market capitalism of the nineteenth century, whose operations were described by the "science" of political economy. The capitalist economy assumed a "philanthropic character," but the new political economy was for Engels a "sham philanthropy," marked by the same greed and avarice that had characterized the earlier stages.[2]

This free-market capitalism was the latest and most sophisticated form the emotions of antisocial envy and cupidity had assumed, even as their rationalization by the political economists was the most hypocritical and, in practice, the most far-reaching and probably the most dangerous. Religious references and metaphors, either direct or by implication, mark Engels's descriptions of these economic stages. While the mercantilists, with "a certain artless Catholic candour" had made no great effort to "in the least conceal the immoral nature of trade," the founder of the economic science, Adam Smith, "the economic Luther," had substituted arguments of "protestant hypocrisy" and had dishonestly depicted trade as "advantageous to all parties" in a transaction and as a bond of international friendship. For Engels, the sham of the free-market system was patent. The capitalists had "civilised the ends of the earth" in order "to win new terrain for the development" of their "vile avarice." While reducing the number of wars so as "to earn the bigger profits in peace," they had intensified "to the utmost the enmity between individuals" by "the ignominious war of competition!" By "dissolving nationalities" and instituting a cosmopolitan world market, "the liberal economic system" had acted "to universalise enmity, to transform mankind into a horde of ravenous beasts." "For what else," Engels inquired, "are competitors?"[3]

Engels clearly agreed with the national economist Friedrich List,

---

though he did not mention him, that the free traders were (in Engels's words) "more inveterate monopolists" than the mercantilists had been. The "sham humanity" of the new economics hid a barbarism greater than that of their mercantilist predecessors, and the "conceptual confusion" of the latter was "simple and consistent" when "compared with the double-tongued logic" of the enemies of the old system. While acknowledging that the new political economy was "the shortest road to wealth," Engels saw the "inconsistency and ambiguity" of free trade as necessarily producing either the return of monopolies or socialism and the end of private property. The free-market utopia was doomed to failure. This was as certain, he added, as that "theology must either regress to blind faith or progress towards free philosophy." The supposed opposition of competition ("the battle-cry of the liberal economists") and monopoly ("the war-cry of the Mercantilists") was "quite hollow." "Free competition" was "an impossibility." Each competitor, whether worker, capitalist, or landowner, "*cannot but* desire to have the monopoly," and consequently "competition passes over into monopoly."[4]

In this essay, Engels joined his endorsement of the charges mounted by the national economists with the critique of the industrial system of the heterodox school of political economy of Malthus, Chalmers, and Wakefield. The two theories fit nicely together, the latter helping to substantiate the charges made by the former. Like the heterodox school, Engels rejected (though without naming) Say's Law: supply and demand never meshed, and there was "a constant alternation of over-stimulation and flogging." Anarchic production produced trade crises in which each would be "more universal and therefore worse" than the previous one. Like Wakefield (and later Carey), he described a "law of the centralisation of private property" whereby large capitalists would "swallow" small capitalists, and large landowners would devour small proprietors. And like Wakefield, Engels foresaw the disappearance of the middle class and a world "divided into millionaires and paupers." The result would be an inevitable "social revolution." Wakefield had believed empire building a possible alternative, whereas Engels saw the victory of socialism as the only solution.[5]

In 1892, nine years after Marx's death, Engels surveyed the preceding forty years in much the same spirit, again combining the perspective of the national economists and heterodox political economy. He saw the repeal of the protectionist Corn Laws in 1846 as having made Great Britain the "workshop of the world"; all countries became for Britain markets for its manufactures, and suppliers of food and raw materials. The country was poised as "the great manufacturing centre of an agricultural world, with an ever-increasing number of corn and cotton-growing Irelands revolving around her, the industrial sun."[6] But this had proved an unstable situation. The 1850s and 1860s, although interrupted by minor crises, had been prosperous, Engels noted, but the 1870s began "a dull depression, a chronic glut" in all branches of industry. Despite the assumption of the free-trade theorists that Britain would perpetuate its position as the chief manufacturer, other nations (notably the United States and Germany) saw no gain in "being turned into Irish pauper-farmers merely for the greater glory of English capitalists." The nations began not only to manufacture for their own needs but also to compete with one another for a world market.[7]

At this point, Engels's argument took on more of a distinctly "Marxist" tone. New markets were becoming "scarcer," and now even the blacks of the Congo were "forced into civilisation" by "Manchester calicos, Staffordshire pottery, and Birmingham hardware." "Capitalist production *cannot* stop," he continued; "it must go on increasing and expanding, or must die." Already Britain had experienced "stagnation, distress, excess of capital here, excess of unemployed work-people there." This was capitalism's "heel of Achilles," and when "constant expansion" became impossible, then either Britain "must go to pieces, or capitalist production must." Again, as in his 1844 essay, he predicted the decisive confrontation of capitalism and socialism, but this time Engels seemed, implicitly, to argue that the discovery of new markets overseas would delay the final struggle.[8] Nonetheless, the end result must be the propagation of socialism among the working classes and the overthrow of the capitalist system.[9]

Although Marx in 1859 was apparently sympathetic to Engels's Listian analysis of 1844, as early as the 1830s he had described Germany's moves toward a revival of mercantilism as a comic "anachronism" and "a flagrant contradiction of generally recognized axioms." Rather than approach the great question of economics and politics in the modern manner, Germany wished to return to the world of *"protective duties, of the prohibitive system, of national economy."* Here one may see Marx in agreement with the liberal social theorists, indeed anticipating the position of Veblen (as well as that of the neo-Marxist Hilferding) with respect to Germany, which Marx labeled "the modern *ancien régime.*" "Cotton barons and iron champions" turned themselves into "patriots," Marx wrote, and argued that Germany ought to return to the "old corrupt condition" of monopoly, against which France and England were rebelling. For the moment, this theory "hardly dares" to

---

move from "cunning" (in German, *listig*, possibly a punning allusion to List) to "ruthless practice." Germans were backward in all matters but philosophy; the country's political development expressed "the *perfection of the ancien régime*," and a German could no more "participate in the problems of the present" than could a Russian.[10]

One may argue that this was not necessarily in contradiction to Engels's subsequent position, for Germany's posture, however reactionary, might well be an immediately realistic response, even if doomed to ultimate failure by the laws of historical progress. Britain's support for free trade, though on the right side of history, might nonetheless be a hypocritical defense of British interests. In 1848, in an address to an association of revolutionary workingmen in Brussels, Marx, indeed, saw British free trade as "cosmopolitan exploitation" disguised as "universal brotherhood." He, however, wanted to be on the right side of history. For Marx, the system of protection was likely to preserve the present order whereas that of a more progressive free trade "works destructively," dissolving old nationalities into a cosmopolitan frame and pushing the class war between bourgeoisie and proletariat to "the uttermost point." "In a word," he concluded, "the Free Trade system hastens the Social Revolution." It should therefore be welcomed.[11]

In the Marxist journal *Neue Zeit* in 1888, forty years later, Engels attempted to set Marx's position in a context more congenial to his own views. For Marx, free trade was the "normal condition" of modern capitalist production, Engels explained, one that would "the sooner and the more fully" realize its "inevitable results" of glut, crises, class struggle, and social revolution. But Engels (again like List and Carey) wished to stress that protection had assisted Britain in achieving its early industrial monopoly, as had the British wartime naval strategy of cutting off the country's competitors from their colonial markets. Great Britain had then "forced" free trade on its overseas customers and, "thanks to this happy mixture of both systems" had secured by 1815 a "virtual monopoly" of world trade. With the beneficial results of such a commercial and industrial monopoly in hand, it became the further advantage of the industrial capitalists—the class representing "the chief national interests" in Great Britain—to impose free trade on the landed aristocracy and to convert other countries to the "gospel of Free Trade." This would make them "dependent" on Britain and compel them to submit to a state of affairs that "degraded them to be mere agricultural appendages" of a British "workshop of the world."[12]

While the founders of communism had somewhat divergent views concerning the analysis of the national economists, both Marx and Engels joined the liberal social theorists in denouncing the persistence of the feudal policy of force. Both were acutely conscious of the survival of the feudal spur to aggression, one with no relationship to capitalism. This factor, they believed, was most evident in the czarist policy of expansion, but it was apparent also, with qualifications, even in Britain's rule in Ireland and India, as their *Tribune* articles argued.

Marx and Engels were convinced that, at least from the time of Peter the Great, czarist Russia had followed a consistent policy of expansion. This consistency was the product of Russia's "historical past" and her "geographical conditions," notably her need for open seaports.[13] The communist theorists pictured Russia as an aggressive state of the preindustrial, feudal type and contrasted its irrational drives to expansion with Britain's nineteenth-century commercial necessities. The clash of the new and old had led to the Crimean War. Two-thirds of Europe (its central and eastern parts) depended on the free use of the Black Sea for trade, Marx observed, and this constituted an ever growing market for British manufactures; if Russia possessed Constantinople, the Black Sea would become "a Russian lake," and easy commercial intercourse would be impossible—another step, and hardly a progressive one, to Russia's "way to universal empire." Should Russia conquer Turkey, moreover, its strength would become "superior to all the rest of Europe put together," "an unspeakable calamity to the revolutionary cause." Thus, the "interests of the revolutionary Democracy and of England go hand in hand," Marx concluded in one of his *Tribune* articles.[14]

Both Engels and Marx, over a period of several decades, described a vast czarist conspiracy aimed at world domination—a demonic empire of force. A Turcophile Scotsman, David Urquhart, had as early as the 1830s written of a European cabal of statesmen and journalists, hoodwinked or bribed, who acted to advance Russian expansionist objectives. (This was much like List's portrait of the fools and hirelings on the Continent who worked to promote free trade and Britain's demonic empire of fraud.) Urquhart saw even the hawkish British prime minister Lord Palmerston as among the dupes of the czar. Marx became acquainted with Urquhart and was converted to his theories of conspiracy, even to seeing Palmerston as a Russian agent.[15] After Marx's death, in articles for *Die Neue Zeit* in 1890, Engels, following Urquhart and Marx, continued to endow czarist foreign policy with the diabolic dimensions of international conspiracy. Every Russian "land-grab" was "carried out under the pretext of enlightenment and national liberation," Engels observed, and the "childish Western Euro-

---

pean liberals," particularly Gladstone, had accepted these justifications for conquest and earned the Russian contempt for the "'educated' West."[16]

Yet after its defeat in the Crimean War, Engels continued, Russia had turned to the building of railways and the establishment of heavy industry, seemingly a progressive policy. But this had in good part taken place because of "purely military" considerations. Because of the abolition of serfdom, the granting of railway privileges, and the enactment of protective tariffs, a Russian bourgeoisie and proletariat had developed, and Russia was "becoming daily more westernized." Such a modern society was certainly in the long run incompatible with the czarist autocracy, and Engels predicted that the Russian people would at some future time enter onto the political stage, and internal struggles between classes would then leave no "time or inclination" for conquest. Far from seeing a monopoly finance capitalism leading to war, Engels in this article of 1890 declared that the "entire danger of a world war" would disappear when the Russian people put a halt to the "traditional policy of conquest of the czars" and gave up "phantasies of world conquest."[17] Such a discussion might easily have been found in Spencer and, with particular reference to Germany, would be implicit, as we have seen, in Veblen.

The feudal element of conquest and repression, Engels maintained, persisted in an advanced capitalist Britain that continued to rule Ireland along quasi-feudal lines. Ireland, he wrote in 1856, was "governed exactly in the old way" by an exploitative landed aristocracy and a heavily armed constabulary.[18] Some years later, Marx argued that the "*prime condition* of emancipation" for the English proletariat was the overthrow of the landed aristocracy.[19] Writing in 1870 to two colleagues on the general council of the recently formed International Working Men's Association, Marx pictured Ireland as not only the greatest "material" but also the greatest "moral" bulwark of the British landed aristocracy, enabling it to maintain "*its domination in England itself*." The interest of Great Britain, of its aristocracy as well as its bourgeoisie, was to turn Ireland from tillage to pasture and to the production of cheap wool and meat.[20]

Marx observed in 1867 that "everytime Ireland was about to develop industrially, she was crushed and reconverted into a purely agricultural land." In a somewhat unusual borrowing from the national economists, he concluded that only independence and a protective system could bring about needed Irish industrialization.[21] Was this a concession to Engels's sympathies for the national economists or a consequence of Marx's wooing at this time of the anti-free-trade Irish members of the International, who regularly employed this argument?

The Liberal Ideal and the Demons of Empire

In an article on India for the *Tribune* in 1853, Marx denounced the landed aristocrats of Britain, who had mastered war, "the Science of Barbarians," and by that science had conquered over a hundred million people in India. Members of noble families had rejected productive work, indeed all careers outside those provided by the Church or state, and found employment in conquering and governing overseas nations. The eighteenth-century British conquest of India, motivated by a mercantilist desire to secure markets as well as an aristocratic interest in providing jobs for "privileged orders," was "without figure of speech, infernal," an exercise in "plunder," and the horrible sufferings inflicted on the Indian people was "as hideous as the Slave trade."[22] These were the fruits of the union between mercantile colonialism and the aristocracy. Here we have the charges of Cobden and Bright that were repeated a half-century later by Hobson.

While Marx believed that the mercantilist East India Company of the eighteenth century had been rapacious and cruel, the nineteenth-century free-trade empire of industrial capital won his praise. "The aristocracy wanted to conquer India," the "moneyocracy [mercantilist finance capital] to plunder it, and the millocracy [industrial capital] to undersell it." Wherever the "moneyocracy" (elsewhere Marx spoke of it as "the haute finance") established itself to promote trade, "we find backward conditions"; "merchants' capital in its supremacy everywhere stands for a system of robbery." Though deploring the suffering caused by the underselling of Indian industries by Manchester and Birmingham, Marx nonetheless saw Britain's role in Asia as a progressive one. He did not, as he had in the case of Ireland, propose a protectionist system for India. The "millocracy," in transforming India into a productive country, not only had destroyed Indian feudalism but had also endowed that country with improved systems of irrigation and transportation. Though it was true that British capital had built railways for its own purposes, primarily to secure cheaper raw materials for British manufactures, these railways were nonetheless "the forerunner of modern industry" and performed a "regenerating" function.[23]

Marx and Engels were prepared to extend this *mission civilisatrice* to other advanced nations of the West. In 1848, for example, a *Tribune* article (probably written by Engels) denounced the brutal methods pursued in Algeria by the French General Bugeaud as "highly blameable," but saw the struggle of the Bedouin as "a hopeless one" and "the conquest of Algeria . . . [as] an important and fortunate fact for civilisation." While expressing some sympathy for the loss of Bedouin liberty, Engels reminded his readers that "we must not forget" that the Bedouin were "a nation of robbers," as much "ruled by the lust of gain" as the more civilized Europeans, except that the barbarians employed "ruder and more cruel means." "And, after all," he concluded, "the modern *bourgeois*, with civilisation, industry, order, and at least relative enlightenment following him, is preferable to the feudal lord or to the marauding robber, with the barbarian state of society to which they belong." So far as the piracies of the Barbary states were concerned, the only solution was the conquest of one of the offending states; this would compel the others to find other employment than piracy and other ways of replenishing their treasuries than "tributes."[24]

But Marx and Engels were hardly apologists for capitalism, and they argued that its defects (glut and the fall of the rate of profit) necessarily led to an expansion of trade and colonies. In a *Tribune* article in 1853, Marx observed that Britain labored under "the supreme necessity" of a "never-ceasing expansion of trade—this *fatum* which spectre-like haunts modern England, and, if not appeased at once, brings on those terrible revulsions which vibrate from New York to Canton, and from St. Petersburg to Sidney—this inflexible necessity."[25] It is in this "inflexible necessity" that we may see the roots of later neo-Marxist theories of imperialism.

Marx's explanation of the contradictions of capitalism differed considerably from those of either the mainstream or the heterodox political economists. One writer has attempted to uncover Marx's inconsistent and "complicated position on Say's Law," but the confusion persists.[26] Marx had his own theory of gluts, of the falling rate of profit and industrial crises: he saw the exploitative profits (surplus value) of the capitalist as originating entirely in the capital used to employ living labor; with sharply increased competition, the capitalist was compelled to invest more heavily in labor-saving machinery to reduce costs, and the greater weight given constant (machinery, etc.) over variable (labor costs) capital within the total composition of capital reduced proportionately the rate of profit. There was, then, a glut of capital that led to an overproduction of commodities and an "overpopulation of laborers." Export of capital and foreign trade were the means employed by capitalism to ward off this inevitable fall of the rate of profit. Though foreign trade tended at first to remedy the situation by increasing the rate of surplus value and permitting an expansion of production, in the long run this only hastened the "process of accumulation," reducing the variable as compared to the constant capital and bringing about a further fall in the rate of profit.[27] Marx's theory of surplus value was the basis for his further conclusion that colonies were useful for capitalism because investment in colonies usually yielded a higher rate of profit both "on account of the backward development of the colony," and because "slaves, coolies, etc., permit a better exploitation of labor."[28]

Toward the end of his life, Marx came to view Western advances into Asia and Africa with distinctly less favor than he had in the 1850s. He became upset with instances of brutality in the colonies and laid increasing stress upon the usurious "tribute" with which colonies were burdened, devices of the older, repressive "moneyocracy" of mercantilism. "India alone," he observed, "has to pay 5 millions in tribute for 'good government,' interest and dividends of British capital, etc., not counting the sums sent home annually by officials as savings of their salaries, or by English merchants as a part of their profit in order to be invested in England." Britons owned foreign securities, European and American, upon which they drew similar "tribute" in the form of interest and dividends.[29] If much might be said for industrial capital, finance capital had little to recommend it.

In an article in 1852, Marx saw the Glorious Revolution of 1688 as having been achieved by an alliance between the landed aristocracy and finance capital ("the Bankocracy"), whereas the equally revolutionary repeal of the Corn Laws in 1846 was primarily the victory of industrial capital, the "millocracy." On both occasions, the Whigs had served as the political agency for change. Marx described the Whigs as "feudalists," "money-mongers with feudal prejudices," "aristocrats without point of honor," and "bourgeois without industrial activity." What the Tory landowners and the British masses had in common was "the hatred against the 'money-monger' "; the ordinary people hated both "the landlord who oppresses, and the money lord who exploits it"[30]—the last, perhaps, an echo of the slogan of a "new feudalism" mounted by Fourierist writers.

Like Henry Carey and, later, Brooks Adams, Marx, in an article in the *Neue Oder Zeitung* in 1855, attributed the passage of the British Specie Act of 1819 (which had revived the gold standard) to the devices of the "financial aristocracy." Both Tories and Whigs had supported this legislation, which paid back in undepreciated currency government debts contracted in inflated currency, to the great advantage of the financial classes. In return the financial aristocracy had for a quarter of a century supported the Corn Laws protecting British grain growers: a "fraudulent increase of government *rentes* for fraudulent increase of ground rents—such was the bargain concluded between financial and landed aristocracy."[31] But by the 1840s, industrial capital in Britain had become dominant, and the repeal of the Corn Laws was the victory of the capitalist manufacturers over both the landed classes and their longtime allies, the usurious "bankers, stock-jobbers, fundholders, etc."[32] Writing in 1849, Marx declared that in Britain industry now controlled finance, while "in France the bank rules over industry."[33]

In the first volume of *Capital*, in 1867, Marx discussed the links of capitalism (even industrial capitalism) with the usury of earlier times. The capitalist "shares with the miser the passion for wealth as wealth," but what was "mere idiosyncracy" in the miser was "in the capitalist, the effect of the social mechanism, of which he is but one of the wheels." Competition and the development of capitalist production made it necessary to increase continually the sums of capital in an industrial enterprise. This competition "compels him [the capitalist] to keep constantly expanding his capital, in order to preserve it," to accumulate more and more wealth. "That is Moses and the Prophets." The capitalist did not enrich himself through his own labor and abstinence: "he squeezes out the labour-power of others, and enforces on the labourer abstinence from all life's enjoyments." Yet the vulgar bourgeois economist spoke of the capitalist robbing himself "whenever he 'lends (!) the instruments of production to the labourer,' that is, whenever by incorporating labour-power with them, he uses them to extract surplus value out of that labour-power." Unlike the miser, who merely accumulated, then, the capitalist like the usurer could accumulate more only by the exploitation of the labor of those to whom he lent—by extracting the last drop of surplus value.[34]

If the virtual (though hardly complete) identification of the industrial capitalist and the usurer were not sufficiently apparent from this portrait, Marx eased the reader's burden by a footnote that drew upon the writings of the sixteenth-century Protestant reformer Martin Luther. Marx, noting that Luther took the usurer, "that old-fashioned but ever renewed specimen of the capitalist for his text," then proceeded (for some three dozen lines) to quote Luther's denunciation of the usurer as a murderer "who starves a man" as he "sits the while safe on his stool, when he ought rather to be hanging on the gallows." Luther had further written that there was "no greater enemy of man (after the devil)" than the "usurer and money-glutton" who "would have the whole world perish of hunger and thirst, misery and want, so far as in him lies, so that he may have all to himself, and every one may receive from him as from a God, and be his serf forever." For Luther (and Marx clearly found this lengthy excerpt from Luther's diatribe appropriate for his own purposes), the demonic usurer was "a great huge monster, like a were-wolf, who lays waste all," though he "would deceive the world, as though he were of use." Luther concluded by calling on all to "hunt down, curse and behead all usurers."[35]

There was no specific mention of the Jew as usurer in Marx's selection from Luther's piece. However, German readers, as well as, of course, the better informed more generally, could not fail to know that the Protestant leader had explicitly damned the Jews in this well-known diatribe. Anti-Semites, indeed, from the sixteenth century to the National Socialists of the twentieth century continued to quote from Luther's tract with its fierce command to "hunt down, curse and behead all usurers."

Elsewhere in this volume, Marx depicted the "credit system" of finance capital in more pragmatic, even somewhat approving terms. The function of finance was to draw "by invisible threads" the money diffused through the economy into the hands of capitalists who were prepared to use it productively; "the world would still be without railways, if it had been obliged to wait until accumulation should have enabled a few individual capitalists to undertake the construction of a railway."[36] This somewhat resembled, though without their extravagant praise of bankers, the position taken earlier by Saint-Simon and Comte.

In the third volume of *Capital*, published by Engels after Marx's death, however, Marx described the joint stock company as having transformed the owners of capital into "mere money-capitalists," while the "functioning capitalist" became a "mere manager, an administrator of other people's capital"—an anticipatory view of what twentieth-century writers would call "the managerial revolution." Monopolies were thereby created which had abolished the "capitalist mode of production" and produced "a new aristocracy of finance, a new sort of parasite in the shape of promoters, speculators and merely nominal directors." There had come into being "a whole system of swindling and cheating by means of corporation juggling, stock jobbing, and stock speculation." The result was "private production without the control of private property."[37] This analysis looked forward to Hilferding, though stressing certain populist themes that Hilferding would resist.

Engels noted the later period of capitalist colonialism and consolidation. In a supplement of 1894 to the third volume of *Capital*, Engels described colonization as "purely a subsidiary of the stock exchange." It was in the interests of the stock exchange that the division of Africa had taken place, the French had conquered Tonkin, and the British had assumed control of Mashonaland and Natal.[38] Even earlier, in response to a piece Karl Kautsky had written on colonization in 1883,

Engels complained that Kautsky might have made the piece more lively by stressing "colonization in the interests of stock exchange swindles," noting particularly French activities in Tunisia and Tonkin.[39]

Since the time of Marx's writing, Engels noted further in his 1894 supplement, production had continued to outstrip the expansion of markets. Tariff protection by foreigners against British industry had had the effect of increasing production even more "by artificial means," resulting in "a chronic overproduction, depressed prices, falling or disappearing profits." The "long cherished freedom of competition" had "reached the end of its tether." The "great captains of industry" meet in a cartel to regulate production, Engels observed, and he noted the prevalence of such cartels in America.[40] Yet again, we see an anticipation of Hilferding and the neo-Marxists.

Rudolf Hilferding

The leading economist of the Austro-Marxist school, Rudolf Hilferding, studied medicine at the University of Vienna, where he joined the student socialist society. In 1902, at twenty-five, he began to write for Karl Kautsky's *Die Neue Zeit,* the principal theoretical organ of Marxist orthodoxy in Germany; and in 1904 he published his rejoinder to the Austrian marginalist economist Eugen Böhm-Bawerk's critique of the Marxist theory of labor value. Hilferding's best-known work, *Das Finanzkapital,* published in 1910, was the most thoroughgoing neo-Marxist investigation of imperialism. We may see in his analysis an implicit evaluation not only of the theories of Marx and Engels but also of those of a number of other writers we have discussed.

Hilferding's intellectual posture in his work on Böhm-Bawerk foreshadowed the outlook of the developing Austro-Marxism. For the Austro-Marxists, orthodoxy's insistence on economic relationships as the basis on which all politics and ideology depended was a dangerous distortion. In the real world all three factors operated, each influencing the others. For the Austro-Marxists—for Otto Bauer in his work on nationalities, Karl Renner on law, and Max Adler on philosophy— Marxism had to move from mere party doctrine to genuine social science. These characteristics of the new school were to be found in Hilferding's study *Das Finanzkapital* as well as in his subsequent thinking about imperialism.[41]

Hilferding's scientific intention, seriously pursued, would separate his theory of imperialism from the polemical and partisan theory subsequently offered by Lenin. For Lenin the goal of a proletarian revolution, immediate and necessarily violent, would be the principal objective; for Hilferding and the Austro-Marxists, the possibility of a gradual evolution, in which the bourgeois state would step by step assume the role of the regulator and director of economic life in the interest of all classes, and with the electoral and moral support of a majority of citizens, appeared not only more desirable but more likely. For Hilferding, though not for Lenin, the move of modern capitalism to imperialism appeared a choice, not a necessity; for the Austro-Marxist, the new conditions of capitalist development had undoubtedly provided the grounds for such a reorientation but had not, in rigidly determinist fashion, excluded other possibilities.

The bulk of Hilferding's study concerned the profound changes which had transpired in the capitalism of the preceding decades. Some had been mentioned by Marx and Engels. Chief among them were the growth of the joint-stock company, which enlisted the savings of all classes, and the salient role taken by the banks, which led in mobilizing much of this capital and in unifying the hitherto separate spheres of industrial, commercial, and bank capital. This unification had led to finance capital's direction of industry, giving rise to the separation between ownership and management, which Hilferding, like Marx, saw as typical of the latest stage of development. Since the late 1870s, in Germany (which nation served as Hilferding's prime model) high finance, in alliance with the state bureaucracy, had turned to a program of steep protective tariffs, monopolies, and cartels, all of which produced heightened profits, as well as a parallel policy of imperial expansion to maintain and expand these gains.[42]

Hilferding stressed the qualitative differences between British conditions and those of Germany or of the United States. Britain had remained preeminently the country of the liberal ideal, of individualist, laissez-faire, free-trade capitalism. The British bourgeois view of the state's role in economic life had evolved out of the struggle of factory owners against a mercantilist regime that sanctioned monopolies and special privileges. The new political economy provided the intellectual basis for this effort, which soon extended into a fight for individual liberty as well. Britain had, of course, also favored free trade because its lead in industrial and commercial development made such a policy advantageous, and industrialists in Germany and in America had demanded and received tariff protection against British competition. German landowners, after the decline of their agricultural exports, joined industrialists, particularly the iron and steel magnates, in seeking protection. For a period, German commercial and banking interests continued to favor free trade, as their British counterparts still did; but unlike the situation in Britain, where small individual capitals had become greater ones, enabling individual capitalists to predominate in manufacturing, German industry had required the services of bankers to raise smaller amounts from a greater number of individuals. Through such means, German finance capital had come to own much of German large-scale industry and to assume responsibility for its direction. Financiers then joined industrialists and landowners in seeking tariff protection.[43]

The combination of industrial and finance capital, with finance in the driver's seat, produced cartels whose interests ran powerfully in favor of very high tariffs, a protection seen not as a temporary means to an end but as a permanent system. Indeed, the most competitive and powerful industrial cartels saw in such tariffs the basis for dividing the domestic market while maintaining a price for domestic consumers considerably higher than the international market price. The higher the tariff, the greater the "extra profit" resulting from a difference between domestic and world market prices. This extra profit was not derived from the surplus value produced by living labor, in the usual manner of exploitation depicted by the Marxists, but was "a tribute," "an indirect tax" on the domestic consumer, all the more useful when the growing strength of trade unions made it difficult to raise the rate of profit by lengthening working hours or lowering wages. The decline in the domestic market resulting from higher prices would be made up, and more, by the cartel's ability, due to the economies secured by large-scale production, to sell its goods on the world market. The cartel could even afford to dump its products abroad below their costs of production, thus underselling and possibly eliminating foreign competitors.[44]

In the preceding three decades, Hilferding continued, protectionist countries like Germany and the United States had become "the model states of capitalist development"—in their adoption of high tariffs, in the ability of their finance capitalists to impose an "organizational superiority" on industry, and in their success in exporting their excess capital.[45] Protection had become not merely a method of defending the home market but a way of conquering foreign markets; thus "what was once a defensive weapon of the weak has become an offensive weapon in the hands of the powerful." When a nation responded to such devices as dumping by raising its tariffs, the invaders simply transferred production to that country, that is, they exported capital. This was a process that took advantage of cheaper labor and ground rents in less developed countries. (Britain, as well as other capital-exporting nations, he also noted, often preferred to invest, in the manner of the earlier mercantilism, in the production of raw materials needed by their domestic industries rather than in the production of consumer goods that would compete with their own manufactures.)[46]

Hilferding described certain benign effects of capital export for both advanced and less developed economies, but he stressed the injuries suffered by the more backward regions. The opening of new markets helped to moderate crises, prolong periods of prosperity, and end depressions in advanced countries. All this made less likely "a conscious awareness of the ills of capitalist society," and produced "an optimistic view of its viability." Hilferding observed, moreover, that in part because of capital export "the tendencies towards pauperization inherent in capitalism appear to be overcome in the advanced capitalist countries." The export of capital also promoted the "maximum development" of the productive forces of less developed countries. But there was a less pleasant aspect of the relationship. Colonial trade, long "associated with robbery and plunder," continued to employ "violent methods"; these were, indeed, "the essence of colonial policy, without which it would lose its capitalist rationale." The shortage of wage laborers in less developed countries, furthermore, compelled the capitalists to secure the necessary proletariat by expropriating the lands of the natives and by money taxation. Perhaps even more vicious and violent was the importation of Asian coolie labor, as had recently taken place in South Africa, and the reinstitution of virtual slavery in the Belgian Congo.[47]

Finance capitalists almost always insisted that their states take formal possession of less developed colonial areas to safeguard their investments against local uprisings. This had been a leading factor in Britain's war against the Boers. In most cases, these financiers also wished to exclude the competition of foreign capital. They mobilized all the resources of the state and its armed forces to obtain cheap raw materials, cheap labor, and cheap land, as well as markets for the huge outputs of their nation's cartels.[48] Protection and cartelization had, furthermore, increased the importance of the markets protected by tariff walls and intensified the "ever-present drive of capital towards a constant expansion of its territory."[49]

Even when there was no formal takeover, finance capital would create informal colonies of less developed territories. (This was Argentina's position, for example, with respect to Britain.) Financiers sometimes made loans on condition that they be used to purchase the commodities of the lending country, the customer thereby becoming "a debtor and hence a dependent who must accept the conditions imposed by his creditor." While the building of a transport system in a backward country might to some extent have helped that country's development, the channeling of most of the profits abroad had slowed accumulation and further development. The sites of capital investment became "economic tributaries of foreign capital" and "second-class states." The competition for markets was now one between "national banking groups over spheres for investment of loan capital," and since competition equalized interest rates, the "economic struggle" had become a "power struggle."[50]

Britain's adoption of protectionism and organization of an imperial trading bloc, which Hilferding believed must soon come to pass, would sharpen its rivalry with Germany and make Germany's situation so difficult that there had to be "a solution by force." The United States was fortunate in already possessing an extended continental market; and an economic federation of Britain and its colonies would provide British industry with a considerable imperial market. But Germany required wider territories for markets and raw materials and was preparing itself to seize them at British expense.[51]

Germany was better able to wage such a struggle with Britain than France had been a century earlier, for Germany had developed a powerful weapon—a "new ideology." In the decades that followed the 1789 revolution, France had led the Continent against both feudalism and Britain's "new empire of world capitalism." It had lost that struggle. At present, the Continental states, this time under German leadership, were once again drawn up in opposition to Great Britain and its empire. However, now Germany had at its service an ideology of imperialism to inspire its crusade. This ideology was the opposite of the liberal ideal: it favored not "freedom, but domination"; it sought not competition, but organization; it required a strong state to protect its domestic market while it assisted in the takeover of foreign markets; and in order to "transform the whole world into a sphere of investment," it favored a state "strong enough to pursue an expansionist policy." German finance had allied itself with large landowners to support these policies, and a vigorous imperial expansion was their "common interest."[52] The new doctrine was, moreover, a "racist ideology, cloaked in the garb of natural science," one that justified finance capital's "lust for power" as part of a Darwinian struggle in which superiority in weapons would be "the final arbiter." The class struggle of socialism had yielded to "a common goal of national greatness," which provided "a new bond for the strife-ridden bourgeois society."[53] The middle class of artisans and small businessmen, understanding their subordinate position, no longer had a policy independent of finance capital and fell "victim" to a militarist and imperialist "demagogy" that exploited their "hostility" to the workers and their fear of a descent into the proletariat.[54]

The true policy of the proletariat was one of opposition to imperialism: like Hobson, whom he probably had read, Hilferding declared that it was in the interest of the working class to expand domestic industry and consumption, not to turn to foreign markets. While temporary "'educational' tariffs" furthered industrial development and thereby helped the worker, the cartel tariff, in association with a tariff to protect agriculture, injured the worker as both producer and consumer and led inevitably to expansionism, international war, and "the unleashing of revolutionary storms" that would bring about the collapse of capitalism. The proletariat must continue its opposition to militarism and expansion if it were to become the "beneficiary" of this collapse. The workers must fight not for an antiquated policy of free trade but for socialism as "the only alternative to imperialism."[55]

Finance capital had performed an essential function in establishing "social control" of production by an oligarchy; it now remained for the working class to "dispossess this oligarchy," take over large-scale industry, and establish a proletarian order. Once the opening of new fields of overseas exploitation tapered off, and this was bound to happen, the concentration of wealth and the concomitant distress of increasing numbers of people would proceed at an even more rapid pace. "Finance capital, in its maturity, is the highest stage of the concentration of economic and political power" at the disposal of the "capitalist oligarchy," Hilferding declared; it marked "the climax of the dictatorship of the magnates of capital." In the war among the "capitalist lords" of each power, and in the revolutionary clashes within each nation, the capitalist dictatorship would "finally be transformed into the dictatorship of the proletariat." Here was rhetorical Marxism at its most orthodox, and a clear anticipation of the Lenin theory. More modestly, and in a decidedly more revisionist spirit, Hilferding suggested that a takeover of the six largest Berlin banks might provide a reasonable and more immediate alternative.[56]

Hilferding approached the question of usury and capitalism in more sober, and more Hegelian, terms than had Marx in *Capital*. In the early development of the industrial system, he wrote, usurer's capital had played an important part in transforming handicraft production into capitalism. But there arose "a resistance of 'productive' capital" ("the profit-earning capitalists" of "commerce and industry") against unproductive "interest-earning capitalists." Industrial capital then took command of usurer's capital, and bank capital, arranging credit for industrial capitalists, soon supplanted usurer's capital. But the banks became increasingly powerful, and in the end emerged as the "founders and eventually rulers of industry." The banks, then, appropriated for themselves a major portion of the profits of industry,

---

"just as formerly the old usurer seized, in the form of 'interest,' the produce of the peasants and the ground rent of the lord of the manor." Hilferding invoked the negation of the negation of the Hegelian dialectic: with usurer's capital as thesis being negated by the antithesis of bank capital, which in turn was negated by finance capital. This last was the "synthesis of usurer's and bank capital" at "an infinitely higher stage of development."[57] Subsequent Marxist writers were to ignore much of Hilferding's dialectical refinements and were, we shall see, to speak simply of the usurious imperialism of finance capital.

Hilferding saw Europe at a crossroads, but as a social scientist rather than a Marxist polemicist, accepted the possibility of the continued survival of capitalism. The mechanism for this was "the internationalization of capital."[58] War might have occurred earlier, he wrote, had it not been for the countervailing force of multinational exploitation of many territories. In South America, for example, the British and the French supplied loan capital in the same countries where the Americans and Germans supplied industrial capital. In this way, British and French capital had acquired "an interest in the progress of German industries in South America, etc." Hilferding was uncertain as to which of the opposing tendencies—war or multinational imperial development—would win out.[59]

Hilferding may have been following Hobson's suggestion of an international imperialism, though the English writer had cast such an eventuality in a more villainous role; more directly, Hilferding was foreshadowing Karl Kautsky's "ultra-imperialism," which, we shall see in the following chapter, the German Social Democrat in 1914 and 1915 would view as implying the peaceful continuance of a revivified capitalism. In the 1920s, Hilferding would accept Kautsky's sanguine view of future capitalist development, for which he himself had prepared the way in his 1910 book. In this he may be seen as, once again, acknowledging that capitalism might choose its political and economic policies and not be compelled onto a predetermined course and as further asserting that, in fact, Germany and America (Hilferding's model states of the new capitalism) had earlier made such a choice, which they might reverse in the future. Such thinking, as we shall see in more explicit fashion in Kautsky's writings, carried with it a somewhat disguised sociological theory. Hobson had written in those terms, and, more reluctantly, so would Kautsky. Other Marxists, however, like Rosa Luxemburg, N. I. Bukharin, and V. I. Lenin were to understand matters quite differently. For them, a more rigidly deterministic, purely economic theory predominated.

The Liberal Ideal and the Demons of Empire

Rosa Luxemburg

In 1913, the Polish-born Marxist economist Rosa Luxemburg published her *Accumulation of Capital,* which added further variations to the Marxist view of imperialism.[60] In an extension of the Wakefield school's insistence on the need for undeveloped lands to extend the field of production—an argument she may have borrowed from the quasi-Marxist Italian economist Achille Loria, who in turn owed much to Wakefield[61]—Luxemburg argued that capitalism was dependent for its continued existence on trade with noncapitalist areas. When these areas became in their turn capitalist, as they necessarily would, for capitalism broke down less advanced economies, the system could no longer survive. Since the number of noncapitalist regions was limited, the new imperialism insisted on a system of protective tariffs to join the newly established colonies firmly to the metropolis. Wakefield had not carried his analysis to this apparently logical conclusion, but, we recall, Torrens had.

Luxemburg also emphasized the need of capitalists for an ever growing quantity of exploitable labor. Capitalism had developed historically in "a feudal environment" of peasants and artisans and, in its search for a labor force, had freed the European peasant from the serfdom or quasi-serfdom of traditional society.[62] A dynamic European capitalism was now "impelled" into a global expansion to "appropriate [further] productive forces for purposes of exploitation."[63] Capitalism's "permanent" device in the process of modern imperialism was to dispossess the Asian and African peasantry by force. Britain's tactics in India were typical: tax the peasantry, drive them into debt, appropriate their lands, and compel them to offer their labor.[64]

Luxemburg wished to investigate what she regarded as the inevitable disturbances, caused by overproduction, in the regular processes of capitalist production and distribution. She examined at some length the ideas not only of the physiocratic and classical schools and those of Marx himself, but also those of underconsumptionists like the nineteenth-century German socialist economist K. J. Rodbertus. She gave special attention to the analysis of underconsumption by the Russian populist economist V. Vorontsov. Vorontsov had developed in another direction the idea of the unproductive consumer, earlier stressed by physiocratic writers like Quesnay and Malthus. The physiocrats saw only agriculture as genuinely productive and postulated that unproductive classes (manufacturers, merchants, members of the professions), who consumed without producing, would be needed to maintain a harmonious circulation of wealth. Vorontsov assigned this role of the essential, unproductive consumer to militarism. The production of military supplies restored to the economy that surplus portion of the capitalist's income that he could not consume, and this in the form of wages given to the workers in the armaments and munitions industries. Without this outlet, overproduction would bring about a glut of capital, depressing the rate of profit, and endangering the harmonious operation of the system. For Vorontsov, these military expenditures, although they performed a necessary role, were not an inevitable accompaniment of the capitalist process. The capitalist could find other means of returning his surplus to healthy circulation. Moreover, for the Russian populist it was necessarily the capitalist who paid the cost of armaments.[65]

Luxemburg adapted this idea of Vorontsov's to her own purposes. She saw militarism as absolutely necessary to the workings of capitalism, and, setting aside Vorontsov's logic, she saw the financial costs of armaments not as a burden on the capitalists but as derived entirely from indirect taxes imposed on the working class. Armaments manufacture gave capitalists a further occasion for accumulation, she argued, and also helped to increase the concentration of industry so profitable to the larger capitalists. Indirect taxes also provided a mechanism for expropriating part of the income of noncapitalist sectors (such as the peasantry) for circulation in the capitalist economy. Quite naturally for Luxemburg and for certain later Marxists, militarism was also necessary to capitalism as "a weapon in the competitive struggle between capitalist countries for areas of non-capitalist civilisation." Militarism, furthermore, helped to bring about the destruction of noncapitalist economies both at home and abroad, and the ruin of these economies, so necessary to the continued existence of capitalism, she argued, would bring about the breakdown of the capitalist system.[66]

For Rosa Luxemburg, then, modern imperialism was the final phase of a long historical process. It was the political consequence of the excessive accumulation of capital. From the time of the primitive accumulation of the first phase of capitalism, this process had been marked by "a series of mass murders of primitive peoples . . . and large-scale slave trading." In the final phase at hand, the "decisive struggle for expansion" was set in the imperial metropolises themselves, and this struggle must end in either "the decline of civilization" or the triumph of socialism.[67]

In her *Anti-Critique*, written in 1915 in response to Marxist critics of her theory of imperialism, Luxemburg was particularly disturbed by the position of the Austro-Marxist Otto Bauer. Bauer had noted that Luxemburg had not given sufficient attention to Hilferding's analysis. She had neglected entirely the role played by finance capital. Moreover, Bauer, like Hilferding, believed capitalism viable without expansion. Imperialism was not the "historical necessity" depicted by Luxemburg, he argued, but "the wicked invention of a small group of people who profit from it." Such a view resembled that of Cobden, Hobson, and the British Radicals. Bauer and the mainstream of Austro-Marxism sought to convince the bourgeoisie that colonialism and militarism were in fact injurious to its interests. This analysis was entirely unacceptable to Luxemburg; the "final confrontation" between the working and bourgeois classes "to settle their world historical contradiction," she complained, was thus transformed by Bauer into "the utopia of a historic compromise" between the proletariat and the capitalists. Such a view was wrong and profoundly subversive of the Marxist vision.[68]

N. I. Bukharin

The Russian Marxist economist N. I. Bukharin was a leading Bolshevik theoretician from the time of the Revolution until his execution in Stalin's purges of 1938. In his *Imperialism and World Economy*, published in 1915, Bukharin employed Hilferding's analysis of finance capital to reach a conclusion perhaps somewhat closer to Luxemburg's than to that of Hilferding. Buhkarin took up Luxemburg's linking of capitalism and armaments, though without her peculiar economic analysis. His description of the world war then in progress, and of imperialism, closely anticipated the one Lenin would employ two years later.[69]

For Bukharin, "the rule of finance capital" throughout Europe implied "both imperialism and militarism." (He rejected Hilferding's view that Britain represented a different economic type from Germany and the United States, citing, however, only instances of industrial concentration, not finance's control of industry.) The middle-class pacifists were wrong to believe military and naval expenditures to be examples of a "bourgeois 'stupidity' . . . blind to its own interests." Now that capitalism had reached its "highest stage," an international struggle among state trusts, armies and navies had become the most essential instruments. This new stage created a demand for the products of heavy industry and raised the importance of armaments manufacturers like Krupp. But the armaments makers did not cause wars, as some bourgeois radicals argued. The capitalist system itself was "unthinkable" without armaments and wars. Rather than see the internationalization of capital as making a pacific capitalism possible, as did Hilferding (and, we shall see, Kautsky), he prophesied that, even

---

were all European trusts to become one, this would mean only an increase of militarism with Europe pitted in a struggle against American and Asian trusts. Bukharin concluded that imperialism was "the most essential element" of modern capitalism, against which the international working classes, who bore the burdens of war and armaments, would soon revolt.[70]

In a later work, in 1924, several years after the Bolshevik triumph, Bukharin took specific issue with the way in which Luxemburg had framed the issue of imperialism. He warned Marxists against the heresy to which the views of Luxemburg (who had been assassinated in 1919 during a crackdown on the communist Spartacist league by the forces of the postwar German republic) might lead. Bukharin found the "basic fault" of Luxemburg's discussion of imperialism, as Bauer had earlier, in her having omitted the role of finance capital, her neglect of the way in which monopolies and cartels, under the control of banks, had given a special character to the new era. The important distinctions between "trade capitalism and mercantilism, industrial capitalism and liberalism, finance capitalism and imperialism—all these phases of capitalist development disappear or dissolve" for Luxemburg "into 'capitalism as such.'" There were still other faults in Luxemburg, whom Bukharin associated with such "renegades" as at one time orthodox Marxist Kautsky. Kautsky, like Luxemburg, had also defined imperialism as a fight for agrarian territories; neither, Bukharin observed, had perceived that imperial powers also wished to expand into "capitalist territories," as the recent war among European powers had demonstrated. The conflict was not merely for agrarian areas but for a "division of the world."[71]

Bukharin noted that Luxemburg, in arguing that capitalism required the existence of noncapitalist "third persons" to survive, had adopted the position of the German Social Democrat Heinrich Cunow. Cunow had observed that more than half the world's population were peasants (even in Europe nearly half of the population was rural), and these consequently constituted such noncapitalist third persons. With such "enormously large . . . reserves" of noncapitalist populations, Cunow had concluded, capitalism would have "such a colossal field of activity at its disposal" that "only utopians" could seriously expect a proletarian revolution." For Bukharin such a "Cunowist" and thoroughly un-Marxist conclusion was the inescapable consequence of Luxemburg's analysis and was clearly unacceptable.[72]

But Bukharin was at least content that Luxemburg, as opposed to reformist Marxists and the "quasi-orthodox" Kautsky, had insisted on "the historical necessity of imperialism." While founding her analysis of the problem of imperialism upon incorrect theory, Luxemburg

The Liberal Ideal and the Demons of Empire

had, unlike Kautsky, "answered it properly." Bukharin was especially disturbed by Kautsky's discussion of "an 'English style' reformed 'ideal capitalism'" and was content that Luxemburg had avoided this trap.[73] Bukharin did not note that the Austro-Marxists Hilferding and Bauer might have been caught in the same snare.

A perceptive political economist, A. O. Hirschman, has recently speculated as to why Marx—who was undoubtedly familiar with a certain two-paragraph passage in Hegel's *Philosophy of Right* (1821)—did not follow its hints in constructing a theory of economic imperialism like those of Hobson and Luxemburg. Hirschman sees in Hegel's remarks prescient insights on excess production and underconsumption that would, as Hegel wrote, by an "inner dialectic" drive a civil society to establish colonies and to "seek markets, and so its necessary means of subsistence, in other lands, which are either deficient in the goods it has overproduced, or else generally backward in industry." Finally, he believes Britain was the civil society Hegel had in mind when he expressed these "premature" thoughts and suggests that Hegel had arrived at this view by his "imaginative use" of the dialectical method.[74]

We have seen that, far from being "premature," these ideas were well worn. Both the mercantilists and the physiocrats, as well as Adam Smith, who owed much to both schools, had written of colonies as a market for surplus production. In line with more advanced thinking, opponents of the Corn Laws of 1815 had also argued that Britain would do well to exchange her manufactures for food grown in less advanced agricultural countries. There was nothing in Hegel's paragraphs to which Cobden would have objected. We know, moreover, that Hegel was familiar with the writings of the chief economists and could not have supposed himself presenting anything startlingly original. Hegel's remarks probably were, we may speculate, a reply to Fichte's protectionist tract of 1800, *Der geschlossene Handelsstaat,* the "closed commercial state," with Hegel arguing that the inner dynamics of a civil society led to openness and to international trade, not to Fichte's autarchic model. As such, we may more readily understand them, in the spirit of Kant, as the acceptance of an international division of labor which constituted a base of the liberal ideal.

For Hirschman, the "most intriguing" question was why Marx, who "did not have any theory of imperialism," neglected this portion of Hegel's book. Invoking Freud, he suggests that Marx repressed these passages because he did not wish to believe that such overseas opportunities might delay the revolution. Luxemburg, "obviously influenced" (Hirschman writes) by Hegel's dialectical method, revived the theory when these opportunities were drying up for a mature capi-

---

talism and revolution seemed more assured.[75] One may reply that Hegel's brief allusions were hardly a theory of imperialism, and the answer was less Freudian repression than Marx's general agreement with liberal efforts to create an international economy, as may be seen in his approval of free trade and the activities of the "millocracy" in India as necessary stages of historical development.

One may more reasonably ask why Marx, who devoted a chapter of the first volume of *Capital* in 1867 to a discussion of Wakefield's theories of colonization, did not apprehend a complete theory of imperialism, one so clearly anticipatory of those of Hobson and the neo-Marxists. Wakefield, we recall, writing in the hard times of the 1830s and 1840s, even saw the roots of difficulty in the capitalist system and believed colonial and commercial expansion to be the only alternative to social revolution. Can we attribute Marx's neglect of Wakefield to his having written his chapter in the most prosperous decade of the century, when an ambivalent Marx may have suspected the liberal utopia feasible, even while still believing that the shifting composition of capital in favor of its constant component would in the long run doom the rate of profit? With the return of hard times in the 1870s and 1880s, the grounds of ambivalence slipped away.

But this uncertainty was to reassert itself in the thinking of Karl Kautsky, much to the irritation of V. I. Lenin. By the first decade of the twentieth century, the capitalist world was fast recovering from the great depression that marked the end of the previous century. In the undeveloped world the European powers were sharing imperial tasks: in many parts of China and Latin America, for example, German firms controlled the merchandising of British goods. Such developments could not but affect the thinking of Marxist theorists. Kautsky foresaw the era of imperialism ending not in a series of international wars, finally leading to a proletarian revolution, as Lenin would predict in 1917 in his tract on imperialism, but in a relatively peaceful "ultra-imperialism." Schumpeter in 1919, in a reply to neo-Marxists like Hilferding, remodeled the sociological thesis; though taking the new role of finance capital into account, he continued to trust to the fundamental truth put forward by the nineteenth- and early twentieth-century liberal social theorists. Like them he would offer hope for the decline and fall of imperialism (with its premodern roots), and like Kautsky he foresaw the rise of pacific international cartels. All three, then, from their quite different positions, predicted the end of imperialism.

The Liberal Ideal and the Demons of Empire

8   The End of Imperialism:

Kautsky, Lenin, Schumpeter

When World War I was in progress, V. I. Lenin, the leader of the Bolshevik wing of the Russian Social Democratic party, was among the left-wing socialists who met at Zimmerwald in 1915 and at Kienthal in 1916 to denounce the war as imperialist. The so-called Zimmerwald International directed a fierce attack both at the European socialists who had joined the bourgeoisie in support of the war and at those like the antiwar German Marxist Karl Kautsky whom it believed to be at bottom merely bourgeois pacifists. In 1916, Lenin wrote a tract on imperialism, published the following year, that would in the next half-century be the standard Marxist treatise on the subject and whose influence, we know, extended well beyond Marxist circles. The tract, in the spirit of Zimmerwald, was directed in large part against Kautsky.

We will see, in the writings of Kautsky, the makings of a very different theory of imperialism, one that combined the analytical insights of the neo-Marxists with those of the liberal sociologists. This hybrid would be Lenin's special target. A number of the points in Kautsky's analysis had already been made by Eduard Bernstein, a founder of a reformist, revisionist Marxism. In 1917, the Austrian economist Joseph Schumpeter would present a theory of imperialism that also combined sociological and neo-Marxist elements, stressing— as Bernstein and Kautsky did not—the centrality of the sociological factor. But Bernstein and Kautsky undeniably had at least one foot in the sociological camp. A student of Bernstein's writings has noted "a striking parallel" between Bernstein's views and those of Schumpeter,[1] and Kautsky's grandson has called attention to his grandfather's and Schumpeter's "parallel theories of imperialism," even going so far as to call Kautsky "a Schumpeterian Marxist."[2] Schumpeter could not have known of Lenin's tract, which appeared almost at the same time as his own and was not translated until 1920; but more likely than not he had read some of Kautsky's many writings on imperialism, particularly two articles published in the early years of the war.

Karl Kautsky

Before turning to Kautsky, we must briefly consider Eduard Bernstein, who converted him to Marxism. Bernstein, born in 1850, was for a time the editor of the *Sozial-Demokrat,* an organ of the German Social Democratic party published from exile, first in Zurich and then in London, during the period when Bismarck's antisocialist legislation made the party illegal in Germany. In London, Bernstein became an intimate of Engels. In the late 1890s, after a long stay in England and a friendly association with a reformist British labor movement and a gradualist Fabianism, he became the advocate of a nonrevolutionary revisionist Marxism. Bernstein argued that Marx's theory of increasing misery and the orthodox view that capitalism would collapse because of its inner contradictions had proved false and that the German socialists should campaign as a party of reform, not revolution. Kautsky in this period took up the standard of Marxist orthodoxy against revisionism. In 1914, Bernstein, like Kautsky and Hilferding, joined the minority Independent Social Democratic party in opposition to the war.[3]

Behind Bernstein's revisionism and antiwar position, it has been argued, was his acceptance of the pacifist internationalism associated with the British Radical bourgeoisie and Richard Cobden. Bernstein's cosmopolitanism and antimilitarism were clearly linked to his antipathy to a "reactionary" German protectionism and his wholehearted approval of free trade, not as a stage to be passed through (as in Marx's 1848 address), but as an ideal to be realized. Bernstein believed protectionism, which he denied had any genuine connection to capitalism, to be pernicious on economic, political, and ethical grounds. Bismarck had installed this atavistic remnant of the mercantilist system not only to prop up his fellow quasi-feudal Junkers, but primarily to insulate Germany from the "mutual dependence" of a free international economy. Germany's autarchic state, if it could be achieved, would act as a serious obstacle to social and political reform at home and sow "stupidly barbarous mistrust" and wars. In the best Cobdenite fashion, Bernstein defended free trade as the best method of achieving international peace and prosperity and the most reliable means of fostering liberty and cultural progress.[4] Kautsky would write along similar lines.

Kautsky was born in 1854 in Prague, and he studied at the University of Vienna, where he joined the Austrian Social Democratic party. In the two prewar decades, Kautsky, as editor of the *Die Neue Zeit,* published in Stuttgart, was the leading theoretician of an orthodox Marxism in its resistance to reformism, though something of Kautsky's ambivalence in this matter may be seen in his approving description of the German Social Democratic party as "a revolutionary party but not a party which makes revolutions." Kautsky began to discuss imperialism in 1897 in an article comparing the "Old and New Colonial Politics." This was followed in the years before World War I by more than a dozen articles and a book which touched upon the subject. In these writings, one may find not only discussions of colonial questions as they emerged in the international politics of the period but a number of different theoretical approaches to the problem of imperialism not unlike those we have observed in the writings of Marx and Engels.[5]

Certain of Kautsky's earlier insights may be seen as anticipations of Hobson and Hilferding, presented more impressionistically; later articles testified to the strong influence of Hilferding. Still others, as Kautsky's grandson has noted, were shaped more in the manner of the liberal sociologists. A detailed examination of the various formulations and qualifications would not prove particularly illuminating either in themselves or for our subject. What particularly merits our notice, however, are two articles published after the war had begun. In these, Kautsky, in the midst of the great conflagration that the left-socialists of Zimmerwald would call imperialist, speculated that the period after the war might witness the end of competing national imperialisms and the arrival of an international, capitalist ultraimperialism.

We must first note that, to a much greater extent than Marx and Engels, Kautsky in his earliest writings made use of the ideas of the liberal social theorists which linked the new colonialism to preindustrial forces. He stressed the tendencies of aristocracies, in modern times as earlier, to support aggressive policies. Present-day aristocrats did so because they benefited from jobs in the army and in the state and also because, as he wrote, "the psyche of the landed aristocracy" preferred warfare to labor. In the mercantilist period, commercial and banking interests had allied themselves to the monarch's and the aristocracy's policy of colonial expansion. The motive power of the new imperialism was similarly lodged in the class of large landowners, militarists, state bureaucrats, churchmen—and in the increasing influence of a high finance with historical ties to the landed aristocracy. Industrial capital, which was capitalism in its purest form, Kautsky believed, was antiimperialist. Late nineteenth-century imperialism, he wrote in 1897, like protectionism, was a reactionary development, a product of the more socially backward nations of the continent, not of British industrial capital, which remained both free-trade and pacifist in sentiment and practice, and whose colonialist activities were more defensive than aggressive. While industrial capital no doubt sought to profit from the new colonial policy, he added, it was not its driving force.[6]

For Kautsky, we see, imperialism was not a necessity for industrial capitalism; it was a policy that capitalism had adopted, not an inevitable stage in capitalist development. Such a position, of course, was abhorrent to the revolutionary wing of Marxism. In an article in *Die Neue Zeit* in September 1914, a few weeks after the beginning of World War I, Kautsky would describe a capitalist ultraimperialism that would prove even more unacceptable to revolutionary Marxists.[7]

The first part of Kautsky's piece concerned the failure of capitalism to maintain a proper proportionality of production between the industrial and agricultural sectors. Industrial production outran agricultural, he observed, noting the classical laws of the declining returns from agriculture and rising returns from industry. The periodic crises of capitalist industry were the market's efforts to restore an equilibrium between the two. Another method of restoring this proportionality was expansion into the undeveloped agrarian regions of the world: this would provide the industrial nations with needed food and raw materials and also with a market for the overproduction of their industry. In this argument, Kautsky, like Wakefield and Luxemburg, saw the drive of the advanced powers toward undeveloped agrarian areas as necessary to the existence of capitalism.

Yet, Kautsky continued, if this expansion was a necessary condition for capitalism, there were relatively peaceful methods of satisfying this need for agrarian areas. A capitalist Britain relied on a system of free trade. In the early years of its industrial predominance, the country had sought to become the workshop of the world, with agricultural countries supplying it with grain and cotton in exchange for manufactures. Such a system had for long been agreeable to both Britain and to the agriculturists of the countries that supplied it. In pursuing this goal, however, Britain had prepared these states, notably those in Western Europe as well as the United States, for industrialization. Cheaper and better British goods had undermined the native, precapitalist handicraft industry, and the unemployed artisans now formed a substantial labor pool that a native entrepreneur might tap. Like Marx, Kautsky noted that Britain had built railways in overseas regions in order to make the production of raw materials more efficient. These railways had served to speed the less developed area's economic advance, even as other industrial enterprises, also often largely dependent on British capital, came into existence to take advantage of the improved transportation.

Kautsky went on to describe the imperialism that had replaced free trade. As it became clearer that an industrial state like Britain would dominate an agrarian one and that the latter in consequence would tend toward political and economic decay, formerly agricultural states like Germany and the United States turned to protection in order to build an industrial base. In time these new industrial states, accumulating great capital reserves, turned to foreign and overseas sites for investment of their excess capital. In the case particularly of overseas regions in Asia and Africa, the capital-exporting state sought to impose its political control. In this way, it might protect its investments in railways, in the growing of commercial crops, in irrigation works, and in mines. It might also prevent these areas from establishing their own industries.

Since capitalism relied so heavily on the continuing economic relationship between industrial and agrarian regions, it appeared to socialist observers like Luxemburg as if imperialism, and with it the reduction of native populations to virtual slavery, was a necessary characteristic of capitalism. The competition for agrarian regions had, moreover, led to an arms race, and many socialists believed that wars over imperial spoils were inevitable under capitalism. The viability of the system seemed to them as much threatened by such colonial conflicts as by the growing proletarian dissatisfaction and unrest that were caused by tax burdens swelled by arms-production costs. Kautsky declared in the early days of World War I that "damit grabt der Imperialismus sein eignes Grab": thus imperialism, with its arms races and wars, was digging its own grave. This was a frequently repeated socialist view well before Lenin's tract.[8]

Kautsky, however, challenged large parts of this analysis. In contrast to Luxemburg and others, Kautsky saw no economic necessity for capitalism to produce armaments. Nor was capitalism as a system approaching a catastrophic end, for there were still fresh agrarian regions to develop. While the present form of imperial exploitation, the effort of each state to expand its own colonial empire, could end only in national bankruptcy and self-destruction, capitalism could move in another direction. What Kautsky discerned as a future possibility was that the imperialist powers, renouncing the arms race, might unite their activities. In this way they could successfully oppose the growing anger in the colonies against the imperialist states. Following the model of industrial monopoly, he added, capitalism might well be entering still another phase, "the translation of the policy of cartels into foreign policy, a phase of ultra-imperialism." But the danger of this new phase lay not in militarism and war but in a wholly different and in many respects more pernicious direction.[9] In April 1915, Kautsky—with obvious ambivalence—described this ultraimperialism as introducing a policy of "common exploitation of the world" by a united finance capital, replacing the "mutual rivalries" of the separate national finance capitals—now more decidedly stressing the need for socialists to fight as energetically against ultraimperialism as they had against imperialism.[10]

V. I. Lenin

Vladimir Ilyich Lenin, the son of a middle-rank Russian bureaucrat, was born in Simbirsk in 1870. Soon after passing his bar examination, he joined the Marxist Social Democratic party, and in the late 1890s he served a term in Siberian exile for his activities on its behalf. Many of the leaders of the party were faithful to Marx's theory of history and believed that Russia must pass through the stage of bourgeois capitalism before it could achieve socialism; they consequently allied themselves with the liberals in a struggle against czarism and were prepared to support social reforms that might better the condition of the working classes. Others, among them Lenin, however, rejected this reformist program, favoring instead one of class war and immediate proletarian revolution.[11]

Lenin's tract *Imperialism: The Highest Stage of Capitalism* was published in Russia a few weeks after the democratic March revolution of 1917 that ended the rule of the czar. With German assistance, Lenin had returned from exile to conduct a campaign to replace Kerensky's provisional government with a proletarian dictatorship that would remove Russia from the war. The publication of the tract provided one of the theoretical bases for this effort. Its preface, written in April 1917, attacked the "social-chauvinism" of those socialists who supported the continuation of the capitalist war; it noted as well the "inconsistency" with which Karl Kautsky regarded such "deserters."[12]

This somewhat gratuitous sneer, since Kautsky was not a supporter of the war, was amplified in the preface to the French and German editions in 1920. By this time, there had been a successful revolution by the Bolshevik faction of Russian Social Democracy, and the war had ended. The enemy now was no longer merely social chauvinism but "the utter falsity of social-pacifist views and hopes for 'world democracy' "—the "Kautskyism" of the leaders of the Second International, which Lenin's Third (Communist) International, the successor to the Zimmerwald International, was attempting to displace. Lenin charged that Kautsky (now joined by "ex-Marxist" Hilferding) had renounced the "revolutionary principles of Marxism" which he had earlier defended against the "socialist opportunism" of Bernstein and the revisionists.[13] But even in the 1917 edition of the tract, the "theoretical errors" of Kautsky and his followers, a sympathy for pacifism and democracy that had "no claim to Marxism whatever," had been a vital theme.

The main lines of Lenin's tract of 1917 are fairly easily described. Lenin skillfully drew on the writings on imperialism of Hobson and the neo-Marxists to synthesize what would become the best-known and most influential theory of imperialism, one that was purely economic and entirely deterministic in character (and consequently, in Lenin's view, authentically Marxist). The tract presented no new theoretical contributions of importance, but then again its purpose was not to advance Marxist social and economic analysis but to win converts. In this Lenin was successful. Less noticed was Lenin's underlying purpose, perhaps his principal one: to save the soul of Marxism from the bourgeois reformism of such Marxists as Kautsky.

Lenin's tract paid tribute to both Hobson and Hilferding but found both wanting, Hobson for being a mere pacifist and reformist and the supposedly Marxist Hilferding for at bottom sharing these sentiments.[14] The first several chapters of the work relied on Hilferding's analysis. Lenin described at some length the new role of the banks in directing large-scale industry, which gave finance capital an overpowering influence on a nation's economic life.[15] Unlike Hilferding, he chose to pass over lightly the fact that a free-trade Britain did not reveal the growth of monopolies that was to be found in protectionist countries such as Germany and the United States (from whose experience virtually all Lenin's examples were drawn); nor did he note that Britain's banks remained commercial institutions, suppliers of short-term credit rather than large-scale investors and managers of industrial combines. Like Hilferding and Hobson, Lenin described the export of capital as a leading characteristic of a now "over-ripe" capitalism, plagued by overproduction and an overaccumulation of capital.[16]

Since all the advanced nations suffered in this way, the monopolistic capitalist cartels and trusts, having divided the internal market, now turned to the division of the world.[17] No longer would a capitalist nation like mid-Victorian Britain proclaim colonies "millstones round our necks," as Disraeli once had. Now Britons saw the imperialists Cecil Rhodes and Joseph Chamberlain as heroes and the exploitation of colonies as the way to solve social problems. The world was now divided between imperialist powers and colonies; even supposedly independent countries were in truth dependencies. One might, for example, describe Argentina as "so dependent financially" on London that it was "almost a British commercial colony."[18]

Capitalism, then, had entered a new stage, its highest (as the tract's title put it) and last, that of imperialism. The older capitalism had been one of individual enterprise and free competition, whereas monopoly characterized the contemporary system of imperialism, as did the merging of bank and industrial capital, the rule of a financial oligarchy, the export of capital, and the division of the world among the great powers and their monopolies.[19] In this stage, capitalism no longer was a progressive force even in the development of technology.[20] A trait of monopoly was "the *tendency* to stagnation and decay."[21]

The export of capital had produced a "usurer state," a creditor state drawing "tribute" in "parasitic" fashion from its debtors. The non-Marxist Hobson had done rather better in understanding this development than the Marxist Hilferding, Lenin observed. Great Britain, once an industrial state, was the most obvious example of a usurious imperialism, although all the more economically advanced countries were on the same track. Since Hobson had explored the subject in 1902, Lenin continued, "the term 'rentier state' [*Rentnerstaat*], or usurer state is passing into current use in economic literature that deals with imperialism." The world had "become divided into a handful of usurer states on the one side, and a vast majority of debtor states on the other." Countries like Britain, the Netherlands, Belgium, Switzerland, France, and Germany were the chief creditor nations. Lenin cited Hobson's warning of a Western alliance of creditor states organized to draw a "vast tribute from Africa and Asia."[22] (After World War I, of course, America would enter more prominently as a prime creditor state, and a Germany beset by reparations payments would become a debtor state, an often repeated ground for complaint among German writers and politicians of the interwar period.)

A "moribund capitalism" had divided the world, but, given the uneven development of their national economies, capitalist states must fight again and again for redivisions corresponding to changing economic and political power relationships. In the end, the concentration of industry and wealth in ever fewer hands and the continual struggles for the division of the world among the nations must lead to an international proletarian revolution and the destruction of a parasitic, monopoly capitalism.[23] This was a conclusion far different from Kautsky's.

The Kautsky articles had so provoked Lenin that much of the Bolshevik leader's tract may be understood as a fierce polemic against Kautsky and his outlook. Those of Lenin's arguments which did not heavily bear the mark of either Hilferding or Hobson concerned the absolute necessity of capitalism to pursue the economic policies that led to imperialism, policies that would inescapably bring about war and proletarian revolution. Lenin passionately insisted on the impossibility of Kautsky's vision of ultraimperialism. On this matter, Lenin was under obligation, though he did not acknowledge this debt, to Bukharin's 1915 work on imperialism, to which Lenin had written the introduction.

Bukharin, in an argument somewhat resembling one mounted by List and Carey concerning a future universal adoption of free trade, had suggested that Kautsky's ultraimperialism could emerge only when all nations had reached a stage of economic and political equality. But to expect such an eventuality was unrealistic, Bukharin had argued. There would continue to be disparities in national strength, and the state or states occupying more favorable positions in the international economy or having greater political or military force would use their power to secure more advantageous trade treaties, establish higher tariffs, and control markets for sales, raw materials, and capital investments. "Peaceful rivalry" was characteristic only of "the epoch of free competition," a period before the cartelization of industry, which necessarily produced imperialism. Bukharin had concluded that to "imagine," as Kautsky did, that these trusts—"this embodiment of monopoly"—could become "the bearers of the free trade policy" was "a deeply harmful Utopian fantasy."[24] (Lenin's introductory comments followed Bukharin in condemning Kautsky's "dream" of the peaceful and "progressive nature of capitalism," and the German Marxist's "semi-philistine 'paradise' of free competition.")[25]

In his *Imperialism,* Lenin denounced Kautsky as a renegade who had abandoned his earlier Marxism. The German socialist, Lenin observed, had described imperialism not as a phase or stage of capitalism but as a "policy 'preferred' by finance capital." But imperialism was not merely a striving by capitalist powers to annex agrarian regions, as Kautsky argued; it aimed at annexing industrialized ones as well, and he cited Germany's "appetite" for Belgium and France's for Alsace-Lorraine. Kautsky's understanding of imperialism was "not only wrong and un-Marxian"; it also served as "a basis for a whole system of views" which opposed Marxist theory and practice. Kautsky had detached politics from economics, believing it possible for a finance capital that sought "monopolies in economics" to follow "non-monopolistic" and "non-annexationist methods" in international politics. Such a position was not Marxism but "bourgeois reformism and 'pacifism.'" Lenin was disturbed as well by Kautsky's view that the development of agrarian regions lessened the "unevenness" in development and "contradictions inherent in world economy," when in fact it only increased them. And capitalism knew only one way of resolving contradictions—"by resorting to *violence*."[26]

Lenin had nothing but contempt for the bourgeois ideas that Kautsky valued. In his 1920 preface to *Imperialism*, he decried the middle-class professors and "petty-bourgeois philistines" who saw the building of railways as a "civilising enterprise" rather than "an instrument for oppressing *a thousand million* people (in the colonies and semi-colonies)."[27] (Lenin may not have been aware that Marx and Engels had written in much these terms.) The petty bourgeois liberals, as good free traders, had even argued that capitalist countries could procure raw materials in the "open market without a 'costly and dangerous' colonial policy." They went so far as to suggest that capitalism could increase the supply of raw materials by investing in agricultural improvements. But monopoly, not free trade, characterized modern capitalism; and to improve agriculture meant the favoring of wages over profits. "Where except in the imagination of the sentimental reformists," Lenin inquired, "are there any trusts capable of interesting themselves in the condition of the masses instead of the conquest of colonies?"[28] He granted that, if capitalism turned to the development of agriculture, and thus to raising the living standards of the masses, who were "everywhere still poverty-stricken and underfed," there would no longer be an excess of capital. "But if capitalism did these things it would not be capitalism," he declared.[29] Lenin also derided Hobson's antidote to imperialism—the raising of domestic consumption—as impossible under capitalism.[30]

What specifically did Lenin have to say about Kautsky's ultraimperialism? For Lenin, Kautsky's naive forecast of the end of imperialism, a partial realization of the liberal utopia deeply embedded in the bourgeois world-outlook, was "ultra-nonsense." It was ludicrous to believe, as Kautsky and the reformers did, that international cartels were "the most striking expressions of the internationalisation of capital" and promised world peace.[31] This was an abstraction that had "an exclusively reactionary aim: that of diverting attention from the depth of *existing* antagonisms."[32] Kautsky's concept of ultraimperialism, like his theory of imperialism as a whole, was "permeated *through and through* with a spirit, absolutely irreconcilable with Marxism." It was "the cant of English parsons." Such alliances among national capitalisms as Kautsky envisioned would prove temporary, and, given the uneven development of capitalist states, there would soon be a cry for new terms and new divisions. Imperialism would soon come to an end, indeed, but by a proletarian defeat of capitalism.[33]

The Austrian liberal economist J. A. Schumpeter, writing in 1919, emphasized the sociological factor, though without neglecting the core of the neo-Marxist, particularly Hilferding's, analysis. Like Hilferding, and like Kautsky and many reformist Marxists, as well as of course Hobson, Schumpeter saw imperialism (and for him its inescapable companions, protection and militarism) as options, not necessities for capitalism. Again like Kautsky and, later, Hilferding, he suggested that the internationalization of capital was a way out for the troubled system.

J. A. Schumpeter

Joseph A. Schumpeter was born in Triesch, Austria, in 1883, into a well-to-do middle-class family. Taking his degree in Vienna in 1906, Schumpeter was a member of the Austrian economist Eugen Böhm-Bawerk's famous seminar of 1905 and 1906, as were the socialists Otto Bauer and Rudolf Hilferding. He soon established himself as a *Wunderkind* in economic circles both on the Continent and in England and the United States, a young man from whom much was expected. Schumpeter had an unusual career. His first teaching post was at the University of Czernowitz, in an eastern province of the Hapsburgs, and then he went to the University of Graz. In 1919, he served briefly as minister of finance in the postwar Austrian government, and he was for several years president of a Viennese bank. In 1925, he was appointed to a chair at the University of Bonn, and from 1932 until his death in 1950 he was professor of economics at Harvard. A professional colleague who delivered the 1979 Ely Lecture before the American Economic Association would describe him as "America's most brilliant economist."[34]

Schumpeter wrote a lengthy essay, "The Sociology of Imperialism" (1919), shortly after World War I, in which his country had fought as Germany's ally against Britain, France, and the United States. (After its 1951 translation into English, the essay would be cited as the *locus classicus* for the sociological theory of imperialism.) Schumpeter refrained at the time of the writing of the essay from specifically naming Germany or Austria as examples of the dynastic states that carried the legacy of a pernicious feudalism and a mercantilistic export monopolism into the modern world. However, he repeatedly referred to Great Britain as the model capitalist state, where public opinion was normally pacifist, free trade inhibited the consolidation of industry, and banks continued their ordinary commercial role and did not, as in Germany or America, engage in a monopolistic restructuring and control of industry. Schumpeter adapted for his own purposes the

---

neo-Marxist analysis of finance capitalism, even as he disputed the Marxist theory of imperialism, and in so doing carried the sociological theory to its most fully rounded form.[35]

Schumpeter distinguished between the belligerence of a state produced by "concrete interests," whether economic or political, a belligerence that ceased as soon as these interests were attained, and an imperialism that he defined as an "aggressiveness" or "expansion for its own sake," an interest in "hegemony" or "world dominion." This was "the objectless disposition on the part of a state to unlimited forcible expansion." While acknowledging the truth of the neo-Marxist view that contemporary imperialism was "the reflex of the interests of the capitalist upper stratum," he noted that such a view did not "of logical necessity" stem from an economic (and, therefore, rational) interpretation of history.[36] Though there were differences among the various imperialisms of the past, they had a common trait, one also present in modern imperialism—an irrational, illimitable will to conquest. This common trait in itself excluded the possibility that the contemporary imperialism was the "product" of capitalism.[37]

First of all, Schumpeter dismissed the so-called British imperialism of the nineteenth and early twentieth centuries as a mere political "catch phrase" free of practical meaning. Disraeli had employed the term in his support of imperial federation, whose aim was not expansion but consolidation. Chamberlain's tariff proposals of 1903 were more properly imperialism because of their protectionist and warlike sentiments, but an antiimperialist electorate had rejected them. Schumpeter attributed the dominance of antiimperialism in Britain to the victory of the people over the Crown in the seventeenth century, a victory that had saved the country from the absolutism and military rule that prevailed on the Continent. The British parties, dependent on public opinion, agreed then in opposing a large professional army. In the early eighteenth century, the Tories were the peace party, while the Whigs, the party of the aristocratic magnates and of the merchants and bankers of London's City, were ready for foreign adventures. But colonial possessions in the eighteenth century *were* valuable, and consequently war was "good business," not the "objectless expansion" of true imperialism; moreover, independent adventurers, not the state, were the principal conquerors of Britain's colonial empire. The economic conditions of the nineteenth century had elevated the captains of industry over the earlier trade monopolists, and the posture of a British industry dependent on a free trade was noninterventionist and pacifist.[38]

But the "instincts of dominance and war" embedded in "the distant past" had not vanished even in Britain. At their core were "the dark powers of the subconscious" called into play by the appeal to national sentiment: "driven out everywhere else, the irrational seeks refuge in nationalism—the irrational which consists of belligerence, the need to hate." Disraeli and Chamberlain's ideal of imperial federation drew strength not only from this source, but also from the mercantilist conviction that formal colonies might be more profitably exploited. Schumpeter also noted "the instinctive urge to domination" which made London beggars speak of " 'our' rebellious subjects" at the time of the Boer War. Though such instincts and sentiments were undoubtedly present in Great Britain, there were no "powerful interests" in the social structure prepared to embrace them, and consequently aggressive feelings were "condemned to political impotence." This was hardly the case elsewhere, he observed.[39]

Schumpeter made a historical survey of imperialisms past, beginning with those of the ancient and medieval Near East. The century-and-a-half war by which the ancient Egyptians expelled the Hyksos invaders had created a professional army, a "war machine" that could maintain its preeminence only by continuous aggression: "Created by wars that required it," Egypt's war machine "now created the wars it required." The Assyrians were a warrior people whose wars of enslavement, exploitation, and often annihilation were commanded by their god Assur. For them, war was a sport, stemming from inclinations once necessary to survival, though no longer so; their conquests were "not means but ends," instances of "brutal, stark naked imperialism."[40] For Persia, surrounded by hostile neighbors, "war was the only method for keeping alive," and the "psychological dispositions and organizational forms" so produced "persisted, continuing in an 'objectless' manner," until undermined by centuries of peace.[41] The Arabs of the seventh century and after were a warrior people, who had been given a special direction by a religion that proclaimed a continuous holy war against the infidel. In their great imperial movement after the death of Mohammed, Schumpeter saw "a typical case of 'objectless,' violent expansion, born of past necessities of life, grown to the proportions of a powerful drive by virtue of long habit, persisting to the point of exhaustion."[42]

The Roman empire presented Schumpeter with a more complex problem. Roman imperialism of the time of Augustus and his successors was not truly imperialism, he argued, for the wars of the empire were carried on merely to secure imperial frontiers. Earlier, however, under the Republic, from the Punic Wars in the third century B.C. until the principate of Augustus, there had been an "unbounded will to conquest." The class committed to imperialism was that of the owners of the large latifundia who had seized public lands, dispossessed the small peasant holders, and replaced Italian farm laborers with slave captives of foreign wars. The great landowners chose an expansionist course both because they required slaves and also because without the glory of war there would have been a social revolution. Subordinate groups like army suppliers or corrupt provincial officials tapped the economic spoils of war. For Schumpeter, then, the history of republican Rome was an example of "imperialism rooted in the domestic political situation and derived from class structure."[43]

The Germanic tribes of Europe, the Salian Franks excepted, did not possess "the imperialist elan." From the end of the fifth century onward, the Salian monarch Clovis I and his successors, without regard for " 'interests' or 'pretexts,' " were "driven forward by instincts of war and power," much as the Assyrian kings had been. Theirs, too, was a "popular imperialism," and the king was merely the leader of a "widespread disposition." But the "habit of conquest" of the Salian Franks was not so old as to become "enduringly fixed," and they returned to agriculture and had to be goaded by the Carolingians into resisting the Arab invasion of the eighth century. Charlemagne and his successors had to create a class of professional knights endowed with feudal benefices to perform the military function after the end of the earlier Salian popular imperialism. With the help of his military vassals, Charlemagne erected a royal imperialism, but his successors largely failed in similar efforts because they were unable to subdue independent-minded nobles. German emperors, most prominently Frederick II, moved their armies into Italy, where they could rule directly, unencumbered by feudal restraints. But none of these imperial efforts secured a lasting success because, Schumpeter suggested, it was the imperialism of a ruler, and not of either the people or the nobles, both of whom opposed it, an example of "an anti-imperialist warrior aristocracy."[44]

The expansionist wars of the absolute monarchies of the European continent during the seventeenth and eighteenth centuries marked the climax of the process by which the kings and their armies imposed a centralized rule on the nobility and the feudal estates. Louis XIV was the heir to the royal armies built up in the centuries-long struggles of French kings against the feudal nobility. His absolutist state was based upon the war machine he had inherited, and which, though the monarchy was now supreme and its foreign enemies no longer threats, could not be easily dismantled. The king thought himself first of all a warlord, and a good portion of the nobility was still closely tied to "a warlike past, martial ideas and phrases, bellicose instincts." Louis gave the nobility the foreign wars it so wanted and used victories to maintain his domestic position.[45]

The Liberal Ideal and the Demons of Empire

Schumpeter explained the bellicose policies of the absolute monarchies by the requirements of their "social structure" and the "inherited dispositions" of their ruling classes rather than by any commercial advantages that might be secured from conquests. The kings were relatively unconcerned with the mercantile profits sought by the bourgeoisie. European industry was still in its craft stage; production was so small that the need to export a surplus was hardly an element in formulating policy. Schumpeter did not deny that mercantilist theory justified many wars and that the powers took care to protect their economic interests. Industry, however, remained subordinate in state policy. What determined events was "the traditional habit of war," with a war machine ready for use. The imperialism of Louis XIV was thus "in its innermost nature" like that of the Assyrians, with mercantilist writers and statesmen attempting to supply rational motives for what was at bottom irrational.[46]

Schumpeter concluded, much as Saint-Simon (with his "vestiges") and Spencer had some decades earlier, that this later imperialism of mercantilist times, like that of the nineteenth and twentieth centuries, was "atavistic in character": it was an "element that stems from the living conditions, not of the present, but of the past—or, put in terms of the economic interpretation of history, from past rather than present relations of production." In earlier centuries, peoples and classes became warriors to preserve themselves, and the "psychological dispositions and social structures acquired in the dim past in such situations, once firmly established," tended to continue after they lost their original meaning. The survival of these sentiments and institutions was facilitated by the interests of the traditional ruling classes and of groups like the makers of armaments, who stood to gain from a policy of war. The imperialist tendencies that survived in the capitalist world were the legacy of the period of the absolute monarchies. They would soon disappear because of "the progressive rationalization of life and mind in the modern era."[47]

Capitalism began to shape a pacific society in the last half of the eighteenth century, producing new classes (the bourgeoisie and the working classes) and broadening the base of the older intellectual classes. In time, Schumpeter observed, these classes were "democratized, individualized, and rationalized," and they applied the same processes to the larger society. The "impulse" to imperialism was a victim of both the reasoned extermination of purposeless instinct and the absorption of previously idle energies by the competitive market system. Wherever capitalism was strongest, there antiimperialism was most influential, as in Britain, where a free-trade capitalism was quite early associated with modern pacifism. Modern wars had to be justified to a peace party in every country, a party that accepted only self-defense as a ground for conflict. The industrial worker was anti-imperialist, as was the modern socialist. Schumpeter noted that the United States, "least burdened with precapitalist elements," was least warlike and the most fervent advocate of disarmament and arbitration and, despite the war of 1898 and the blusterings of Theodore Roosevelt, the least interested in colonial empire. Though capitalism appeared to have a stake in an imperial policy, for war in its early phase frequently produced high wages and high profits, the burdens of war soon outweighed its advantages, except for those industrialists who produced arms.[48]

Schumpeter was convinced that under a free-trade system "*no* class has an interest in forcible expansion." Under free trade, both people and goods could move freely across frontiers, and it was a matter of perfect indifference which nation assumed the jobs of colonization, of patrolling the seas, or of building railways. The premier capitalist nation, Britain, was not protectionist, sufficient proof that protectionism was not a necessary condition of capitalism. Protective tariffs divided countries, placing their entrepreneurs in national "battle formation," and making it easier for imperialist-minded governments to prepare their peoples for war. But even under protection, Schumpeter insisted, capitalist interests as a whole received no genuine economic benefit from imperialism. Neomercantilism merely made it possible to separate the national economy from the international market and place it in the service of the state. Entrepreneurs might benefit if their own products were protected, but these advantages declined when other countries erected countertariffs and when their own nation imposed tariffs on goods they used in production. Still, many entrepreneurs tended to favor tariffs, hoping "to score special gains." Entrepreneurs generally, and even the working class, might be seduced by a protectionist spirit stemming from a minority of entrepreneurs and certain noncapitalist elements, particularly large landowners, for whom, Schumpeter conceded, protectionism might be a considerable advantage.[49]

Schumpeter agreed with Hobson and Hilferding that protectionism had spurred the organization of cartels and trusts, and a new expansionism. Though a "typical and fundamental" conflict of capitalism was one between capitalists and entrepreneurs, "monopoly capitalism" on the Continent and in America had "virtually fused the big banks and cartels into one." In this "close alliance" between high finance and the cartel chiefs, capitalism had established a "central organ" to replace the free market. But the policy of high finance was no more in the

The Liberal Ideal and the Demons of Empire

interests of most capitalists than that of the cartel magnates was to the advantage of most entrepreneurs. Under these new conditions, however, the international competition to dispose of surplus capital and goods—the question of who built a railway or owned a mine—was no longer unimportant. Every market, no matter how trifling, became an object of contention. Nations turned to military force for "relief" from what they believed "economic aggression" or to secure for themselves monopolistic control over colonial markets. Writing just after World War I, Schumpeter, like Lenin two years earlier, discussed the eventuality, relatively unexplored by previous theorists of empire, of one advanced European country conquering and making a colony of another.[50]

The strength of imperialist forces even in an "export-dependent monopoly capitalism" was overestimated, Schumpeter argued, for the industry and commerce of every nation were conscious of interdependent interests. The only parts of the community whose outlook and interests favored protection, export monopolism, and aggressive expansion without reservation were high finance and the entrepreneurs of the cartels. All others were "victims" of imperialist policy. This was particularly true of the proletariat. Certainly the "popular imperialism" of the past, one similar to that of the Assyrians or the Salian Franks, could not be revived. Schumpeter decried the offers of protectionists, like Joseph Chamberlain in Britain, to improve the condition of the working classes by social welfare schemes as merely the "exploitation of the consumer." Schumpeter's conclusion, similar to those of Hobson and Hilferding, was that monopolies and cartels did "*not* grow from the inherent laws of capitalist development," from the "automatism of the competitive system," but from a system of tariff protection, the consequence of political action by an interested minority. It was therefore "a basic fallacy" to see either protection or imperialism as "a necessary phase of capitalism, or even to speak of the development of capitalism into imperialism," as did most Marxists.[51]

Modern imperialism, then, Schumpeter concluded, like the "soul" of modern Europe, was the product of two entirely different eras, the feudal (and mercantile) and the bourgeois. Capitalism was "by nature anti-imperialist," and existing imperialist tendencies were "alien elements, carried into the world of capitalism from the outside" and supported by "non-capitalist factors in modern life," the remnants of both feudalism and mercantilism.[52] Feudal forces, possessing an established ideology, a solidity of social position, a social and economic base in the possession of land, and an unimpaired self-confidence, continued to govern in most European countries. Tariffs, Schumpeter observed, were originally employed by absolute monarchs to exploit the merchant in the interest of the crown. The bourgeoisie of the early modern world, understanding its dependence on the monarch, dutifully supported mercantilist policies. Where royal power receded, as in the Netherlands and Britain, the bourgeoisie began to insist on free trade, but elsewhere the precapitalist ethos survived, shaped by the association of early capitalism with "the spirit of guild and monopoly" espoused by the absolutist monarchies. The Continental commercial and industrial classes were the "creatures of mercantilism," and most of them persisted in their demands "for paternalism, for protection, for forcible restraint of strangers, and above all for tariffs." They followed the monarchs in their "bullionist prejudices," in their view of international trade from the standpoint of the exporter, not the consumer, and in their paranoid view of the bellicose intentions of foreign states.[53]

This divided character of the bourgeois mind was apparent in its view of nationalism and militarism. "Pure" capitalism, by its inner logic, ought to be cosmopolitan, yet the middle classes had made nationalism their very own. But in the contemporary world it was not business and industry that were "carriers of nationalist trends" but middle-class intellectuals, and they not because of class interests but "from chance emotion and individual interest." Militarism, a system rooted in autocracy, where military leaders possessed considerable political power, was similarly uncongenial to the pacifist bourgeois. In Britain the antimilitarist bent of a pure capitalism was readily apparent, but the Continental bourgeois saw the army "almost as a necessary component of the social order." Thus, "nationalism and militarism, while not creatures of capitalism, became 'capitalized' and in the end drew their best energies from capitalism."[54]

Similarly, Schumpeter argued, along lines resembling Hilferding's discussion of the ideology of imperialism, the old export monopolist policies of the absolute monarchies became merged with modern nationalism and militarism to produce the new imperialism. Historically then, he maintained, modern imperialism was "a heritage of the autocratic state." Export monopolism by itself would not be imperialism. What made it imperialism was the precapitalist heritage of "the war machine, together with its socio-psychological aura and aggressive bent, and because a class oriented toward war maintained itself in a ruling position." The alliance of this governing feudal and military class with bourgeois "pro-military" groups had preserved long-obsolete "war instincts and ideas of overlordship, male supremacy, and triumphant glory."[55]

The Liberal Ideal and the Demons of Empire

While Schumpeter acknowledged the continued strength of these forces, he was convinced that "the climate of the modern world must destroy them." In a probable allusion to liberal and socialist discussion of ultraimperialism, Schumpeter suggested that the future might witness the rise of "*international* cartels" that united capitalists of several advanced nations: then there could be no economic conflicts among nations, and capital and commodity exports would have no "aggressive character." The heritage of imperialism would consequently be "overcome in time," he concluded, and would "wither and die."[56]

In his study *Business Cycles* in 1939, Schumpeter cryptically remarked that "a glimpse of a view that now seems to the writer to be nearer the truth than either the Marxist or his own theory [of imperialism] is embodied in Karl Renner's concept of Social Imperialism."[57] He would make a similar disavowal in his Lowell Lectures of 1941 (not published until 1991) when he suggested that the economic theory of an imperialism emerging from late capitalism and the sociological theory of imperialism as an atavistic survival of feudalism and mercantilism were both wrong.[58] Exactly what Schumpeter meant by Renner's concept of social imperialism—an imperialism that coopted the proletariat by offering it benefits from imperial spoils—is uncertain. (Like most socialists, Renner had written of the error of social imperialism and counseled the "positive interest of the working class" in international socialism.)[59] Was Schumpeter abandoning his previous position that the working class could not profit by imperialism and that a modern people's imperialism was impossible? The apparently successful efforts of the German National Socialists of the 1930s to arouse popular enthusiasm in favor of an expansionist program could well have altered this earlier view. His later writings do not enlighten us. He would return to the subject only to condemn the Leninist theory of imperialism.

In his *Capitalism, Socialism, and Democracy*, written in 1942, Schumpeter called attention to the "almost universal hostility" that capitalism produced, a hostility that also marked imperialism as the supposed fruit of capitalism. On purely utilitarian, rational grounds, the case for capitalism was strong, Schumpeter argued, but rational rebuttals did not prove persuasive to those whose critiques, however rational in appearance, had their source in an "extra-rational driving power."[60]

Schumpeter was dismayed by the widespread acceptance of the Leninist theory of imperialism, particularly on the part of intellectuals, and found its popularity explicable on the same grounds as the appeal of Marxism generally. For believers, "the whole maze of international politics seems to be cleared up by a single powerful stroke of analysis."

"No longer . . . content with giving technical answers to technical questions," the Marxist economist "teaches mankind the hidden meaning of its struggles." This accounted for the popularity of Marxism among those who formed public opinion.[61] But in its distorted conception of events, Schumpeter concluded, "Marxism degenerates into the formulation of popular superstitions." This was particularly the case of the common Marxist view of a conspiracy of businessmen behind policies of export monopolism, one akin to there being "somewhere a committee of supremely wise and malevolent Jews who behind the scenes control international or perhaps all politics." Schumpeter hastened to observe that the Marxists were "not victims of this particular superstition," adding that "theirs is on no higher plane."[62]

The discoveries of Schumpeter's recent biographer, making use of the economist's private diaries, put into some doubt the usual view of the economist as a quintessential liberal. Although his published works offer no substantiation, these diaries reveal Schumpeter to have favored the victory of Nazi Germany during World War II, fearing that a German defeat would mean a Europe dominated by communist Russia. More startlingly, however, he saw the war as essentially one between the Jews and Hitler, and he preferred the latter. Schumpeter's anti-Semitism, grounded on race, had a curious perspective. He depicted Jews as the true "master race," citing as proof their considerable contribution to the founding of modern capitalism, but unlike Sombart and the Fourierists, who had written on similar lines, Schumpeter saw capitalism as "the greatest achievement of our civilization." In a surprising reversal of his sympathies during World War I and of the liberal conclusions of his published writings, Schumpeter also pronounced himself the enemy of "English ideas," among which one might presume the liberal politics and economics with which he himself had become identified.[63] Schumpeter's apparent readiness to embrace—if only in private diaries—the ideas and demonology of the Nazis is a puzzling and chilling coda to a discussion of his life and thought.[64]

The Liberal Ideal and the Demons of Empire

9 The Idea of Imperialism:
Some Concluding Remarks

During the 1930s, the great powers deserted the liberal ideal. Both Britain and the United States abandoned the gold standard, which had achieved a measure of monetary stability, and other nations followed their example. Britain gave up free trade in favor of a program of protection and imperial preference in 1932, and states already protectionist adopted even higher tariffs. The international economy imagined by Adam Smith and the nineteenth-century Cobdenites appeared lost beyond any possibility of reclaiming. Trade dislocations put all economies under increased strains, with the poorer debtor nations feeling especially anxious and oppressed.

The demons of empire described by writers of the previous century were enlisted. The Axis powers during World War II saw themselves as fighting not only communism but the usurious creditor nations of the West. German propaganda easily linked the Kremlin, a sinister British aristocracy, and international Jewish bankers.

Western capitalism, German and Italian writers asserted, possessed the money and controlled the colonies and natural resources vital to the economic well-being of their own have-not nations. The West had employed its power, military and naval as well as financial, to prevent Germany from creating a *Mitteleuropa,* a Central and Eastern European market and source of raw materials sufficiently large to accommodate Germany's economic requirements. (The Marxist Hilferding described Imperial Germany's need for such a market in 1910.) Italy felt excluded by France and Britain from the profitable imperial role it coveted. Similarly, a resource-poor Japan believed it was fighting a battle to free colonial Asian nations, and their rich natural resources, from the clutches of a racist Western imperialism and to organize these colonies into a "coprosperity sphere" that would serve the same purposes as Germany's *Mitteleuropa*. (Veblen had foreseen the likelihood of an alliance of semifeudal Germany and Japan, with their militant ethos and in possession of an advanced technology; and a war against Britain and international finance had been anticipated by both national economists and usury theorists for over a century.) The Axis believed itself to be revolting against the Western empires of capitalist fraud; the West, for its part, saw the Axis as waging war to establish demonic empires of force.

After 1945, largely under the influence of the United States, which emerged from the war as the strongest economic and military power, the nations of the noncommunist world began the construction of an international economy again founded on a relatively free trade. (It did not go unnoticed that this course was as much in America's interest in the mid-twentieth century as it had been in Britain's in the mid-nineteenth.) In the late 1940s, and in the 1950s and 1960s, moreover, the great imperial nations, some more, some less voluntarily, divested themselves of their former colonial possessions in Asia and Africa without experiencing undue economic hardship. Whatever the motives and expectations, and very much in accord with the operation of the free-market ideal of the nineteenth-century classical economists and their Cobdenite allies, the results of the reduction of tariff barriers and decolonization have proved, on the whole, good. The regime of competition that followed the American-aided economic recovery of Western Europe and Japan saw an immense absolute increase of wealth throughout the world, though not one that was equally distributed, or, as many maintained, equitable. Certain nations, notably Germany and Japan, developed economies that could and did compete with that of the United States. By the 1980s, in fact, if not earlier, an observer might argue that by entirely peaceful means those nations had achieved all that their countries had fought World War II (and Germany World War I as well) to secure—again as the Cobdenites might have predicted.

As remarkable, perhaps, was the apparent triumph in the early 1990s of the free-market ideal throughout the world. Statist, right-wing Latin American military dictators (as in Chile) and, with the collapse of communism and its economies in Eastern Europe and the Soviet Union, formerly Marxist-Leninist states struggled painfully to move toward a free market. In the West, even left-liberals who for decades had denied both the viability and the justice of such a market smothered previous doubts and became ostensible converts. The liberal economic ideal, perhaps only for a brief time, appeared to have been largely accepted, though hardly achieved in fact, throughout the world. (We will recall Adam Smith's calling its full realization a utopia.)

Were the world's states at last preparing to accept the free market, both at home and internationally, and thus justify the authentic anti-imperialist, liberal character of capitalism so sanguinely described by its early proponents in nineteenth-century Britain?

Capitalism and Imperialism

A leading theme of this study has been the relationship between capitalism and imperialism. For the classical political economists, both orthodox Ricardians and heterodox Malthusians, there were serious contradictions within capitalism. The Ricardians pointed to the declining rate of profit and the declining returns from agriculture; the Malthusians wrote of the inevitable tendencies to glut of production and capital, as well as population. Both groups saw colonization and foreign trade as ways of postponing, perhaps for a long time, a serious crisis for the system.

Simultaneously, and more optimistically, the orthodox held to Say's Law (denying the possibility of overproduction and glut of capital) and to the law of comparative advantage (arguing the benefits for all in an international division of labor). For the Cobdenites, an expanded foreign trade, made possible by the repeal of the Corn Laws, would restore what at times seemed the uncertain operations of Say's Law during the three decades after Waterloo. The great depression of the 1870s, following the prosperity of the 1850s and 1860s, persuaded the advocates of the "new liberalism" of the early twentieth century (which accepted a greater role for the state in promoting social welfare) that a system of redistribution would divert spending power from the rich to the poor and make Say's Law, which the depression of the end of the century had again called into question, once more workable.

Cobden and Bright had seen in a free-market capitalism of the liberal ideal not merely the end of war, which they as Christians and pacifists believed a sufficiently grand outcome, but a system by means of which all the world would be able to experience the relative prosperity enjoyed by an industrial Great Britain. Hobson would describe Cobden as an "international man," and, indeed, Cobden had complacently envisioned a future in which American industry would eclipse that of Britain, just as in time America itself would in certain of its pursuits fall victim to foreign competition. Britain and America would then turn to other activities, such as commerce and finance. A global free market would see a true international division of labor, in which by the law of comparative advantage each nation would benefit by doing what it could do best. And Say's Law, which might run into friction when restricted by national frontiers, would operate successfully on a world scale. Although Cobden and Bright and their followers were decided opponents of aggressive colonial activities, they supported the nonviolent expansion of a free commerce throughout the undeveloped world so as to produce the harmony and prosperity that an interdependent international economy would bring.

The Marxists were the least optimistic of the theorists. Whereas the liberal economists, despite qualified, long-range pessimism, usually saw some immediate remedy for prolonging the life of the capitalist economy in extending the sway of the new system to noncapitalist regions abroad or widening the number and appetites of consumers at home, most Marxists, in apocalyptic fashion, saw the end as both inevitable and near. For Marx and Engels, in their later years, and, of course, more insistently for Lenin and his followers, the contradictions of capitalism were moving the system to a great smash-up. The wars of imperialism were the birth pangs of the proletarian revolution, and the colonial peoples would join in the revolt against capitalism. Capitalism, obsessively amassing and concentrating its wealth, was incapable of enlarging the base for consumption and must disintegrate under the weight of its many contradictions.

But the Marxists were not unanimous in their portrait of the future of capitalism. Most Marxists of the early decades of this century may have seen the protectionism, cartels, and imperialism of *fin-de-siècle* capitalism not as distortions that could be ameliorated by a better-conceived political and economic program but as consequences of the inevitable development of a capitalism that was unable to alter the necessary conditions of its existence. This was the argument of Lenin's deterministic and purely economic theory of imperialism, one that he and his followers regarded as authentically Marxist. However, there were orthodox Marxists like Kautsky and Hilferding, not to speak of revisionists like Bernstein, who joined liberals like Hobson and Schumpeter in seeing the possibilities for the reform of capitalism. Neither Kautsky nor Hilferding saw in the development of later monopolistic and protectionist capitalism the system *in extremis*, the Leninist last stage in which a final series of bloody confrontations over the sharing of colonial booty would result in a proletarian revolution. They depicted, rather, an ultraimperialism that would not only solve, for many decades, the problems that capitalist development had produced but would so internationalize capital that the economic causes of war, whose existence was critical to the theories of other Marxists, would be considerably weakened and perhaps disappear. Such a final state, dimly, uncertainly, and sometimes reluctantly foreseen by Kautsky and Hilferding, might appear like a fulfillment of the dream of the liberal, Cobdenite ideal. Bukharin and Lenin denounced such a vision as an impossible utopia.

With the improvement in economic conditions in Europe after 1900, it became more politically useful for Marxists to depict the ugly consequences of capitalism hundreds or thousands of miles overseas than to address the failure of communist prophecies of growing immiseration. Early twentieth-century Marxist theories of imperialism were in good part motivated by a need to prove that a capitalism that was clearly succeeding in raising domestic living standards and disseminating progressive economic techniques overseas was demonic and approaching its final days. Without this faith, there could be no basis for expectations of a proletarian revolution—and the realization of the communist utopia.

The sociological theorists were liberals, defenders of the industrial system and opponents of the "feudal," mercantilist, militant ethos. In the view of both the earlier and later sociological schools, capitalism, that is, the "true" or ideal type of capitalism, was by its very nature an opponent of mercantilism and imperialism. But the later sociological school, as we have seen, worried that the model industrial capitalism, on which the ideal had been founded, was giving way to a revival of the old system. Capitalism might well be reverting to a preindustrial socialist and militant model (for Spencer); or it might become both imperialist and protectionist because of a corrupting, neomercantilist finance capital (for Hobson and the later Veblen); or might succumb to the still potent influence of the quasi-feudal aristocratic classes (for all the social theorists). For this school, capitalism appeared as imperialism only when, corrupted by the atavistic forces of feudalism and mercantilism so persuasively described by Schumpeter, it behaved contrary to its true nature. Certain Marxists, like Kautsky and Hilferding, borrowed substantially from this school and at times seemed to accept the latent reality of a true, ideal-type capitalism, which only awaited the final defeat of its enemies before revealing itself.

One might argue that the sociological theory was more acceptable when it appeared that the liberal capitalist ideal might yet be realized—once time had eliminated the residues of feudalism and mercantilism—whereas the eager reception of the economic model accompanied the growing conviction that critical, possibly insurmountable, difficulties existed within capitalism itself. Even defenders of the liberal ideal acknowledged the imperialist role of a portion of the financial and entrepreneurial classes. They speculated that the quasi-feudal, landed classes, still influential throughout Europe, were constructing an alliance with selfish, export-oriented industrialists and the financial interests that dominated industry. (In the case of Germany, this alliance had been sealed by the tariff of 1879.) Such a hypothesis may be considered a more sophisticated version of the sociological theory since it predicated a rogue neomercantilism (not true capitalism) in alliance with the surviving feudal interest, seeking both illicit (i.e., non-free-market) profits at the expense of the rest of the nation and power rather than plenty.

For the national economists, the relationship of capitalism and imperialism had a different meaning than it did for liberal economic or sociological theorists. The ideal of a cosmopolitan capitalism was abhorrent to the national economists and their Fourierist and populist allies because they believed its free-trade foundations favored an advanced Britain over less developed nations. They saw Britain's campaign to achieve worldwide acceptance of the free-trade doctrine as a way of preventing other countries from using the mercantilist methods by which Britain had achieved its own predominance. The national economic model, as opposed to the cosmopolitan one of the liberal schools, was essentially mercantilist, one that frankly sought power more than plenty, although both List and Carey believed the growth of industrialism would promote both.

The national economists and the populist usury theorists defended productive industrial capital against the international financiers of the City of London who represented the worst elements of an evil system: the parasitic commercial and financial capitalism of the cosmopolitan republic of merchants and bankers. Quite early, capitalism was associated with usury, which did not improve its ability to produce moral sympathy; a usurious finance capital was regarded, particularly in France, as a new feudalism and doubly venomous. For the Fourierists and populists, with their sentimental ties to the preindustrial community, capitalism was essentially identical with exploitative British and Jewish moneylenders. Like most of the national economists, the populists sought to rescue their more virtuous nations from the foul stench of a demonic usury.

While Cobden and Bright might see the free-market principle of the buying of goods at the cheapest price and their sale at the dearest as virtually a scriptural injunction, many, probably most people were dissatisfied by a system motored by greed which turned a blind eye to the poverty and squalor in which a good part of the industrial working classes seemed to be trapped. The stereotypical capitalism of its critics was an unlovely and, like the stereotypical feudalism, even a wicked system. Colonialism and imperialism appeared as the export

The Liberal Ideal and the Demons of Empire

of the distasteful characteristics of the new market economy to other countries. A predatory capitalism in Europe became a predatory imperialism abroad, marked by the cruelty and violence that public opinion would no longer tolerate at home.

Colonialism: Apologists and Critics

It proved impossible to create an international market without sporadic violence and exploitation, and without the destruction of the traditional societies of the less developed world. This process brought incalculable pain to great masses of people. While King Leopold's system of terror in the Congo may have been an extreme case, it was in its essentials hardly unique. Sir Roger Casement's exposés of the enormities inflicted by the white traders in exploiting native labor in the Congo (1904) and in Peru (1912) became especially well known— and won him a knighthood, a testimony, perhaps, to the sensitivity of public opinion to imperial outrages, once they became widely understood. But more often than not, there was no outcry, as the English Radical E. D. Morel observed in his horrifying 1920 discussion of the activities of Europeans in Africa for the preceding four centuries, *The Black Man's Burden*.[1]

In this study, we have not discussed the issue of racism as contributing to the idea of imperialism. This is a large subject that deserves, and has received, considerable attention from a number of writers. The subject includes the condescension of Kipling's "white man's burden" to bring law to the "lesser breeds." Kant, as we have seen, had dismissed the ethics of such a mission a century before Kipling. There was also the social Darwinist faith that nature and history intended the rule of superior Europeans over inferior colonial races. If, in the transmission of a higher civilization, the argument ran, a less advanced people was trampled upon or even made extinct, this was the way in which a scientific progress operated.[2] Such a view, as the Nazi regime of the 1930s and 1940s proved, was capable of extension to Europe itself.[3]

Few would suggest that the creation of an international economy and society by Western imperialism can be unequivocally defended, and yet one may contend, though hardly without objection, that the material conditions of the great masses in the underdeveloped countries, the so-called Third World, have improved because of the economic expansion of the West. The most rudimentary measures of this are the great explosions of population and the remarkable extensions of life expectancy in most of Asia and in Africa, although neither in these features nor in material progress have these countries yet come up to the standards of the West. (One may further argue, of course, that such population growth might bring even greater misery in its trail.) Yet can we justify the sufferings of the working population during the first decades of British industrialization in the early nineteenth century or of that of Soviet Russia in the early twentieth century by the relative well-being of children or grandchildren of the pioneers of "progress"? By what right, it can be similarly argued, following Kant, can the West justify its claim to have acted as an agent of this progress in Asia and Africa, given the pains of imperialism?

What deserves some notice, certainly, is that once the colonies overthrew their imperial masters, they made no attempt to revert to the society or polity that preceded the coming of the intruders. Their new leaders hoped to accomplish more equitably and expeditiously the programs pursued by their old colonial governors—essentially one of industrialization and Westernization. This might suggest that the process of colonization, which the later term *imperialism* transformed into an unmitigated evil, was a mixed affair. Some critics might, of course, blame the "false consciousness" of the Western-educated Third World leaders for the policies of "modernization" being followed at present.

Marx and Engels, given the spirit of their writing about the issue in the 1850s, might well have pronounced this modernization of the world to be justified by history; a similar argument has been made by a number of recent non-Marxist writers. Herbert Lüthy, a liberal Swiss economic historian, has written that "the history of colonization is the history of humanity itself": colonization was a process that opened and made safe for humans "closed continents"; it made available to all "new techniques, new customs, new knowledge and new forms of social organization." For Lüthy, European expansion into Africa and Asia was the modern "world revolution," one that "for the first time made it possible to think of mankind as a single whole, and of history as universal history."[4] For the American sociologist Lewis Feuer, imperialism is a universal historical theme and not merely a spawn of modern capitalism. Feuer distinguishes between a "regressive" imperialism (like that of the Mongols, the Spaniards, and the Nazis) and the "progressive" Western imperialism of the late nineteenth and early twentieth centuries, one that resembled the earlier progressive imperialism of Alexander the Great and Rome. Denouncing the "ideology of Imperialist guilt" that obsesses Western public life, Feuer is particularly severe on Hobson, the Marxists, and Schumpeter for their role in forming the "anti-imperialist psyche."[5] For both Lüthy and Feuer, the West has successfully engaged in a historic *mission civilisatrice*.

When examined by the test of history, the various theories of a capitalist imperialism have different evaluations. Luxemburg was not mistaken, nor were the orthodox defenders of comparative advantage and the heterodox Wakefield, in seeing the usefulness to advanced nations of trading partners at different levels of economic progress. In 1874, Cairnes expressed a somewhat exaggerated view of this principle when he wrote that "the great trades of the world are carried on between countries pretty widely removed from each other either in the scale of civilization or in respect to their natural resources and productions." The more closely "countries approximate to each other in natural resources or in industrial qualities," he added, the more "the scope for foreign trade is narrowed: it is even possible it should fail altogether." For Cairnes, as for Wakefield, the most valuable trade was between an industrial Britain and a predominantly agricultural United States.[6] This view reflected the long period when Britain was virtually the only industrial power and the principal trading country.

By the 1890s, however, when other nations had become industrialized, a different pattern emerged. Hobson noted that the most valuable trade had regularly proceeded among advanced industrial countries, countries that Britain regarded as its "industrial enemies," and not between industrial and agricultural countries.[7] Another writer of the time, a liberal and pacifist, cited the trade statistics employed by Hobson as proof that wars between advanced nations were no longer advantageous even to the victors.[8] Though overseas colonies have certainly proved useful for a number of capitalist economies, in other cases colonial possessions have been a burden, as Hobson argued and documented.[9] A number of more recent scholars have maintained persuasively that the possession of formal colonies was never *necessary* to European or American economic development.[10]

Nor do the liberal and neo-Marxist arguments concerning the relation of finance capital, protectionism, and imperialism entirely hold up, given Britain's peculiar position as a free-trade and yet an imperial power. When particular cases of imperial expansion are examined— and this may be the only sound way of proceeding—it would certainly appear that economic reasons were important and sometimes critical. As often, or more often, however, as certain historians have demonstrated, political and strategic considerations proved decisive in the creation of the empires of both the old colonialism and the new imperialism.[11]

Much confusion still exists as to just what properly constituted imperialism, or, when the older hallmarks of imperialism vanished, what has been described as an even more insidious "neo-colonialism." When a capitalist First World country invested in a Third World country, Marxists often denounced the capitalist country as imperialist; when it did not invest, the capitalist state was excoriated for depriving the less advanced nation of much-needed development capital so that a neocolonialist West might continue to exploit it. When the United States imported Cuban sugar at a price higher than the prevailing market price (in the pre-Castro period) it stood accused of an imperialist effort to confine Cuba to a stagnant monoculture. When America abrogated this arrangement after the establishment of the communist regime, the charge against it became neocolonialism.[12]

For much of this century, both the left and the right accepted the essential reality of a purely economic description of imperial exploitation. Masses of evidence were assembled to justify the indictment, and despite considerable gaps in the proofs, sensitive men and women, more guiltily conscious of the ugly aspects of the system than of its accomplishments, were persuaded. The theory provided a way of understanding complex phenomena, past, present, and future, as successful ideologies must, as well as a slogan that could be immediately understood by the simplest citizen.

Imperialism and colonialism became metaphors for the kinds of injustice associated with historic oppression, drawing as they did on the images of the violent and rapacious feudal lord and merciless and parasitic usurer. And their success in evoking ancestral memories was all the greater because people still seemed able to recognize modified forms of the old villains. What might have seemed abstract and theoretical became real and tangible because it had been assimilated into our heritage, giving form to what would otherwise be beyond immediate comprehension. Not only liberals and socialists but also German, French, and Italian right-wing writers and politicians were captivated by what appeared an uncovering of the secret lever of events. It bore the aura of conspiracy, always attractive to the popular mind — of the secret machinations of the Elders of Zion, the nefarious Freemasons, and the British Secret Service. And despite these demonic trappings, the plot draped itself in the clothes of economic rationality, which made it irresistible.

Theories of Imperialism since Lenin and Schumpeter

The nineteenth-century theories of imperialism which we have examined survived into the twentieth, and many "classical" liberals in the period between the wars followed with few variations the pattern established by the earlier sociological theorists. Among these writers were the British economist Lionel Robbins and the American Jacob Viner, who retained their faith in the liberal ideal. For Robbins, writing

The Liberal Ideal and the Demons of Empire

on the eve of World War II, the condition that led to war was the political division of the world into national states; this was "the root disease of our civilization." But even given this, if a free market and a free trade prevailed, as the Cobdenite liberals ("probably the most disinterested body of men who ever influenced the policy of a great nation") had urged, peace would be assured.[13] During World War II, Jacob Viner wrote along similar lines. "It was for the most part aristocrats, agrarians, often the urban working classes, who were the expansionists, the imperialists, the jingoes," not businessmen, he observed, as Schumpeter had a quarter of a century earlier.[14]

Schumpeter's sociological theory, the most carefully drawn and inclusive of the genre, was largely forgotten until revived in 1951 by the unearthing and translation of his articles of 1919, which were introduced by one of his Marxist students and admirers, Paul Sweezy. Sweezy was of course impressed by Schumpeter's borrowings from the neo-Marxist writers but took no notice of the fact that Schumpeter had cleared capitalism of the charge of imperialism, nor of the apparent agreement of Marxists like Kautsky and Hilferding with the more important of Schumpeter's conclusions. One must assume that for Sweezy, as for others, these pieces were interesting if peripheral additions to the Schumpeterian system but afforded no real challenge to the Leninist theory.[15] Certainly Sweezy did not alter the conclusions of his own writings on imperialism, which persisted in offering the Marxist-Leninist interpretation.[16] (A Marxist historian, on the other hand, has recently written a Schumpeterian study of "the persistence of the old regime," to which he attributes the coming of war in 1914.)[17]

It would be tedious to list the many books and tracts supporting Lenin's theory which have been written in the years since its original publication in 1917. Most prominent were those emanating from official state publishers in the U.S.S.R. The Soviet Union maintained the Leninist position as the theoretical underpinning of its international policy well into the 1980s. A manual of 1972 which was prepared by high army officers teaching at Soviet war colleges, for example, restated Lenin's argument while hitting at "modern bourgeois ideology" and its "anti-scientific sociological theories about the cause and essence of wars." The psychological school of bourgeois sociology, the manual declared, insisted that irrational "striving for violence and the thirst for wars" were inherent in human nature, and had "roots in man's subconscious strivings." Such theories, based on idealism, were "beneath all scientific criticism," for they recognized no "objective laws of social development." Bourgeois theories were designed not only to deny the inevitable triumph of communism, but to call into question the view that the elimination of capitalism would bring about an era

---

The Idea of Imperialism

187

of perpetual peace. The conclusion of the Marxist-Leninist military thinkers was that, whereas the struggle among animals was "dictated by biological laws," wars among men resulted from "the division of human society into classes."[18] (A materialist philosopher might well discover the germ of idealist heresy in a view of mankind being removed from the operation of biological laws.)

Yet even in the interwar heyday of the Leninist theory, and more frequently after, there were critics as well as supporters. One may note in particular the Marxist Fritz Sternberg, who in his *Der Imperialismus* (1926) found Luxemburg's argument more acceptable than Lenin's.[19] There were other writers of the interwar period who took exception to the specifically Marxist formulation but still stressed economic factors, at times to the exclusion of all others.[20] For two decades after World War II, of course, Marxist-Leninist writers in the West persisted in defending the essentials of the Lenin theory against those, both Marxist and non-Marxist, who questioned it.[21] Certainly Soviet and Chinese writers continued to make it the cornerstone of their position against Western capitalism and the basis for their hopes of capitalism's imminent disintegration. Since the mid-1960s, however, many Marxist-Leninist theorists have found Lenin's theory of imperialism no longer generally relevant.

Their new theory, somewhat surprisingly, appears to resemble that of the national economists with which Marx and Engels had flirted, and which had figured marginally in the analysis of certain of the neo-Marxists. What prompted this new view was the dominant position—both politically and economically—that America enjoyed after 1945, although rival capitalist powers, in Western Europe and Japan, came into prominence in the past quarter of a century. List and Carey, we recall, saw Germany and America as exploited and reduced to dependence by an economically advanced Britain and subject to the manipulation of the Bank of England. In the period between the wars, as we have already noted, this position became that of German and Italian fascists, who described their countries as proletarian nations exploited by the plutocratic capitalist nations of the West. Just as the imperial nation condemned by the national economists of the last century had been Britain, so the demonic villain of fraud (and force) for twentieth-century Marxists was to be the United States.

These attempts of recent Marxist theorists to transcend Lenin's theory of imperialism because of its failure to deal persuasively with the relationship between the metropolitan core and the peripheral colonial sectors have already received considerable attention by scholars.[22] What many of these theories have in common is what one economist has called their "sloganistic generalisations."[23] Most prominent among these is the assertion that the deliberate impoverishment of the peripheral satellites has largely created the wealth of the Western capitalist metropolis, that is, the United States.[24] These writers are generally labeled dependency theorists,[25] and certain of them, following the example of writers like Carey, have detailed the ways in which the metropolis fixed the terms of trade to the disadvantage of the periphery;[26] on rare occasions, there have been brief references to the ideas of List and Carey, though without any substantial acknowledgment of the extent of the debt owed to these earlier formulations.[27] (One of these writers did suggest a partial return to the conceptions of Hobson's 1902 work, even as he embraced the previously forbidden ones of Kautsky.[28])

The national economists of the last century had asserted that an advanced, capitalist Britain would maintain its dominant position until the dependent nations established their own industries behind tariff walls; today's dependency theorists, in Marxist-Leninist fashion, see the United States holding the masses of the Third World in a subservience from which only a socialist revolution can remove them. Easily dismissing internal reasons for underdevelopment, the dependency theorists have largely ignored instances of economic success in the Third World, for example, in such states as Taiwan, South Korea, and Singapore, and have chosen to stress instances in which the gap between the core and the periphery has been the greatest and is increasing. Some of these writers, in examining individual colonial examples, have gone astray when generalizing from the not-always-persuasive results of their local studies.[29]

But non-Marxist, even anti-Marxist, writers have also, without acknowledgment, borrowed the essential argument of the national economists. In 1974, for example, the well-known French political theorist Raymond Aron, a liberal who described Marxism as "the opium of the intellectuals" and criticized "the Leninist myth of imperialism," wrote in similar terms, and likewise without any recognition of either his Marxist contemporaries or his national economist predecessors. Aron explored at some length how the advanced countries, particularly the United States, engaged in an exploitation (his term) of the Third World, entitling his Listian analysis "Towards a New Theory of Capitalist Imperialism."[30] Such extensions of the theories of the national economists may well be the most widely accepted view of imperialism today.

The Triumph of the Liberal Ideal?

Nineteenth-century opponents of imperialism had described two types of empire, one erected primarily on force and the other on fraud, and such a distinction has continued into the present century. Both in the interwar period and in that after 1945, a Marxist-Leninist Soviet Russia, in agreement with the German National Socialists, saw a capitalist empire of fraud controlled by Wall Street and the City of London. (Before 1945, the Nazis saw international Jewish finance as the ally of the plutocrats; in the 1950s and afterward, the Soviets assigned this role to international Zionism.) Western critics of the Soviet Union, agreeing that contemporary Russia was backward, from an economic, political, and cultural point of view, saw it as an empire of force. Its modern nuclear arsenals and enormous standing armies, they argued, embodied a threat of brutal conquest not unlike that posed by the prerevolutionary czarist regimes, against which Marx and Engels had warned.

The Soviet Marxist-Leninist leadership insisted that Russia as a communist state could not be guilty of imperialism since that phenomenon was produced by a moribund capitalism in its last stage. The nuclear power of the United States, Soviet Marxists added, had made it an empire of force as well as fraud. The "adjustment" of Russia's western frontiers and the assurance of friendly states in central and eastern Europe by the stationing of large and powerful armies were necessary to defend communist Russia against capitalist encirclement. A similar explanation accounted for the Soviet invasion of Afghanistan and for Soviet and Cuban military presences in Ethiopia and Angola in the 1970s and 1980s.

It is by now clear that the various theories of imperialism, particularly when employed by nations competing for power, were and are not always impartial efforts to define a phenomenon. Each of the theorists had and has a particular target and a special position to defend. The West could only see the Soviet role in Eastern Europe or Africa as naked aggression; the East denounced any Western commercial involvement in the Third World as colonialism. More often than not, writers found the mote in their opponent's eye, though some, almost exclusively in the West, concentrated on the beam in their own.

Theories of imperialism, one may suggest, depicted a social, economic, or political institutional home for what was long believed a deep-lying human inclination, what Freud called "the greatest hindrance to civilization—namely the constitutional inclination of human beings to be aggressive towards one another."[31] But critics and theorists of imperialism persuaded themselves that Freud's was a faulty explanation. Often with images of quite different ideals in mind, they were confident that, if one eliminated the aggressive feudal or mercantilist atavism or the usurious capitalist virus of greed, there would be a millennial final victory of the spirit over the flesh; the lion would certainly lie down with the lamb. It was antiscientific to think differently.

In 1914, we recall—in a formulation resembling the liberal ideal more than the Marxist utopia—the German Marxist Karl Kautsky foresaw an era of ultraimperialism. This would be marked by the union of capitalists from the advanced countries into international cartels that would develop and modernize the world and might well bring about an epoch (though perhaps only of limited duration) of international peace and prosperity. For the moment, at least, especially since the collapse of European communism, capitalism appears to have triumphed, although to many liberals, both in the United States and in Europe, it remains an unprepossessing system with an uncertain record for justice, despite its undeniable achievements in both producing wealth and, with the assistance of trade unionism and reform legislation, distributing it widely. While one cannot easily cheer the decidedly unlovely multinational corporations, these conglomerates constitute a considerable step in the denationalization of capital, thereby cutting away another ground for international conflict. (Of course, we are still uncertain as to how fully denationalized these international corporations really are.) Despite sometimes serious setbacks, material progress moves steadily forward almost everywhere, even if that in the advanced nations seems to proceed at a more rapid rate than that in the Third World.

We must remember, however, that we still live in a world in which human avarice and aggression persist. We are not faced with the "end of history," as a Hegelian commentator has recently argued. Francis Fukuyama has described the collapse of communism in eastern Europe and the admissions of its failures in China and Russia as "the total exhaustion of viable systematic alternatives to Western liberalism" and "the triumph of the West, of the Western *idea*." While its victory was not yet complete in the real world, liberalism had won the war of ideas and had clearly become "the final form of human government." What Fukuyama was clearly celebrating was the achievement, in ideas at first, but to be followed in the real or material world, of the major parts of the liberal ideal. (The great failure of liberal societies in the nineteenth century, he noted in Kantian fashion, was to believe in "the legitimacy of imperialism.") Both political liberalism (liberty and equality) and the free-market system had displayed their superiority to fascism and communism. The result was "a de-ideologized world." From this time forward rational economic concerns would dominate world thinking and behavior. Economic calculation would supplant the readiness to go to war on behalf of an emotion-laden ideological goal. Men and women would turn their attention to solving technical or environmental problems and to satisfying consumer demands. The great aim of the eighteenth-century thinkers would be realized as the passions at last yielded to the interests.[32]

The nineteenth and twentieth centuries, we have seen, produced many writers who argued, falsely as it turned out, that a rational age that would reject war was at hand. A few years before 1914, an observer alluded to earlier declared that a violent conflict between Great Britain and Germany would not occur since each was the other's best customer and each would lose more by war than it could gain by victory.[33] The premise was true, but not the conclusion. Two world wars, the Holocaust, dozens of minor conflicts in our century testify to the continued strength of the passions, particularly when allied with interest—the passion of nationalism, most dramatically. Power, it may be argued, will always manifest itself as long as there are considerable differences in development.

Given human limitations, there continues to be a danger stemming from the hubris of economic power, even when held as a consequence of free competition; it is easy to self-righteously abuse power, however based, and the less powerful, as the history of the past century has taught us, will not fail to resist. (Nearly a century ago, Hobson warned of the danger of a parasitic "pax Europoea"[34]; today that combination would include both the United States and Japan, and recent writers have sounded an alarm about an economic conquest of the West by Japan.[35]) It is difficult to imagine that the world of the multinational corporation is the ultimate synthesis of liberty triumphant. There is already enough known of the activities of the multinationals to worry us about their future potentialities when they may become even more free of the restraints imposed by nation-states. The double perils of empires of force or fraud and, more likely in the modern world, of both force and fraud allied, still exist. The danger persists of a power akin to a Wilhelmine or Nazi Germany, or a czarist or Stalinist Russia, in possession of the most advanced technology, including the nuclear bomb, but with a polity that is quasi-feudal or worse. Nor is empire building an enterprise open only to superstates, as the recent example of Iraq demonstrates.

But such a cautious view cannot deny the reality of a continued— to use a word fallen into a frequently merited disfavor—progress, which despite wars and holocausts, the unveiling of the ugliest aspects of man's selfishness, stupidity, and sadism, can still be discerned in the history of the past century. To dare to say this no doubt displays the difficulty of even the wary to resist parts of the liberal synthesis. We owe much to the creation of an international economy, however imperfect, to the advance of science that has accompanied it, and to the growth of sympathetic feelings. A continued movement to limited goals may be all that humans can expect. If we persist in this course, we may be judged by future generations to have done quite enough.

Notes

Chapter 1   Imperialism and the Liberal Ideal

1. See the perceptive study of A. O. Hirschman, *The Passions and the Interests: Political Arguments for Capitalism before Its Triumph* (Princeton: Princeton University Press, 1977).

2. Immanuel Kant, *Kant's Political Writings*, ed. H. Reiss (Cambridge: Cambridge University Press, 1970), 44, 46, 50–51, 90–92, 94–96, 99–100, 103, 106–7, 174. See also W. B. Gallie, *Philosophers of Peace and War: Kant, Clausewitz, Marx, Engels, and Tolstoy* (Cambridge: Cambridge University Press, 1978), 8–36.

3. Ferdinand Tönnies, *Community and Society* (originally 1887), trans. C. P. Loomis (New York: Harper Torchbooks, 1957); and, of course, for the antimony of reason and emotion, see Max Weber, *From Max Weber: Essays in Sociology*, ed. H. H. Gerth and C. W. Mills (New York: Oxford University Press, 1946), esp. 267–333. Also T. Parsons and E. A. Shils, *Toward a General Theory of Action* (Cambridge, Mass.: Harvard University Press, 1962), esp. 77–91.

4. F. Engels, *Anti-Dühring: Herr Eugen Dühring's Revolution in Science* (Moscow, 1962), 239–40.

5. See Richard Koebner and H. D. Schmidt, *Imperialism: The Story and Significance of a Political Word, 1840–60* (Cambridge: Cambridge University Press, 1964).

6. See George Lichtheim, *The Concept of Ideology and Other Essays* (New York: Random House, 1967), 3–46.

7. G. I. Langmuir, *Toward a Definition of Antisemitism* (Berkeley and Los Angeles: University of California Press, 1990), 263–81, 305–10; also G. I. Langmuir, *History, Religion, and Antisemitism* (Berkeley and Los Angeles: University of California Press, 1990), 266–67, 298–300, 305.

8. Christopher Frayling, *Vampyres: Lord Byron to Count Dracula* (London: Faber, 1981).

9. See H. D. Schmidt, "The Idea and Slogans of 'Perfidious Albion,'" *Journal of the History of Ideas* 14, no. 4 (1953): 604–16.

10. Karl Marx, *Capital; A Critique of Political Economy* (New York: Modern Library, n.d.; reprint of C. H. Kerr ed. of 1906; originally 1867), 645n.

11. J. A. Schumpeter, *Capitalism, Socialism, and Democracy* (New York: Harper, 1947), 45–49.

12. Adam Smith, *The Wealth of Nations* (New York: Modern Library, 1937; originally 1776), 437–38.

Chapter 2   The Political Economists, Free Trade, and Empire

1. See Jacob Viner, "Power versus Plenty as Objectives of Foreign Policy in the Seventeenth and Eighteenth Centuries," *The Long View and the Short: Studies in Economic Theory and Policy* (Glencoe, Ill.: Free Press, 1958), 277–305.

2. For Smith, see R. H. Campbell and A. S. Skinner, *Adam Smith* (New York: St. Martin's Press, 1982); Samuel Hollander, *The Economics of Adam Smith* (Toronto: University of Toronto Press, 1973). Also see discussion in Bernard Semmel, *The Rise of Free Trade Imperialism: Classical Political Economy, the Empire of Free Trade, and Imperialism, 1750–1850* (Cambridge: Cambridge University Press, 1970), 24–30.

3. Adam Smith, *An Inquiry into the Nature and Causes of the Wealth of Nations*, ed. E. Cannan (London: Methuen, 1930), 1:343–54, 459–60; 2:101–4.

4. See G. H. Guttridge, "Adam Smith on the American Revolution: An Unpublished Memorial," *American Historical Review* 38, no. 4 (July 1933): 714–20.

5. Smith, *Wealth of Nations,* 2:95–96.

6. Ibid., 160, 96–109, 111–13, 115–16.

7. Ibid., 125–26; 1:413–14.

8. Ibid., 2:127; see also 120.

9. Ibid., 116–17.

10. For Tucker, see W. George Shelton, *Dean Tucker and Eighteenth-Century Economic and Political Thought* (New York: St. Martin's Press, 1981), esp. 126–32.

11. Josiah Tucker, *A Series of Answers to Certain Popular Objections Against Separating from the Rebellious Colonies* (Gloucester: R. Raikes, 1776), 6, 30–31, 41–45.

12. Josiah Tucker, *Cui Bono? Or, An Inquiry, What Benefits Can Arise Either to the English or the Americans, the French, Spaniards, or Dutch, from the Greatest Victories, or Successes, in the Present War* (London: T. Cadell, 1782), 5, 16–19, 36, 129.

13. Josiah Tucker, *The Respective Pleas and Arguments of the Mother Country, and of the Colonies, Distinctly Set Forth* (Gloucester: R. Raikes, 1776), 59–60.

14. For a historical discussion of Say's Law, see Thomas Sowell, *Say's Law: An Historical Analysis* (Princeton: Princeton University Press, 1972).

15. See William Spence, *Britain Independent of Commerce* (London: Cadell and Davies, 1808), 75, 27–32; for James Mill's reply, see his *Commerce Defended* (London: Baldwin, 1808), 79, 81–84, 90, 86–87.

16. See historical discussion of the law of comparative advantage in Jacob Viner, *Studies in the Theory of International Trade* (London: Allen & Unwin, 1955), 441–44; also, Lionel Robbins, *Robert Torrens and the Evolution of Classical Economics* (London: Macmillan, 1958), 31–35.

17. Quoted in Leone Levi, *The History of British Commerce and of the Economic Progress of the British Nation, 1763–1878* (London: John Murray, 1880), 294–95.

18. *Parliamentary Debates,* House of Commons, 3d ser., 81, 10 June 1845, 349. Hereafter cited as *PD.*

19. Quoted in John Morley, *Life of Richard Cobden* (London: Fisher Unwin, 1903), 561.

20. For a recent life of Malthus, though less sure on his ideas, see Patricia James, *Population Malthus: His Life and Times* (London: Routledge, 1979). Briefer and more trustworthy is Donald Winch, *Malthus* (New York: Oxford University Press, 1987).

21. T. R. Malthus, *Essay on Population* (London: Johnson, 1803), 443–45, 437; see also T. R. Malthus, *The Grounds of an Opinion on the Policy of Restricting the Importation of Foreign Corn* (London: John Murray, 1815). The physiocratic basis of Malthus's political economy has been explored more fully in Bernard Semmel,

"Malthus: 'Physiocracy' and the Commercial System," *Economic History Review,* 2d ser., 17, no. 3 (1965): 522–35.

22. T. R. Malthus, *Principles of Political Economy Considered With a View to Their Practical Application* (London: John Murray, 1820), 413–20.

23. T. R. Malthus, *Additions to the Fourth and Former Editions of An Essay on the Principles of Population* (London: John Murray, 1817), 111–12, 119, 199.

24. [T. R. Malthus], "Political Economy," *Quarterly Review* 30, no. 40 (January 1824): 297–334.

25. On Chalmers and his ideas, see S. J. Brown, *Thomas Chalmers and the Godly Commonwealth in Scotland* (New York: Oxford University Press, 1982).

26. Thomas Chalmers, *On Political Economy in Connexion With the Moral State and Moral Prospects of Society,* in his *Works* (Glasgow: William Collins, n.d.; originally 1832), 19:80–82.

27. On Ricardo and his ideas, see David Weatherall, *David Ricardo: A Biography* (The Hague: Martinus Nijhoff, 1976); for a careful discussion of his economic ideas, see Mark Blaug, *Ricardian Economics: A Historical Study* (New Haven: Yale University Press, 1958).

28. David Ricardo, *The Works and Correspondence of David Ricardo,* ed. P. Sraffa (Cambridge: Cambridge University Press, 1950–66), 4:179.

29. Ibid., 5:180.

30. Robert Torrens, *The Economists Refuted; Or An Inquiry into the Nature and Extent of the Advantages Derived from Trade* (London: Oddy, 1808), 33–35, 37–43. The best work on Torrens and his economic ideas remains Robbins, *Robert Torrens.*

31. Robert Torrens, *An Essay upon the External Corn Trade* (London: Hatchard, 1815), 321–35.

32. For Bentham, see T. W. Hutchison, "Bentham as an Economist," *Economic Journal* 66 (June 1956): 288–306. For a full collection of his works on economics, see Jeremy Bentham, *Jeremy Bentham's Economic Writings,* ed. W. Stark (London: Allen & Unwin, 1952–54), 3 vols.

33. Bentham, *Economic Writings,* 1:211–12, 47–48.

34. Jeremy Bentham, "Emancipate Your Colonies! Address to the National Convention of France, *Anno* 1793," in *The Works of Jeremy Bentham,* ed. J. Bowring (Edinburgh, 1843), 4:410–13.

35. Jeremy Bentham, "Rid Yourself of Ultramaria," Bentham Manuscripts, University College, London, portfolio no. 8, folder no. 1, p. 6, dated 11 July 1818.

36. Bentham, "The True Alarm," in his *Economic Writings,* 3:65–216.

37. Bentham, "Defence of a Maximum," in his *Economic Writings,* 3:301–2.

38. Ibid., 355.

39. See Ricardo, *Works,* 3:260–63.

40. James Mill, "The Article 'Colony,' reprint from the supplement to the *Encyclopaedia Britannica* (London, 1821?), 28–29, 31–33, 24–27, 9–14. For Mill's economic thought, James Mill, *Selected Economic Writings,* ed. and intro. D. N. Winch (Chicago: University of Chicago Press, 1966).

41. On Wakefield, see R. Garnett, *Edward Gibbon Wakefield; The Colonization of South Australia and New Zealand* (London: Fisher Unwin, 1898); Paul Bloomfield, *Edward Gibbon Wakefield, Builder of the British Commonwealth* (London: Longmans, 1961). For Wakefield's ideas, see Bernard Semmel, "The Philosophical Radicals and Colonialism," *Journal of Economic History* 31, no. 4 (December 1961): 513–25; Donald Winch, *Classical Political Economy and Colonies* (Cambridge, Mass.: Harvard University Press, 1965), chaps. 6–10.

42. See E. G. Wakefield, *A Letter from Sydney* (London: Simpkin & Marshall, 1829); E. G. Wakefield, *England and America; A Comparison of the Social and Political*

State of Both Nations (New York: Harper & Bros., 1834; original London edition, 1833).

43. Karl Marx, *Capital; A Critique of Political Economy* (Chicago: C. H. Kerr, 1906), vol. 1, chap. 33.

44. E. G. Wakefield, Papers, British Library, fols. 20, 25, 261.

45. Notes to Adam Smith, *Adam Smith's An Inquiry into the Nature and Causes of the Wealth of Nations*, ed. E. G. Wakefield (London, 1835), 1:243–46, 249–50, 223–24, 253n., 235–36, 75–76, 81.

46. Ibid., 1:238–39.

47. Wakefield, *England and America*, 224–31, 23–24.

48. Ibid., 61–63, 47, 40, 70, 42.

49. Ibid., 120–21, 123–27; also 93–127.

50. Ibid., 130.

51. Ibid., 82–84.

52. See ibid., 252n.; also Jeremy Bentham, Papers, University College, London, folder 8 (dated 1831), fols. 149, 152, 161–91.

53. *PD,* House of Commons, 3d ser., 37, 16 March 1837, 597–601.

54. *PD,* House of Commons, 3d ser., 41, 15 March 1838, 928–32.

55. *PD,* House of Commons, 3d ser., 106, 26 June 1849, 940.

56. On Mill, see Michael St. John Packe, *The Life of John Stuart Mill* (New York: Capricorn, 1970); for his economic ideas, Pedro Schwartz, *The New Political Economy of J. S. Mill* (Durham, N.C.: Duke University Press, 1972).

57. J. S. Mill, *Principles of Political Economy,* ed. J. M. Robson, in J. S. Mill, *Collected Works* (Toronto: University of Toronto Press, 1965; originally 1848), 3:735–36, 745–46, 748–49, 752–57.

58. J. A. Roebuck, *The Colonies of England* (London: Parker, 1849), 153.

59. See Robert Torrens, *The Budget* (London: Smith, Elder, 1844); also Robbins, *Robert Torrens,* chap. 7.

60. J. S. Mill, *Principles of Political Economy,* 3:591–93.

61. For Cairnes, see Adelaide Weinberg, *John Eliot Cairnes and the American Civil War: A Study in Anglo-American Relations* (London: Kingswood Press, 1970).

62. For Olmsted, see Broadus Mitchell, *Frederick Law Olmsted, A Critic of the Old South* (Baltimore: Johns Hopkins Press, 1924). Also L. W. Roper, *Frederick Law Olmsted* (Baltimore: Johns Hopkins Press, 1973).

63. A. M. Schlesinger, introduction to F. L. Olmsted, *The Cotton Kingdom* (New York: Modern Library, 1969; originally 1861), xxv–xxvi.

64. F. L. Olmsted, *A Journey in the Seaboard Slave States in the Years 1853–1854 With Remarks on Their Economy* (New York: Knickerbocker Press, 1904; originally 1856), 1:201–8, 232–36; 2:375–77.

65. Olmsted, *Cotton Kingdom,* 5.

66. F. L. Olmsted, *A Journey Through Texas; or a Saddle-Trip on the Southwestern Frontier* (New York: Dix Edwards, 1857), xvi–xvii.

67. Olmsted, *Journey in the Seaboard Slave States,* 2:310–12.

68. Ibid., 1:265–69, 2:223.

69. Olmsted, *Journey Through Texas,* xx–xxi.

70. Olmsted, *Cotton Kingdom,* 4–5.

71. Ibid., 582–84.

72. J. E. Cairnes, *The Slave Power; Its Character, Career, and Probable Designs* (Newton Abbot: David & Charles, 1968; originally 1862), 52–53, 56. Two American economic historians have discussed at some length the contributions of Olmsted and Cairnes to the shaping of the traditional opinion of the inefficiency of slave labor—a view with which they disagree. See R. W. Fogel and S. L. Engerman, *Time on the Cross: The Economics of American Negro Slavery* (Boston: Little, Brown, 1974),

170–90. See also Eugene Genovese, *The Political Economy of Slavery: Studies in the Economy and Society of the Slave South* (New York: Pantheon, 1967); Genovese has mistakenly accused Cairnes of having offered only a "simplistic and mechanistic" economic view of slavery (243).

73. Cairnes, *Slave Power*, 182, 179. The traditional view of the exhaustion of the soil by the recklessly negligent cultivation of Northern farmers was presented in P. W. Bidwell and J. I. Falconer, *History of Agriculture in the Northern United States 1620–1860* (New York: Peter Smith, 1941; originally 1925), 272. In recent years this opinion has been questioned by a number of historians. See, for example, Jonathan R. T. Hughes, *American Economic History* (Glenview, Ill.: Scott Foresman, 1990), 193–94.

74. Cairnes, *Slave Power*, 162, 185–86, 165–70, 176–78.

75. Ibid., 170, 81–83.

76. Ibid., 199–202.

77. Ibid., 239–45.

78. Ibid., 164–65.

79. Ibid., 277–80.

80. J. E. Cairnes, "The Revolution in America," *Political Essays* (New York: A. M. Kelley, 1967; originally 1873), 60–63, 88.

81. Ibid., 104.

82. J. S. Mill, *The Later Letters of John Stuart Mill, 1849–73*, ed. F. E. Mineka and D. N. Lindley, in J. S. Mill, *Collected Works* (Toronto: University of Toronto Press, 1972), 15:554, 738.

83. Ibid., 750–52.

84. J. S. Mill, *The Contest in America* (Boston: Little Brown, 1862), 27, 29–30.

Chapter 3   Liberal Social Theory and the Persistence of the Feudal Ethos

1. For Saint-Simon's life and ideas, see F. E. Manuel, *The New World of Henri Saint-Simon* (Cambridge, Mass.: Harvard University Press, 1956).

2. Elie Halévy, *The Era of Tyrannies*, ed. and trans. R. K. Webb (New York: Anchor-Doubleday, 1965), 28–30.

3. For the Saint-Simonians and their ideas, see ibid., 21–104; also Frank Manuel, *The Prophets of Paris* (New York: Harper Torchbooks, 1962), 149–93; George G. Iggers, *The Cult of Authority: The Political Philosophy of the Saint-Simonians* (The Hague: Nijhoff, 1958). See also G. G. Iggers, ed., *The Doctrine of the Saint-Simonians: An Exposition; First Year, 1828–29* (New York: Schocken Books, 1972), esp. chaps. 2, 4, 5, 7.

4. See Manuel, *Prophets of Paris*, 103–49.

5. Henri Saint-Simon, *L'Industrie* (1817), in *Oeuvres de Saint-Simon* (Paris, 1868), 18:108.

6. Ibid., 53–55.

7. Ibid., 59.

8. Ibid., 109–13.

9. See Benjamin Constant, *L'Esprit de conquête* (Paris, 1918; originally 1814), 11–15.

10. See Charles Comte, *De l'impossibilité d'établir un gouvernement constitutionnel, sous un chef militaire, et particulièrement sous Napoléon* (Paris, 1815), esp. 18–19. Of course, a number of writers of the eighteenth-century Scottish and French enlightenments had written similarly; e.g., Adam Ferguson, *An Essay on the History of Civil Society* (Philadelphia, 1819; originally 1769), 385–418.

11. For the life and thought of Comte, see Henri Gouhier, *La Jeunesse d'Auguste Comte et la formation du positivisme* (Paris: J. Vrin, 1933–41), 3 vols; also Henri

Gouhier, *La Vie d'Auguste Comte* (Paris: Librairie Philosophique J. Vrin, 1965). A work of the last century by one of Comte's disciples is also useful: Emile Littré, *Auguste Comte et la philosophie positive* (Paris, 1863), who, of course, gave Comte the major credit for positivist ideas.

12. Auguste Comte, *The Positive Philosophy of Auguste Comte*, ed. and abr. Harriet Martineau (London: Trübner & Co., 1875; originally, 1853), vol. 2, chaps. 6–11.

13. Ibid., 145, 148, 183–84.

14. Ibid., 187–99, 145.

15. Ibid., 148.

16. Ibid., 4, 323, 275.

17. Ibid., 276.

18. Auguste Comte, *System of Positive Polity* (New York: Burt Franklin, 1968; originally, 1851–54), 3:491–92.

19. Ibid., 324–25; see also 2:144.

20. See Lewis S. Feuer, *Ideology and the Ideologists* (Oxford: Basil Blackwell, 1975), esp. 1–6, 138–51; see also P. Enfantin, "Des banquiers cosmopolites," *Le Producteur* 2 (1826); Edmund Silberner, *The Problem of War in Nineteenth Century Economic Thought* (Princeton: Princeton University Press, 1946), 227–28.

21. Comte, *System*, 3:519–20.

22. Ibid., 367–69.

23. Ibid., 375–76.

24. Ibid., 294–96; see also 315–16, 327–28, 334, 350–51, 395.

25. Ibid., 46–55; see also 153–56, 168–69.

26. For Buckle's life, see G. St. Aubyn, *A Victorian Eminence: The Life and Works of H. T. Buckle* (London, 1958); the best treatment of his ideas is J. M. Robertson, *Buckle and His Critics: A Study in Sociology* (London, 1895); see also Bernard Semmel, "H. T. Buckle: The Liberal Faith and the Science of History," *British Journal of Sociology* 17, no. 3 (September 1976): 370–86.

27. Bertrand Russell, *My Philosophical Development* (New York: Simon & Schuster, 1959), 35.

28. Shaw to A. J. Marriott, 28 October 1894, in *Bernard Shaw: Collected Letters, 1874–1897*, ed. Dan H. Laurence (New York: Dodd, Mead, 1965), 456.

29. H. T. Buckle, *History of Civilization in England* (London: Longmans, Green, 1871; originally 1857), 1:190–94.

30. Ibid., 195–97.

31. Ibid., 198–99.

32. Ibid., 203–9.

33. Ibid., 210–19.

34. Ibid., 219–21.

35. Ibid., 225–26.

36. For his life, see E. Lecky, *A Memoir of the Right Hon. William Edward Hartpole Lecky* (London, 1909); a tribute to Lecky as a sociologist appears in the sociologist C. Wright Mills's introduction to W. E. H. Lecky, *History of the Rise and Influence of the Spirit of Rationalism in Europe* (New York: G. Braziller, 1955).

37. W. E. H. Lecky, *History of the Rise and Influence of the Spirit of Rationalism in Europe* (New York: Appleton & Co., 1893; originally 1865), 2:205–7.

38. Ibid., 311, 313–14.

39. Ibid., 279–80.

40. Ibid., 316–17, 319.

41. Ibid., 218–19.

42. Ibid., 241–50.

43. Ibid., 255–73.

44. Ibid., 276, 278.

45. Ibid., 323–33.
46. Ibid., 338–39.
47. Ibid., 335–38.
48. Ibid., 341–42.
49. Ibid., 218–20.
50. On Cobden and Bright, see E. Hughes, "The Development of Cobden's Economic Doctrines and His Methods of Propaganda," *Bulletin of John Rylands Institute* 23 (1938): 405ff.; Norman McCord, *The Anti–Corn Law League, 1838–1846* (London: Allen & Unwin, 1958); Donald Read, *Cobden and Bright: A Victorian Political Partnership* (London: St. Martin's, 1967); Wendy Hinde, *Richard Cobden, A Victorian Outsider* (New Haven: Yale University Press, 1987).
51. "The Opium War," *Spectator* 13, no. 613 (28 March 1840): 297.
52. "The Opium War, Its Supporters and Opponents," *Spectator* 13, no. 618 (2 May 1840): 418.
53. Richard Cobden, *England, Ireland, and America* (Edinburgh: Tait, 1836), 11.
54. John Bright, "On the Foreign Policy of England," Birmingham, 29 October 1858, in *Representative British Orators*, ed. C. K. Adams (New York: Putnam, 1884), 3:161, 174, 19.
55. Richard Cobden to John Bright, 31 October 1861, Cobden Papers, British Library, Add. Mss. 43, 651, fols. 276–78.

Chapter 4   The National Economists against Free-Trade Empire

1. *PD*, House of Commons, 3d ser., 83, 27 January 1846, 241–46, 276–80.
2. *PD*, House of Commons, 3d ser., 83, 20 February 1846, 1335–40, 1346–47.
3. For Hume, see E. C. Mossner, *The Life of David Hume* (Austin: University of Texas Press, 1954); Duncan Forbes, *Hume's Philosophical Politics* (Cambridge: Cambridge University Press, 1975). For his economic ideas, see Didier Deleule, *Hume et la naissance du libéralisme économique* (Paris: Aubier Montaigne, 1979); also David Hume, *David Hume: Writings on Economics*, ed. Eugene Rotwein (Edinburgh: Collins, 1955).
4. For a portrait of Tucker as a mercantilist, see W. E. Clark, *Josiah Tucker, Economist* (New York, 1903), 174–76. R. L. Schuyler accepted this view in the introduction to R. L. Schuyler, *Josiah Tucker: A Selection from His Economic and Political Writings* (New York: Columbia University Press, 1931), 13–14; he saw Tucker quite differently, however, in his *Fall of the Old Colonial System: A Study in British Free Trade, 1770–1870* (New York: Oxford University Press, 1945), 42.
5. Josiah Tucker, *Four Tracts Together With Two Sermons, On Political and Commercial Subjects* (Gloucester: R. Raikes, 1774), 20–27.
6. Ibid., 28, 30–36.
7. David Hume, *The Letters of David Hume*, ed. J. Y. T. Greig (Oxford, 1932), 1:271–72.
8. Tucker, *Four Tracts*, 41–47.
9. See A. F. Tytler, *Memoirs of the Life and Writings of the Honourable Henry Home of Kames* (Edinburgh, 1814), 3:160.
10. See Bernard Semmel, "The Hume-Tucker Debate and Pitt's Trade Proposals," *Economic Journal* 75 (December 1965): 762–69.
11. Alexander Hamilton, "Report on Manufactures," *Papers on Public Credit, Commerce, and Finance*, ed. Samuel McKee, Jr. (New York: Columbia University Press, 1934), 182, 192.
12. Ibid., 197–201, 223–29, 234–35.
13. Ibid., 249, 227.
14. Daniel Raymond, *The Elements of Political Economy* (Baltimore: Lucas & Coale,

1823), 2:225–26, 228–29, 240–43, 231–32, 245–46, 250. See also C. P. Neill, *Daniel Raymond: An Early Chapter in the History of Economic Theory in the United States* (Baltimore: Johns Hopkins Press, 1897).

15. On List, see Margaret Hirst, *Life of Friedrich List and Selections from His Writings* (New York: A. M. Kelley, 1965; originally 1909); see also W. O. Henderson, *Friedrich List, Economist and Visionary, 1789–1846* (London: Frank Cass, 1983); Monique Anson-Meyer, *Un Economiste de développement au XIXe siècle: Friedrich List* (Grenoble: Presses Universitaires de Grenoble, 1982).

16. Friedrich List, "Petition on Behalf of the Handelsverein to the Federal Assembly, April 1819," in Hirst, *Friedrich List,* 138, 139, 142, 143.

17. Friedrich List, "Outlines of American Political Economy" (1827), in Hirst, *Friedrich List,* 149, 151–52.

18. Ibid., 153–54.

19. Ibid., 167–68, 174–76, 178; see also esp. 245–62.

20. Friedrich List, *The Natural System of Political Economy* (originally 1837), trans. W. O. Henderson (London: Frank Cass, 1983), 29.

21. Ibid., 46–48, 51–52, 128–40.

22. Friedrich List, *The National System of Political Economy* (New York: A. M. Kelley, 1966; originally 1844), xxx, 171–73.

23. Ibid., 365.

24. Ibid., 189–94.

25. Ibid., 182–85.

26. Ibid., 130–32.

27. Ibid., 218–21, 201, 233, 259–70.

28. Ibid., 300–301, 319.

29. Ibid., 269–70.

30. Ibid., 125–30, 189–94, 269–70.

31. Ibid., 271–82.

32. Ibid., 272–74, 144–45, and passim.

33. Ibid., 144–47.

34. Ibid., 289–90.

35. Ibid., 111, 43.

36. Ibid., 55.

37. Ibid., 115.

38. Ibid., 405, 408.

39. Ibid., 398–99, 402, 388.

40. Ibid., 421–24.

41. Ibid., xxvii–xxviii.

42. *PD*, House of Commons, n.s. 21, 19 May 1829, 1464–78.

43. *PD*, House of Commons, 3d ser., 60, 21 February 1842, 754.

44. *PD*, House of Commons, 3d ser., 83, 27 January 1846, 241, 246, 276–80.

45. *PD*, House of Commons, 3d ser., 41, 15 March 1838, 940.

46. *PD*, House of Commons, 3d ser., 53, 1 April 1840, 53.

47. See A. D. H. Kaplan, *Henry Charles Carey: A Study in American Economic Thought* (Baltimore: Johns Hopkins Press, 1931); J. Dorfman, *The Economic Mind in American Civilization* (New York: Viking, 1946), 2:789–805.

48. H. C. Carey, *Principles of Political Economy* (Philadelphia, 1837–40), 3 vols.; H. C. Carey, *The Harmony of Interests, Agricultural, Manufacturing, and Commercial* (Philadelphia: Skinner, 1851).

49. H. C. Carey, *The Past, the Present, and the Future* (Philadelphia, 1848), chap. 3.

50. H. C. Carey, *Principles of Social Science* (Philadelphia: Lippincott, 1873; originally 1858–59), 1:273–77, 336.

51. Ibid., 260–62, 284.
52. Ibid., xi–xiv.
53. Ibid., 239n., 235–36, 257–60.
54. Ibid., 243–46.
55. Ibid., 246–56.
56. Ibid., 257, 286, 288.
57. Ibid., 290–91, 295.
58. Ibid., 296, 302, 304.
59. Ibid., 307–11.
60. Ibid., 311–20.
61. Ibid., 320–28, 330.
62. Ibid., 361, 340, 353, 358–60.
63. Ibid., 318–20, 380, 335–37, 407–10, 419–22.
64. Ibid., 2:466–70; see also S. G. Checkland, "The Birmingham Economists, 1815–50," *Economic History Review,* 2d series, 1, no. 1 (1948): 1–19.
65. Carey, *Principles of Social Science,* 2:331–34, 345–47, 349–51.
66. Ibid., 366, 244, 359–73, 378–80.
67. Ibid., 460, 442, 445–46.
68. Ibid., 446–47, 452, 417.
69. Ibid., 466–70.
70. Ibid., 72–73, 90–92, 97–98; see also 43–47, 66–71.
71. Ibid., 125; see also 142.
72. Ibid., 176, 1:257.
73. Ibid., 2:208, 228, 242, 182–83, 205–6.
74. Ibid., 239, 250–51, 253.
75. Ibid., 455–58.
76. Ibid., 238–39, 241–50.
77. H. C. Carey, *Letters to the President on the Foreign and Domestic Policy of the Union, etc.* (Philadelphia: Lippincott, 1858), 126, 131; see also 79–86.
78. H. C. Carey, *Review of the Decade 1857–67* (Philadelphia: Collins, 1867), 15, 17, 26–27, 31, 35. See also H. C. Carey, *Commerce, Christianity, and Civilization, Versus British Free Trade: Letters in Reply to the London Times* (Philadelphia: Collins, 1876), 10–11, 35–36.
79. Carey, *Harmony of Interests,* 72.
80. Carey, *Review of the Decade,* 39. See also H. C. Carey, *The Way to Outdo England Without Fighting Her* (Philadelphia: Baird, 1865), 165.
81. [John Austin], "List on the Principles of the German Customs Union. Dangers of British Industry and Commerce," *Edinburgh Review,* no. 152 (July 1842): 521–22.
82. J. S. Mill to John Austin, 7 July 1842, in *The Earlier Letters of John Stuart Mill, 1812–1848,* ed. F. E. Mineka, in J. S. Mill, *Collected Works* (Toronto: University of Toronto Press, 1963), 13:528.
83. J. S. Mill, *Principles of Political Economy,* ed. J. M. Robson in J. S. Mill, *Collected Works* (Toronto: University of Toronto Press, 1965; originally 1848), 3:918–19.
84. For example, see J. S. Mill to Henry Soden, 2 May 1865, in J. S. Mill, *The Later Letters of John Stuart Mill,* ed. F. E. Mineka and D. N. Lindley, in J. S. Mill, *Collected Works* (Toronto: University of Toronto Press, 1972), 16:1043–44.
85. *Times,* 16 January 1847, 46.
86. J. S. Mill to H. C. Carey, 15 February 1845, in J. S. Mill, *Earlier Letters,* 13:659–60.
87. J. S. Mill to Chapman, in November 1845, in J. S. Mill, *Earlier Letters,* 13:686–87.

88. J. S. Mill to Earl Grey, 13 May 1864, in J. S. Mill, *Later Letters*, 15:942; J. S. Mill, *Principles of Political Economy*, 922–26.

89. J. S. Mill to Cairnes, 1 December 1864, in J. S. Mill, *Later Letters*, 15:967–68.

90. J. S. Mill to W. F. Rae, 9 April 1869, in J. S. Mill, *Later Letters*, 17:1589–90.

91. Marx to J. Weydemeyer, 5 March 1852, Karl Marx, *On Revolution*, ed. S. K. Padover (New York: McGraw-Hill, 1971), 134.

92. Marx to Engels, 14 June 1853, Karl Marx, *Karl Marx on Colonialism and Modernization: His Despatches and Other Writings in China, India, Mexico, the Middle East and North Africa*, ed. Schlomo Avineri (Garden City, N.Y.: Doubleday, 1968), 429–30.

93. Karl Marx, *Grundrisse: Foundations of the Critique of Political Economy* (Harmondsworth, Middlesex: Penguin, 1973), 884–89.

Chapter 5   The International Usury of Finance Capital

1. For a history of the changing attitudes toward usury, see Benjamin Nelson, *The Idea of Usury: From Tribal Brotherhood to Universal Otherhood* (Chicago: University of Chicago Press, 1969). See *The Wealth of Nations* (New York: Modern Library, 1937; originally 1776), 339–40 for Adam Smith's opinion of the need to regulate interest. Jeremy Bentham attempted to convert Smith to a free-market view of usury in his "Defence of Usury" (1787), in *Jeremy Bentham's Economic Writings*, ed. W. Stark (London: Allen & Unwin, 1952–54), 1:124–207; and according to one of Smith's biographers, apparently with some success. See John Rae, *Life of Adam Smith* (New York: Kelley, 1965; originally 1895), 423–24.

2. Karl Marx, "On the Jewish Question," in Karl Marx and Friedrich Engels, *The Marx-Engels Reader*, ed. R. C. Tucker (New York: Norton, 1972; originally 1843), 46, 47, 50.

3. For Fourier's life, see Jonathan Beecher, *Charles Fourier: The Visionary and His World* (Berkeley and Los Angeles: University of California Press, 1986). Curiously, Fourier's anti-Semitism is not discussed.

4. Charles Fourier, *Design for Utopia: Selected Writings of Charles Fourier*, ed. Charles Gide (New York: Schocken Books, 1971), 99.

5. Charles Fourier, *Théorie des quatre mouvements*, in his *Oeuvres Complètes* (Paris: Editions Anthropos, 1967), 1:253–54.

6. Fourier, *Design for Utopia*, 100.

7. Ibid., pp. 99–100.

8. Fourier, *Oeuvres*, 1:195–203.

9. Ibid., 206–11, 213.

10. Ibid., 233.

11. Charles Fourier, *The Utopian Vision of Charles Fourier: Selected Texts on Work, Love, and Passionate Attraction*, trans. and ed. by Jonathan Beecher and Richard Bienvenu (Columbia: University of Missouri Press, 1982), 108n., 117, 119n. 122, 199; also Fourier, *Oeuvres*, 1:264. See E. Silberner, "Charles Fourier on the Jewish Question," *Jewish Social Studies* 8, no. 4 (October 1946): 245–66.

12. Fourier, *Oeuvres*, 1:206–7, 209–10.

13. Ibid., 278.

14. Ibid., 211.

15. Ibid., 100–101, 107; also Fourier, *Design for Utopia*, 100–101.

16. Fourier, *Oeuvres*, 1:268–73.

17. Ibid., 1:275.

18. Alphonse Toussenel, *Les Juifs, rois de l'époque; Histoire de la féodalité financière* (Paris, 1845), 128.

19. Ibid., 269–70.

20. Ibid., 279–80.
21. Ibid., 165, 162–63.
22. Ibid., 263–64.
23. Ibid., i–iv, xiii–xix.
24. Ibid., i, vi–viii, 1–2.
25. Ibid., 1–6.
26. Ibid., 11–15.
27. Ibid., 47, 51–52, 49–50.
28. Ibid., 73.
29. Ibid., 49.
30. Ibid., 57, 74.
31. Ibid., 57, 55–56.
32. Ibid., 68–69.
33. Ibid., 72–73.
34. Edouard Drumont, *La France juive* (Paris, 1886), 342–44. For studies of Drumont, see Michel Wincock, *Edouard Drumont et Cie.: Anti-sémitisme et fascisme en France* (Paris: Seuil, 1982); Frederick Busi, *The Pope of Anti-Semitism: The Career and Legacy of Edouard-Adolphe Drumont* (Lanham, Md.: University Press of America, 1986).
35. Drumont, *La France juive*, 345, 419.
36. Ibid., vi–vii.
37. Ibid., 481, 471–73, 450.
38. Ibid., 503–4, ix–xii.
39. Ibid., 41.
40. Brooks Adams, *The Law of Civilization and Decay* (New York: Knopf, 1943; originally 1896), 59–60.
41. Ibid., 277–78.
42. Ibid., 278, 285, 291–96.
43. J. M. Keynes, *A Treatise on Money* (London: Macmillan, 1965; originally 1930), 2:156–57.
44. Adams, *Law of Civilization and Decay*, 58–61.
45. Ibid., 304, 308.
46. Ibid., 304–8.
47. Ibid., 316–18, 320–21.
48. Ibid., 321–24.
49. Ibid., 322–24, 333. We may note in passing that with the coming of the new century, Adams observed that Great Britain had already yielded her economic predominance to the United States, a somewhat bold proposition this early. See Brooks Adams, *America's Economic Supremacy* (New York: Macmillan, 1900), esp. 1–25, 142–92.
50. See Henry Adams, *The Education of Henry Adams* (New York: Modern Library, 1931; originally 1918), 343–44.
51. Henry Adams, *The Letters of Henry Adams*, ed. J. C. Levenson, E. Samuels, C. Vandersee, and V. H. Winner (Cambridge, Mass.: Harvard University Press, 1988), 4:404 (27 July 1896); see also 4:127, 130, 190, 414.
52. On Sombart, see Arthur Mitzman, *Sociology and Estrangement: Three Sociologists of Imperial Germany* (New York: Knopf, 1973), 135–264; esp. 251–55, 258–61.
53. Werner Sombart, *The Jews and Modern Capitalism* (Glencoe, Ill.: Free Press, 1951; originally 1911), 13–21, 29–30, 37.
54. Ibid., 51–55.
55. Ibid., 93.
56. Ibid., 91, 99–101.

57. Ibid., 39–41, 44.

58. Ibid., 108–12.

59. Ibid., 122, 140, 134, 136, 153, 247–49.

60. Ibid., 276–77, 344, 306–7, 310, 189.

61. For critiques of Sombart's treatment of this question and his frequently far-fetched "proofs," see: B. F. Hoselitz, introduction to Sombart, *Jews and Modern Capitalism*, xvii–xxxi; Freddy Raphael, *Judaisme et capitalisme: Essai sur la controverse entre Max Weber et Werner Sombart* (Paris: Presses Universitaires de France, 1982).

Chapter 6 The Later Liberal Sociologists and the New Imperialism

1. Justin McCarthy, review of *History of Civilization in England* by H. T. Buckle, *Westminster Review*, n.s. 20, 7 (July 1861): 193.

2. For Spencer, see J. D. Y. Peel, *Herbert Spencer: The Evolution of a Sociologist* (New York: Basic Books, 1971); Herbert Spencer, *The Social and Political Writings of Herbert Spencer*, ed. David Wiltshire (New York: Oxford University Press, 1978).

3. For a discussion of social Darwinism, see Bernard Semmel, *Imperialism and Social Reform* (Cambridge, Mass.: Harvard University Press, 1960), 29–52; also Gertrude Himmelfarb, *Marriage and Morals among the Victorians* (New York: Knopf, 1986), 76–93.

4. Herbert Spencer, *Principles of Sociology* (New York: Appleton, 1887–97; originally 1876–85), 2:568–602.

5. Ibid., 607–8, 610; and 603–40, passim.

6. Ibid., 584–86.

7. Ibid., 588–90.

8. Ibid., 620–24.

9. Ibid., 626–28, 640.

10. Ibid., 635–36.

11. Ibid., 1:568.

12. Ibid., 569–70.

13. Ibid., 570–730.

14. Herbert Spencer, "Government Colonization," *Social Statics* (New York: Appleton, 1913; originally 1892), 188–99.

15. Herbert Spencer, "The Bias of Patriotism," *The Study of Sociology* (New York: Appleton, 1886), 204–5.

16. Herbert Spencer, "Patriotism," in *The Works of Herbert Spencer* (Osnabrück: Otto Zeller, 1966; reprint of 1902 edition), 19:88–91.

17. Herbert Spencer, "Imperialism and Slavery," in his *Works*, 19:112–14, 117, 118–21.

18. Herbert Spencer, "Re-Barbarization," in his *Works*, 19:122–33.

19. On Hobson, see John Allett, *New Liberalism: The Political Economy of J. A. Hobson* (Toronto: University of Toronto Press, 1981); Michael Freeden, *The New Liberalism: An Ideology of Social Reform* (Oxford: Oxford University Press, 1986); Michael Freeden, ed., *Reappraising J. A. Hobson: Humanism and Welfare* (London: Unwin Hyman, 1990).

20. J. M. Keynes, *The General Theory of Employment, Interest, and Money* (New York: Harcourt Brace, 1936), 364–71.

21. J. A. Hobson, *The War in South Africa* (London: Macmillan, 1900), 189–91, 193–94, 196–97.

22. J. A. Hobson, *Imperialism: A Study* (London: Allen & Unwin, 1948; originally 1902), xvii–xviii. For my earlier (1970) discussion of Hobson as having offered an essentially sociological theory of imperialism, see Bernard Semmel, *The Rise of Free Trade Imperialism: Classical Political Economy, the Empire of Free Trade, and Imperialism,*

1750–1850 (Cambridge: Cambridge University Press, 1970), 222–26. A fuller presentation of this position (and discussion of certain difficulties in Hobson's presentation) may be found in P. J. Cain, "J. A. Hobson, Cobdenism, and the Radical Theory of Economic Imperialism, 1898–1914," *Economic History Review*, 2d ser., 31 (1978): 565–84. This article gave rise to a scholarly exchange: see P. F. Clarke, "Hobson, Free Trade, and Imperialism," *Economic History Review*, 2d ser., 34 (1981): 308–12; and Cain's reply, "Hobson's Developing Theory of Imperialism," *Economic History Review*, 2d ser., 34 (1981): 313–16. See also P. J. Cain, "J. A. Hobson, Finance Capitalism, and Imperialism in Late Victorian and Edwardian England," *Journal of Imperial and Commonwealth History* 13 (May 1985): 1–27. For other discussions of Hobson's work, see H. Mitchell, "Hobson Revisited," *Journal of the History of Ideas* 26 (1965): 397–416; B. Porter, *Critics of Empire: British Radical Attitudes to Colonialism in Africa, 1895–1914* (London: Macmillan, 1968), 207–38; J. C. Wood, *British Economists and the Empire* (London: Croom Helm, 1983), 236–56; Jules Townshend, *J. A. Hobson* (Manchester: Manchester University Press, 1990), 101–15.

23. Hobson, *Imperialism*, 3–13.
24. Ibid., 15–17.
25. Ibid., 38, 41–45.
26. Ibid., 45, 50–51.
27. Ibid., 46–50.
28. Ibid., 53–55.
29. Ibid., 56–61.
30. Ibid., 59.
31. Ibid., 65–67.
32. Ibid., 71–81.
33. Ibid., 100–109.
34. Ibid., 92–93.
35. Ibid., 81.
36. J. A. Hobson, *International Trade: An Application of Economic Theory* (New York: A. M. Kelley, 1966; originally 1904), esp. 1–22; J. A. Hobson, *The Economic Interpretations of Investment* (London: Financial Review of Reviews, 1911), 116–18. See P. J. Cain, "Variations on a Famous Theme: Hobson, International Trade, and Imperialism," in Freeden, *Reappraising J. A. Hobson*, 31–53. Cain attributes Hobson's shifts of position to a pursuit of "a Utopian dream of world prosperity and peace" that caused him to choose arguments that appeared to offer "the best prospect for progress" at a particular moment (52).
37. Hobson, *Imperialism*, 86.
38. Ibid., 91.
39. Ibid., 85.
40. Ibid., 81.
41. Ibid., 88.
42. Ibid., 29–30.
43. Ibid., 81.
44. Ibid., 88–89.
45. Ibid., 85.
46. Ibid., 86, 88, 90, 91.
47. Ibid., 364–67.
48. Ibid., 85.
49. Ibid., 135. See Hobson's 1904 tribute to Spencer, "Herbert Spencer," in *J. A. Hobson: A Reader*, ed. Michael Freeden (London: Unwin Hyman, 1988), 60–64.
50. Hobson, *Imperialism*, 150, 152.
51. Ibid., 213–14.

52. Ibid., 222.

53. For Veblen and his ideas, see Joseph Dorfman, *Thorstein Veblen and His America* (New York: Viking, 1947; originally 1934); David Reisman, *Thorstein Veblen: A Critical Interpretation* (New York: Scribner's, 1960), 133–37; for a more recent, more perceptive and imaginative account, see John Patrick Diggins, *The Bard of Savagery: Thorstein Veblen and Modern Social Theory* (New York: Seabury Press, 1978). See also D. L. Cranmer and C. G. Leathers, "Veblen and Schumpeter on Imperialism," *History of Political Economy* 9, no. 2 (Summer 1977): 237–55.

54. Thorstein Veblen, *Imperial Germany and the Industrial Revolution* (New York: Viking, 1954; originally 1915), esp. 244.

55. See Joseph Dorfman, introduction to Veblen, *Imperial Germany,* xii–xiii.

56. Ibid., esp. 117.

57. Ibid., esp. 127.

58. Ibid., 131n.

59. Ibid., 128–33.

60. Ibid., 59–61.

61. Ibid., 67, 69–70.

62. Ibid., 158, 166–69, 173.

63. Ibid., 174–75.

64. Ibid., 133.

65. Ibid., 183.

66. Ibid., 80–81, 83–84.

67. Ibid., 204–7.

68. Ibid., 220, 238–48, 253.

69. Ibid., 220.

70. Ibid., 228, 239–41.

71. Ibid., 271.

72. Thorstein Veblen, "The Opportunity of Japan," *Essays in Our Changing Order,* ed. Leon Ardzrooni (New York: Viking, 1954), 249.

73. Ibid., 254–55.

74. Ibid., 255, 261–62, 264, 266.

75. Thorstein Veblen, editorial article for *New Republic,* 30 June 1917, *Essays in Our Changing Order,* 245–48.

76. H. J. Mackinder, "The Great Trade Routes," *Journal of the Institute of Bankers,* May 1900, 271. These questions are explored in Semmel, *Imperialism and Social Reform,* esp. chaps. 3, 7.

77. Quoted in Dorfman, *Thorstein Veblen and His America,* 369–70.

78. Ibid., 487.

79. J. A. Hobson, *Veblen* (New York: John Wiley, 1937), 224, 53, 21, 71.

80. J. A. Hobson, *Confessions of an Economic Heretic* (London: Allen & Unwin, 1938), 62–64.

Chapter 7 The Formulation of a Marxist and Neo-Marxist Theory

1. On Marx, see David McLellan, *Karl Marx: His Life and Thought* (New York: Harper & Row, 1973); S. Avineri, *The Social and Political Thought of Karl Marx* (Cambridge: Cambridge University Press, 1968). On Engels, see W. O. Henderson, *The Life of Friedrich Engels* (London: Cass, 1976); for a brief survey of Engels's ideas, David McLellan, *Engels* (London: Fontana/Collins, 1977).

2. Frederick Engels, "Outlines of a Critique of Political Economy (1844)," in K. Marx and F. Engels, *Collected Works* (London: Lawrence & Wishart, 1975): 3:418, 420, 436–39.

3. Ibid., 422–23.

4. Ibid., 421–22, 432–33, 441.

5. Ibid., 433–34, 441–44.

6. Friedrich Engels, introduction (1892) to the English edition of Engels, "The Condition of the Working Class in England (1844)," in K. Marx and F. Engels, *On Britain* (Moscow: Foreign Language Publishing House, 1953), 25.

7. Ibid., 29.

8. Ibid., 29–30.

9. Ibid., 31–32; see also 19–20.

10. K. Marx, "Contributions to the Critique of Hegel's Philosophy of Law (1833–34)," in Marx and Engels, *Collected Works*, 3:178–81. The editor of the volume spotted the pun. An essay by Marx on List has been discovered in a Russian translation: see Roman Szporluk, *Communism and Nationalism: Karl Marx versus Friedrich List* (New York: Oxford University Press, 1988), 1–3, 30–42. The essay, of course, denounced List as a reactionary. Szporluk seems unaware of Engels's Listian sympathies.

11. K. Marx, *Free Trade; A Speech Delivered Before the Democratic Club, Brussels, Belgium, Jan. 9, 1848* (Boston: Lee and Shepard, 1888; originally 1848), 40, 42.

12. F. Engels, "Protection and Free Trade (1888)," in K. Marx and F. Engels, *On Colonialism* (Moscow: Foreign Languages Publishing House, n.d.), 263–66.

13. K. Marx, "Traditional Policy of Russia," *New York Tribune*, 12 August 1853, *The Eastern Question; A Reprint of Letters Written 1853–1856 Dealing With the Events of the Crimean War* (London: Swann, Sonnenschein, 1897), 76–80.

14. Marx, "Eastern Question," *New York Tribune*, 12 April 1853, *Eastern Question*, 14–19.

15. See Marx to Dr. Kugelmann, 11 May 1869, K. Marx, *Letters to Dr. Kugelmann* (London: Martin Lawrence, n.d.), 70; K. Marx, *Secret Diplomatic History of the Eighteenth Century and the Story of the Life of Lord Palmerston* (London: Lawrence & Wishart, 1969), 214–15. See also Bernard Semmel, *Liberalism and Naval Strategy: Ideology, Interest, and Sea Power during the Pax Britannica* (Boston: Allen & Unwin, 1986), 64–65.

16. K. Marx and F. Engels, *The Russian Menace to Europe; A Collection of Articles, Speeches, Letters, and News Dispatches*, ed. P. W. Blackstock and B. F. Hoselitz (Glencoe, Ill.: Free Press, 1952), 26, 32–33.

17. Ibid., 47, 51, 53.

18. Engels to Marx, 23 May 1856, in K. Marx and F. Engels, *Ireland and the Irish Question: A Collection of Writings by Karl Marx and Frederick Engels* (New York: International Publishers, 1972), 83–85.

19. Marx to L. Kugelmann, 29 November 1869, in Marx and Engels, *Ireland*, 281.

20. Marx to S. Meyer and A. Vogt, 9 April 1870, in Marx and Engels, *Ireland*, 292–94.

21. Marx, "Outline of a Report on the Irish Question" (1867), in Marx and Engels, *Ireland*, 132.

22. K. Marx, "Parliamentary Debate on India," *New York Tribune*, 25 June 1853, in *Karl Marx on Colonialism and Modernization: His Despatches and Other Writings on China, India, Mexico, the Middle East and North Africa*, ed. Schlomo Avineri (Garden City, N.Y.: Doubleday, 1968), 76–78.

23. K. Marx, *British Rule in India* (Sydney: Modern Publishers, 193?), 6, 8–9, 18–21; K. Marx, *Capital; A Critique of Political Economy* (Chicago: Charles Kerr, 1915), 3:382, 385, 387–89, 392–93.

24. [F. Engels,] "French Rule in Algeria," *Northern Star*, 22 January 1848, in Marx, *Marx on Colonialism*, 43.

25. Marx, "Eastern Question," 14–19.

26. See Beatrice Shoul, "Karl Marx and Say's Law," *Quarterly Journal of Economics* 71, no. 4 (November 1957): 611–29.

27. Karl Marx, *Capital: A Critique of Political Economy* (Chicago: C. H. Kerr, 1906), vol. 3:294–95, 300–303, 278.

28. Ibid., 279–80.

29. Ibid., 693–94.

30. K. Marx, "The Elections in England—Tories and Whigs," *New York Tribune*, 6 August 1852, in Marx and Engels, *On Britain*, 353–55.

31. Marx, "Lord John Russell," *Neue Oder Zeitung*, 4, 7, 8, 10, and 15, August 1855, in Marx and Engels, *On Britain*, 440n.

32. Engels, introduction (1892) to his "Condition of the Working-Class," 25.

33. Marx to F. Freiligrath, 31 July 1849, in Marx and Engels, *On Britain*, 488.

34. Karl Marx, *Capital; A Critique of Political Economy* (New York: Modern Library, n.d.; originally 1867), 648–55.

35. Ibid., 648–50n.

36. Marx, *Capital* (Kerr ed.), 1:685–89.

37. Ibid., 3:306.

38. Ibid., 3:516–17.

39. Engels to Kautsky, 18 September 1883, in Marx and Engels, *On Colonialism*, p. 342.

40. Marx, *Capital* (Kerr ed.), 3:516–19.

41. See Tom Bottomore, introduction to Rudolf Hilferding, *Finance Capital* (London: Routledge & Kegan Paul, 1985; originally 1910), 1–17; Tom Bottomore, introduction to Tom Bottomore and Patrick Goode, eds., *Austro-Marxism* (Oxford: Clarendon Press, 1978), 1–56.

42. See Hilferding, *Finance Capital*, esp. pts. 2, 3.

43. Ibid., 301–7.

44. Ibid., 307–9.

45. Ibid., 304–5.

46. Ibid., 310, 314–18.

47. Ibid., 319–21.

48. Ibid., 322, 324–26.

49. Ibid., 310–14.

50. Ibid., 328–30, 323.

51. Ibid., 323, 314–18.

52. Ibid., 334–35, 342–43.

53. Ibid., 335–36.

54. Ibid., 344–45, 349–50.

55. Ibid., 364, 366–68.

56. Ibid., 368–70.

57. Ibid., 225–26.

58. Ibid., 310–14.

59. Ibid., 331–32.

60. On Luxemburg, see J. P. Nettl, *Rosa Luxemburg* (London: Oxford University Press, 1966).

61. For Loria and Wakefield, see discussion in Bernard Semmel, *The Rise of Free Trade Imperialism: Classical Political Economy, the Empire of Free Trade, and Imperialism, 1750–1850* (Cambridge: Cambridge University Press, 1970), 212–13.

62. Rosa Luxemburg, *The Accumulation of Capital* (New Haven: Yale University Press, 1951; originally 1913), 368, 362.

63. Ibid., 358.

64. Ibid., 371.

65. Ibid., 48–63; sec. 2, esp. 276–83.

66. Ibid., 454–67.

67. Rosa Luxemburg, *The Accumulation of Capital—An Anti-Critique* (New York: Monthly Review Press, 1972); originally 1915), 147.

68. Ibid., 143, 148.

69. For Bukharin, see Stephen F. Cohen, *Bukharin and the Bolshevik Revolution: A Political Biography, 1888–1938* (New York: Knopf, 1973).

70. N. Bukharin, *Imperialism and World Economy* (New York: International Publishers, 1929; originally 1915), 68, 123–27, 139–40, 170.

71. N. Bukharin, *Imperialism and the Accumulation of Capital* (New York: Monthly Review Press, 1972; originally 1924), 253–54 (in a volume containing Luxemburg's *Anti-Critique*).

72. Ibid., 260–61.

73. Ibid., 268.

74. A. O. Hirschman, "On Hegel, Imperialism, and Structural Stagnation," *Essays in Trespassing: Economics to Politics and Beyond* (Cambridge: Cambridge University Press, 1981), 167–70.

75. Ibid., 170–72.

Chapter 8   The End of Imperialism: Kautsky, Lenin, Schumpeter

1. R. A. Fletcher, "Cobden as Educator: The Free Trade Internationalism of Eduard Bernstein, 1899–1914," *American Historical Review* 88, no. 3 (June 1983): 572n.

2. J. H. Kautsky, "J. A. Schumpeter and Karl Kautsky: Parallel Theories of Imperialism," *Midwest Journal of Political Science* 5, no. 2 (May 1961): 101–28.

3. For Bernstein, see Eduard Bernstein, *My Years in Exile: Reminiscences of a Socialist* (Westport, Conn.: Greenwood Press, 1986; originally 1921); Peter Gay, *The Dilemma of Democratic Socialism: Eduard Bernstein's Challenge to Marx* (New York: Columbia University Press, 1952).

4. Fletcher, "Cobden as Educator," 561–78, passim.

5. On Kautsky, see Massimo Salvadori, *Karl Kautsky and the Socialist Revolution, 1880–1938* (London: New Left Books, 1979), esp. 181–203. Also G. P. Steenson, *Karl Kautsky, 1854–1938: Marxism in the Classical Years* (Pittsburgh: University of Pittsburgh Press, 1978), 174–180, 192–93; D. Geary, *Karl Kautsky* (New York: St. Martin's Press, 1987), esp. 46–59. Geary writes of Kautsky as "the first Marxist to develop a fully coherent theory of economic Imperialism" (46).

6. See Karl Kautsky, "Aeltere und neuere Kolonialpolitik," *Die Neue Zeit* 6 pt. 1, no. 25 (1897–98): 769–81, 801–16; see also discussion in J. H. Kautsky, "J. A. Schumpeter and Karl Kautsky," 110–20.

7. Karl Kautsky, "Der Imperialismus," *Die Neue Zeit* 32 (1914): 908–22; a translation of a part of the article has appeared as "Ultra-imperialism," *New Left Review* 59 (January-February 1970): 41–46.

8. Kautsky, "Der Imperialismus," 921.

9. Ibid., 920–21.

10. Karl Kautsky, "Zwei Schriften zum Umlernen," *Die Neue Zeit* 33, no. 5 (30 April 1915): 144.

11. For Lenin, see David Shub, *Lenin: A Biography* (Harmondsworth, Middlesex: Penguin, 1966); also B. D. Wolfe, *Three Who Made a Revolution* (Boston: Beacon Press, 1955).

12. V. I. Lenin, *Imperialism: The Highest Stage of Capitalism* (New York: International Publishers, 1939; originally 1917), 8. The development of Lenin's ideas on imperialism may be followed in V. I. Lenin, *Notebooks on Imperialism* in his *Collected Works* (London: Lawrence & Wishart, 1968), vol. 39; see also V. I. Lenin, *British*

Labour and British Imperialism: A Compilation of Writings by Lenin on Britain (London: Lawrence & Wishart, 1969).

13. Lenin, *Imperialism*, 9, 12–13.
14. Ibid., 7, 13–15.
15. Ibid., chaps. 1, 2, 3.
16. Ibid., chap. 4.
17. Ibid., chap. 5.
18. Ibid., 85, and chap. 6.
19. Ibid., chap. 7.
20. Ibid., chap. 8.
21. Ibid., 99.
22. Ibid., 99–104; and chap. 9.
23. Ibid., 126; and chaps. 5–9.
24. N. Bukharin, *Imperialism and World Economy* (New York: International Publishers, 1929; originally 1915), 135–43.
25. V. I. Lenin, introduction to ibid., 11–14.
26. Lenin, *Imperialism*, 74, 90–93, 95–97.
27. Ibid., 10.
28. Ibid., 83.
29. Ibid., 62–63.
30. Ibid., 111.
31. Ibid., 74.
32. Ibid., 94.
33. Ibid., 117–19, 122. Lenin's later denunciation of Kautsky may be found in V. I. Lenin, *The Proletarian Revolution and the Renegade Kautsky* (New York: International Publishers, 1934; originally 1918).
34. The Ely lecturer that year was Tibor Scitovsky. Quoted in the new biography of Schumpeter, R. L. Allen, *Opening Doors: The Life and Work of Joseph Schumpeter* (New Brunswick, N.J.: Transaction, 1991), 2:251. For high points of Schumpeter's career, also see E. März, *Joseph Schumpeter: Scholar, Teacher, and Politician* (New Haven: Yale University Press, 1991). Other useful works are Erich Schneider, *Life and Work of a Great Social Scientist* (Lincoln: University of Nebraska, Lincoln, 1975); R. V. Clemence, *The Schumpeterian System* (New York: A. M. Kelley, 1966); S. E. Harris, ed., *Schumpeter, Social Scientist* (Cambridge, Mass.: Harvard University Press, 1951). Unfortunately, this and other works on Schumpeter say little about his sociology. More relevant to Schumpeter as sociologist is J. A. Schumpeter, *The Economics and Sociology of Capitalism,* ed. Richard Swedberg (Princeton: Princeton University Press, 1991), esp. 3–77.
35. Much has been written on Schumpeter's theory of imperialism. See, for example, the favorable E. Heimann, "Schumpeter and the Problem of Imperialism," *Social Research* 19, no. 2 (June 1952): 177–97; and the highly critical M. Greene, "Schumpeter's Theory of Imperialism," *Social Research* 19 (December 1952): 543–63. März's recently published work contains a chapter purporting to discuss Schumpeter's theory but in fact dismissing it routinely in favor of a lengthy updating of the Marxist-Leninist theory. See März, *Joseph Schumpeter,* 62–84.
36. J. A. Schumpeter, *Imperialism and Social Classes* (New York: Meridian, 1974; originally 1919), 3–7.
37. Ibid., 23.
38. Ibid., 10–11, 15, 17–19.
39. Ibid., 11–12, 22.
40. Ibid., 29–33.
41. Ibid., 25–29.
42. Ibid., 34–40.

43. Ibid., 50–54.
44. Ibid., 43–49.
45. Ibid., 54–59.
46. Ibid., 59–62, 33–34.
47. Ibid., 64–66.
48. Ibid., esp. 68–70, 72–73.
49. Ibid., 75–79.
50. Ibid., 79–84.
51. Ibid., 84–89.
52. Ibid., 70–73.
53. Ibid., 89–94.
54. Ibid., 94–96.
55. Ibid., 96–97.
56. Ibid., 75–76, 174n.
57. J. A. Schumpeter, *Business Cycles: A Theoretical, Historical, and Statistical Analysis of the Capitalist Process* (New York: McGraw-Hill, 1939), 2:696n.
58. Joseph Schumpeter, "An Economic Interpretation of Our Times: The Lowell Lectures" (1941), *Economics and Sociology of Capitalism*, 345.
59. Karl Renner, *Marximus, Krieg und International* (Stuttgart, 1917), 323–50.
60. Schumpeter, *Capitalism, Socialism, and Democracy*, esp. 143–45.
61. Ibid., 45–49.
62. Ibid., 55.
63. Allen, *Opening Doors*, esp. 66–67, 90–93, 138–39, 190–91.
64. See Bernard Semmel, "Schumpeter's Curious Politics," *Public Interest*, no. 106 (Winter 1992): 3–16.

Chapter 9   The Idea of Imperialism: Some Concluding Remarks

1. See E. D. Morel, *The Black Man's Burden* (New York: Monthly Review Press, 1969; originally 1920); on the Congo, E. D. Morel, *Red Rubber* (London, 1919).
2. See V. G. Kiernan, *The Lords of Humankind: European Attitudes to the Outside World in the Imperial Age* (London: Weidenfeld and Nicolson, 1969); H. W. Koch, *Der Sozialdarwinismus: Seine Genesis und sein Einfluss auf das imperialistische Denken* (Munich: C. Beck, 1973). Also Bernard Semmel, *Jamaican Blood and Victorian Conscience* (Boston: Houghton, Mifflin, 1963).
3. See Hannah Arendt, *The Origins of Totalitarianism* (New York: Harcourt, Brace, 1951), esp. pt. 2.
4. Herbert Lüthy, "Colonization and the Making of Mankind," *Journal of Economic History* 21, no. 4 (December 1961): 485–86.
5. Lewis S. Feuer, *Imperialism and the Anti-Imperialist Mind* (Buffalo, N.Y.: Prometheus Books, 1986), 3–4, 10–16; 50–56, 104–12; 148–65, 204–15.
6. J. E. Cairnes, *Some Leading Principles of Political Economy, Newly Expanded* (London: Macmillan, 1884; originally 1874), 300.
7. J. A. Hobson, *Imperialism: A Study* (London: Allen & Unwin, 1948; originally 1902), 35.
8. Norman Angell, *The Great Illusion; A Study of the Relation of Military Power to National Advantage* (New York: Putnam, 1913; originally 1909), 71.
9. Hobson, *Imperialism*, 38–40.
10. See, for example, D. S. Landes, "Some Thoughts on the Nature of Economic Imperialism," *Journal of Economic History* 21, no. 4 (December 1961): 496–512; D. K. Fieldhouse, *Economics and Empire, 1830–1914* (Ithaca, N.Y.: Cornell University Press, 1973).

11. See, for example, J. Gallagher and R. Robinson, with Alice Denny, *Africa and the Victorians* (London: Macmillan, 1962).

12. See discussion in Bernard Semmel, "On the Economics of 'Imperialism,'" in *Economics and the Idea of Mankind,* ed. Bert F. Hoselitz (New York: Columbia University Press, 1965), 230–31. We should note that the privileged price was especially prized by large American sugar growers in Cuba, as well as constituting a means of protecting higher-cost domestic sugar producers in the United States.

13. Lionel Robbins, *The Economic Causes of War* (London: Jonathan Cape, 1939), 95, 99.

14. Jacob Viner, "The Economic Problem," *New Perspectives on Peace* (Chicago: University of Chicago Press, 1944), 95, 97, 101–2.

15. Paul Sweezy, editor's introduction to J. A. Schumpeter, *Imperialism and Social Classes* (New York: A. M. Kelley, 1951), vii–xxv.

16. See, for example, P. A. Baran and P. M. Sweezy, *Monopoly Capital: An Essay on the American Economic and Social Order* (New York: Modern Reader Paperbacks, 1968), esp. chs. 7 and 8; and P. M. Sweezy, *The Theory of Capitalist Development: Principles of Marxist Political Economy* (New York: Monthly Review Press, 1956; originally 1942), pt. 4.

17. A. J. Mayer, *The Persistence of the Old Regime: Europe to the Great War* (New York: Pantheon, 1981).

18. B. Byely, G. Fyodorov, V. Kulakov, et al., *Marxism-Leninism on War and Army* (Moscow: Progress Publishers, 1972), 67–85.

19. Fritz Sternberg, *Der Imperialismus* (Berlin: Malik Verlag, 1926); after World War II, Sternberg was to write *The Coming Crisis* (London: Gollancz, 1947), which continued his critique of previous Marxist theories from what was nonetheless an essentially Marxist position. A Marxist attack on Sternberg's first work is H. Grossman, "Eine neue Theorie über Imperialismus und die soziale Revolution," *Archiv für die Geschichte des Sozialismus und der Arbeiterbewegung* 13: 141–92.

20. See, for example, L. S. Woolf, *Empire and Commerce in Africa: A Study in Economic Imperialism* (London: Allen & Unwin, 1920); L. S. Woolf, *Imperialism and Civilisation* (London: Hogarth Press, 1928); P. T. Moon, *Imperialism and World Politics* (New York: Macmillan, 1926); Herbert Feis, *Europe: The World's Banker, 1870– 1914; An Account of European Foreign Investment and the Connection of World Finance with Diplomacy before the War* (New Haven: Yale University Press for the Council on Foreign Relations, 1930).

21. See, for example, Tom Kemp, *Theories of Imperialism* (London: Dennis Dobson, 1967).

22. See, for example, Anthony Brewer, *Marxist Theories of Imperialism: A Critical Survey* (London: Routledge & Kegan Paul, 1980); W. J. Mommsen, *Theories of Imperialism* (New York: Random House, 1980), esp. chaps. 2, 5.

23. Brewer, *Marxist Theories of Imperialism*, 264.

24. For a discussion and refutation of these claims, see P. T. Bauer, *Dissent on Development: Studies and Debates on Development Economics* (Cambridge, Mass.: Harvard University Press, 1972). A closely related debate concerning the relative advantages in the international market of industrial and agricultural nations emerged in a controversy in the 1950s between the Swedish economist Gunnar Myrdal and the American Jacob Viner. See Jacob Viner, *International Trade and Economic Development* (Glencoe, Ill.: Free Press, 1952), esp. 24, 55–62, 142; Gunnar Myrdal, *Economic Theory and Under-Developed Regions* (London: Duckworth, 1957), esp. 149–58. Also see discussion of the Viner-Myrdal controversy in Semmel, "The Hume-Tucker Debate and Pitt's Trade Proposals," *Economic Journal* 75 (December 1965): 759–70.

25. Among the best known of the so-called dependency theorists are A. Gunder

Frank and I. Wallerstein. See particularly A. G. Frank, *Capitalism and Underdevelopment in Latin America: Historical Studies of Chile and Brazil* (New York: Monthly Review Press, 1969); A. Gunder Frank, *Dependency, Accumulation and Underdevelopment* (London: Macmillan, 1978); and see I. Wallerstein, *The Capitalist World Economy* (Cambridge: Cambridge University Press, 1979).

26. See, for example, Arghiri Emmanuel, *Unequal Exchange: A Study in the Imperialism of Trade* (New York: Monthly Review Press, 1972). See also S. Amin, *Imperialism and Unequal Development* (New York: Monthly Review Press, 1977).

27. See Frank, *Capitalism and Underdevelopment*, 163–64, 289; Emmanuel, *Unequal Exchange*, xviii, 260.

28. Giovanni Arrighi *The Geometry of Imperialism* (London: New Left Books, 1978); also see a critical review article, Bernard Semmel, "Arrighi's Imperialism," *New Left Review*, no. 118 (November-December 1979): 73–79.

29. See, as prominent examples of these local studies, G. Arrighi and J. S. Saul, *Essays on the Political Economy of Africa* (New York: Monthly Review Press, 1973); P. P. Rey, *Colonialisme, néo-colonialisme et transition au capitalisme* (Paris: Maspéro, 1971). Also Prabhat Potnaik, "Imperialism and the Growth of Indian Capitalism," in *Studies in the Theory of Imperialism*, R. Owen and B. Sutcliffe (London: Longmans, 1972), 210–29.

30. Raymond Aron, *The Imperial Republic: The United States and the World, 1945–1973* (Cambridge, Mass.: Winthrop Publishers, 1974), 280–82. See also R. Aron, *The Century of Total War* (New York: Doubleday, 1954), 56–73. Acknowledging the arguments of the national economists, I presented a similar theory in the early 1960s; see Semmel, "On the Economics of 'Imperialism,'" 192–232.

31. S. Freud, "Civilization and Its Discontents" (1930), in his *Complete Psychological Works*, ed. J. Strachey (London: Hogarth Press, 1961), 21:141–43.

32. Francis Fukuyama, "The End of History?" *National Interest*, no. 16 (September 1989): esp. 3–5, 13–18.

33. Angell, *Great Illusion*, 71.

34. Hobson, *Imperialism*, 194–95.

35. An American mathematician, who has also written on mathematical economics, has set forth a new economic model (applicable to the high-technology industries of the late twentieth century), one that, he has argued, invalidates the classical free-trade model; and he has called for a return to Alexander Hamilton's 1791 remedies of protection and subsidies to avert the loss of American economic independence to Japan. See J. T. Schwartz, "America's Economic-Technological Agenda for the 1990s," *Daedalus* 121, no. 1 (Winter 1992): 139–65. There have been a number of less theoretical treatments of the subject, among them Clyde Prestowitz, *Changing Places* (New York: Basic Books, 1988).

Index

Index

155–56, 159, 180; on heterodox political economy, 140–41; and national economists, 9, 73, 78, 82, 135–36, 138; positive view of capitalism, 136, 139–40, 160, 184; and sociological theorists, 9, 129, 136–38, 139; on usurious capitalism, 10, 86, 130, 142–43, 149; and Wakefield, 28, 31, 156. *See also* Sociological theory of imperialism

Marxism, 5, 9–10, chap. 7 passim, 157–67, 175–76, 180–81, 187–89, 190, 191

Mercantilism, 1–3, 4, 6, 7, 11, 14, 17–21 passim, 25, 32, 52, 58, 104, 133, 139, 155, 159, 171, 181. *See also* National economists

Mexican War, 33–34, 36, 80

Militant society, 40, 41, 42, 44, 47, 54, 103–10 passim, 120–21, 159, 170–71, 174, 178, 181

Militarism, 7–8, 152–58, 174. *See also* Armaments industry

Mill, James, 7, 21, 26–27, 37, 113

Mill, John Stuart, 7, 31, 32, 34, 36, 38, 43, 48, 119, 121; and Carey, 73, 81–82; on colonization, 31; on free trade, 32–33, 37–38, 82; on glut, 31; on slave economy, 7, 33, 36–37; and Wakefield, 7, 31–32. *See also* Sociological theory of imperialism

Mission civilisatrice, 4, 68, 108, 139–40, 183–84, 191

Molesworth, Sir William, 30–31

Montesquieu, C. L. de S., 3, 47

Morel, E. D., 183

Morgan interests, 114, 116

Multinational corporations. *See* Ultraimperialism

Myrdal, Gunnar, 214n.24

Napoleon I, 5, 9, 18, 39, 42, 43, 46–47, 52, 71, 72, 89

Napoleon III, 5, 46, 90, 106

National economists, 8–9, 13, 55, chaps. 4 and 5 passim, 122, 132, 134, 138, 161, 177, 182, 188, 189

Nationalism, 112, 123, 136, 148, 174

Navigation Acts, 19, 26

Nazism, 99, 102, 129, 143, 175, 176, 183, 188, 190, 192

Neo-Marxism, 134–55, 157–62

Neomercantilism. *See* Finance capital; National economists; Protection

New York Tribune, 82, 90, 132, 137, 139

Olmsted, Frederick Law, 7, 33–35, 37, 80. *See also* Sociological theory of imperialism

Opium War, 54, 74

Overproduction. *See* Underconsumption

Pecuniary society, 121–22, 123–24, 127

Peel, Sir Robert, 57, 72, 77

Pennsylvania, 64, 98

Persian empire, 1, 107, 169

Physiocrats, 18–19, 20, 21, 23, 24, 52, 151, 155

Pitt, William, 61–62

Political economy: heterodox, 23–32, 52, 134, 179; orthodox, 3, 4, 6, 10, 11, 26, 52, 179; science of, 90, 92–93, 133, 134. *See also* Malthus; Ricardo; Smith

Population, law of, 73–74, 79

Populism, American, 95, 97, 98–99, 122

Portugal, 2, 50, 66, 70, 76

Protection, 2, 8, 9, chap. 4 passim, 103, 106, 110–11, 117, 146, 172. *See also* Mercantilism; National economists

Protestantism, 4, 9, 22, 44, 45, 51, 53, 54, 85, 92, 93, 101, 133, 142–43

Prussia, 17, 71, 125, 126, 127

Radicals. *See* Cobdenites

Rate of profit, declining: heterodox, 25; Marxist, 9, 10, 140–41, 156; orthodox, 7, 9, 179

Raymond, Daniel, 8, 63, 73

Renner, Karl, 144, 175

Rent, law of, 39, 73–74, 79, 82, 120

Revolution, social, 7, 29, 30, 136, 149, 164–65, 180, 181, 189

Ricardo, David, 26, 119; on comparative advantage, 21; on declining returns, 37; on free trade, 25; and frugality, 24; on iron law of wages, 23, 25; on rate of profit, 7, 9; on rent, 73, 79; on usury, 86

Robbins, Lionel, 186–87. *See also* Sociological theory of imperialism

Rockefeller interests, 116

Rodbertus, K. J., 151

Designed by Glen Burris
Set in Baskerville text and Galliard display by
Capitol Communication Systems, Inc.
Printed on 50-lb. Glatfelter Eggshell Cream by
The Maple Press Company